(A)

# A FIELD ARTILLERY

# GROUP IN BATTLE.

A Tactical Study based on the Action of 2nd Brigade, R.F.A., during the German Offensive, 1918, the 100 Days' Battle, and the Battle of Cambrai, 1917,

by

COLONEL W. H. F. WEBER, C.M.G., D.S.O., p.s.c.

# PREFACE.

Permission has kindly been given by the Royal Artillery Inst tion to republish in book form the three Articles contained her They were published in R.A. Journal as follows :—I. November 1 to March 1920; II. October and November, 1922; III. July, 1! The first was reproduced, with but little additional comment, in 1 by the American Field Artillery Journal.

Oscar Wilde has written of personal memoirs that either writers appear to have completely lost their memories or they 1 done nothing worth remembering; but another has said that we 1 more autobiographies of nonentities. One object of these articles 1 place on record a set of actual experiences, before we again bec dependent on theory for training. In these days of changes of ar ment, the Press, military and civilian alike, frightens us with p nostications as to the next war; horrors are thrust in our face protagonists of the aeroplane, the tank, and chemical warfare, in t in comparison to which the submarine terror seems quite innocu The writer has no intention to underrate the possibilities of deve ment in these branches of warfare, but would rather leave then more ambitious prophets; his idea in presenting this record of f is to provide a framework on which to consider the practical effec these developments on field artillery in battle.

Official reports have a human tendency towards self-defei war diaries do scant justice to the actors of a battle drama; regime histories are too domestic. An actual record of experiences, o another name for mistakes, should have a certain value, if only as a to the seeming platitudes of the training manuals, the instruct contained in which sometimes get contravened in battle owing pressure of circumstance. Unfortunately, either from modesty, from wisdom, or simply from indolence, few men publish such rece until they have become archaeological studies; in 1918 the metl of 1914 seemed old fashioned; and indeed the writer, recently disc ing his subject with younger and ambitious military enthusia detects already a flavour of antiquity about his experiences as 1 recorded.

In the R.A. Journal for May and June, 1922, appeared exceedingly interesting article by Lieut.-Colonel C. N. F. Bro D.S.O., entitled "The Development of Artillery Tactics 1914—1 which presents the tactical (and indeed strategical) influence of artill upon the Great European War in its true light (the author probably thinking chiefly of Heavy Artillery). The article mentio summarises developments still impending at the end of 1918 follows :—

(a) Improvement in actual battle co-operation by the Royal Air Force.

(b) Introduction of large masses of tanks.

(c) Improvement in all forms of communication.

(d) Increase in mobility owing to cross-country traction.

All these developments find a place in the training of a modern army; what will be their actual effect on field artillery tactics? Will those tactics be materially altered?

There may be criticism contained in the following chapters; it is almost inevitable, however undesirable. The writer can only say that his criticism is directed chiefly against the "Group Commander." For any other criticism he herewith makes apology, as he has always met with the greatest courtesy and consideration from his superiors and the most loyal co-operation from those placed under his command, the vast majority of whom never dreamed that they would one day help make history—no mean task for all that the cynic may say who wrote "Anyone can make history; it takes a great man to write it." The 6th Divisional Artillery was, in truth, a happy family; its chief was one of those who make for happy families, none the less so because he taught, in a kindly manner, that obedience is a soldier's first duty—and practised what he preached. We all recognised good men in our Divisional Commander and his staff, and for our infantry we entertained the most profound respect and affection.

A second object of this book is to provide a souvenir of great days of the past for such officers and others who participated in the events recorded, should they care to obtain it.

The volume is dedicated (by permission) to Lieut.-General Sir E. A Fanshawe, K.C.B., to whom the writer had at one time the honour to be a staff-officer, and to whose training is due anything of the tactical parts of these pages which may be worth reading.

Birkin House,
    Dorchester,
        July 6th, 1923.

---

The author wishes gratefully to acknowledge the help received from Sergt.-Major Bigg, R.E., in the preparation of the maps accompanying Articles II and III.

---

# TABLE OF CONTENTS.

## LIST OF MAPS, DIAGRAMS, ETC.

# ARTICLE I.

# A FIELD ARTILLERY

# GROUP IN RETREAT.

In three parts:

Part I—March, 1918.

Part II—April, 1919.

Part III—Conclusion and some Platitudes.

*Reprinted from the Journal of the Royal Artillery.*
*Vol. XLVI.   Nos. 8, 9, 10, 11 and 12.*
*(By kind permission of the Royal Artillery Institution.)*

# PART I. March, 1918.

An examination of the German criticism that "the British Artillery was splendidly served, but badly directed."

---

## CHAPTER I.

### CONDITIONS PREVIOUS TO THE GERMAN OFFENSIVE ON 21ST MARCH.

THE 1917 fighting, culminating in the battle of Passchendaele, had brought centralised control of artillery to its zenith; there was hardly any initiative left to subordinate artillery commanders except in the choice of gun-platforms and the management of personnel.[1] The offensive reigned supreme in the mind of the rather weary British Army, in a manner suitable to the theory of military training, but possibly unsuitable to the strategical situation.

One should consider this and the following conditions in order to arrive at an estimate of 'moral,' which we are told is the major element of success and should therefore be taken first.[2]

The 6th Division had been engaged during the whole of 1917 in what may be called 'active trench warfare' on the battle-field of Loos. The 6th D.A. (who had been longer 'in' than the infantry) were 'pulled out' early in October after a decision to abandon certain projected operations against Lens; instead of the expected march to the Salient, the division moved south and was heavily engaged at Cambrai,[3] certain phases of which operation were unexpected and were even carried out by some people in 'undress.' After Christmas the 2nd Bde. R.F.A. was relieved (the infantry had been some time) and 'rested' in the snows till 20th January, 1918.

At Cambrai[3] the brigade had suffered considerable casualties, which included a veritable holocaust for the 42nd Battery, its commander (Major N. B. Robertson, D.S.O.) being killed, 7 other. officers wounded, and nearly all its Nos. 1 put out of action; hardly an officer or senior N.C.O. was left whom the men knew.

---

[1] Subordinate commanders posted nearly all officers, men and horses to batteries—which gave those commanders a chance to maintain the efficiency for which they were responsible.

[2] The writer of "Infantry Tactics," in the August 1919 number of the R.U.S.I. Journal, says "It is questionable whether the German offensive would not have been "checked sooner if every moment had been devoted to musketry and training in open "order . . . . A well-trained soldier lying behind what cover he can find . . . . is a "much more formidable obstacle to tackle than an untrained man in a well-dug "trench . . . ." Says Sir John Fisher "Born fools count ships; wise men reckon the ability of the crews."

[3] See Article III.

During the period of rest-and-training, a set of instructions was received outlining a new policy for employment of the artillery in view of the now obvious likelihood of a German offensive on a first-class scale. The change of policy affected all ranks as involving an immense amount of manual labour. The burden of these new instructions was the disposition of the defending artillery in depth, its concealment, and its surprise action in the form of counter-preparation. In practice, the depth of the prepared battle zone was insufficient while concealment in such terrain proved impossible however devotedly 'silent'[1] the batteries. The idea was that by never shooting the guns, the enemy would be unaware how and in what strength they were disposed; in some terrain it is easy to conceal guns, but in such as that round Bapaume one could not, with the material available, conceal the work necessary to dig in a large force of artillery. It is a fable that tactics are initiated by the Higher Command; lessons penetrate from the front line backwards through whatever obstacles are laid out against them; at some cost, these lessons do eventually reach their objective, where they are assimilated and distributed. After our experiences in March and April, and theirs in May and June, the French applied these January principles on July 15, 1918, in a different way; on receipt of warning of attack, they changed many battery positions. On March 21st practically all our would-be concealed gun positions got their share of German shells, and some rather more; on July 15th a combination of the three very same principles enunciated in January, but now applied by the light of experience, resulted in a decision against the Germans of the very highest importance. In March we failed to achieve concealment; in July the French found a successful product of concealment and mobility. We shall return to this point later.

Towards the end of January the 6th Division relieved the 51st across the Bapaume-Cambrai road; there was very little fighting at this period, but an endless amount of manual work in carrying out the new ideas; it was a period heartily disliked by all ranks.

In February the 6th Division side-slipped to the North (left) to allow the 51st to come back to their old line. This system had inconveniences for the 6th Division, but it was instructive to gain touch with several different suggestions as to fighting the forthcoming defensive battle; it is well to know what your next door neighbour is doing. The new ideas had been less drastically applied in the February area and a great deal of work was necessary. The 6th Division completed its three weeks tour on this front, but, though all was supremely quiet at the beginning, the wind got up towards the end, presaging the coming storm; false alarms with much counter-preparation occurred on March 10th, 13th, and other subsequent dates; attempts to relieve the division failed again and again.

---

[1] The name given to positions which were not used except in emergency was "silent positions."

As regards the 2nd Bde. R.F.A., the 21st Battery was lent to the Left Group and emplaced complete in a 'silent' position—as we used to say 'a position of anticipation.'  On 21st March the Right Group consisted of the 42nd, 53rd and 87th Batteries R.F.A.  The 42nd Battery, scarcely recovered from Cambrai, was near completing a new position—a big task; its headquarters and 2 sections had just occupied this new (silent) position, in an endeavour to carry out the principle of depth; unfortunately, with the prospect of relief staring us in the face, determination to calibrate a particular gun before handing over led to there being 3 guns in the (old) forward or 'active' position on 'Zero' day instead of the usual 2.  The 87th (Howitzer) Battery had had rather less to do; it had its headquarters and 2 sections in a silent and really well concealed position (a gully not marked on the map); but here again our luck was out, for the R.F.C. were educating observers, and, to lessen difficulties, the two forward guns in the active position had been increased to three on the 20th March; the B.C. had only just returned from hospital and was not yet well acquainted with the ground.  The 53rd Battery had only arrived on the scene a day or two before the German attack; it had been several weeks at the III Army Artillery School, and was in great form, but had had insufficient time to perfect its acquaintance with the terrain; 3 guns were in a 'silent' position well known to the Germans, 2 in a new forward position and one was an anti-tank gun.  Thus one might say the Right Group was perhaps a shade below normal efficiency; the effort to carry out a G.H.Q. policy as originally interpreted by some-one else had been confusing—drastic alterations had had to be made to that interpretation at a late hour.  The average soldier was below par, for the continual offensive without material progress is neither salubrious nor exhilarating; on the top a change of policy involving heavy manual labour; daily, even hourly, warnings of an overwhelming attack to be supported by tanks of fabulous speed, size, armament, pattern and number.   It was unfortunate that our Intelligence could not get hold of facts[1] or trust us with the truth that the enemy had so few; overmuch talk of tanks occasioned 'nerves' rather than caution—so that our most phlegmatic subaltern awoke one night at the clinking of a passing engine crying "Tanks, Sammy, Tanks"; lastly, the need of employing certain guns to stop tanks robbed each battery of from 10% to 20% of its efficiency.

So much for the human element; let us now consider a natural one in the shape of geography.[2]  First and foremost, our whole area was open country, arable land where agriculture had been suspended, covered with rough grass; dotted here and there with the relics of villages of the usual mud and timber type with an occasional ruin of brick or stone; in the centre of each village a cross-road pitted with shell-holes near which lay generally a heap of white stones which had once formed the walls and tower of the village church.   The area was intersected by long lines of trench and belts of barbed wire (lying S.E. & N.W.) which formed the only obstacle to movement; a country

---

[1] See p. 87, Vol. II.  "Sir Douglas Haig's Command."
[2] See map, Part I., Chapters IV. and V.

well suited to the individual horseman, and to movements on foot on a wide front. The features are shown on the map, but it is necessary to give prominence to certain points :—

(a). The importance of maintaining the III Army position East of Bapaume arose from the lack of communications from Bapaume rearwards; there was only the one great road from Albert across the battlefield of the Somme. Bapaume itself was an important junction of roads and railways; its houses were far more uninhabitable than they looked at first sight—on investigation, it was completely in ruins, but it had a considerable (military) population accommodated in cellars converted into dug-outs, while above ground had grown up quite a little city of canvas and hutting concealed amongst the shrubs and ruins; in the neighbourhood were many big 'Dumps.'

(b). The open nature of the country rendered camouflage most difficult; except when placed in sunken roads, it was practically impossible to hide work from the German air camera.

(c). Our forward zone (facing N.E.) was intersected by a series of depressions of tactical importance running N.E. and S.W., therefore at right angles to our line, so that the enemy on the heights behind Pronville and Queant, where lay the "Hindenburg Line," obtained superior observation.

(d). Observation over the enemy forward system in front of Pronville and Queant could only be obtained from our front or support trenches (Blue or Outpost system) or from the air.

Other topographical features will be noticed as we come to them; let us turn to artificial ones. To obtain a true idea of a minor difficulty of war, it must be understood that, though maps are as common as men in a headquarter office and much cleaner, in the forward area they are hard to come by and often extremely hard to read, as anyone will testify who has tried to refer to the F.O.O's map after a shower of rain.

Between the opposing trench systems was generally a wide No Man's Land, perhaps a mile[1]; the ground went level to varying distances in front of our outpost line (foremost trench) then dropped quickly, thus giving the enemy dead ground on his side of No Man's Land, over which it was very hard and in certain places impossible to obtain ground observation.

Our forward zone combined the first (Blue or Outpost) and second[2] (Red or Reserve) system; these were good trenches in very fair order and gradually becoming well provided with dug-outs; they had been prepared by the British at the conclusion of the German withdrawal in the Spring of 1917, and since then lightly held. They were efficiently wired.

Our battle-zone began with the third[3] (Brown) system, a single

---

[1] But on the left the opposing trenches were almost touching, at a place known as the Birdcage, valuable to the enemy for observation and a marked salient in his "Observation Line."

[2] Between 500 and 1200 yards behind "outpost line."

[3] Approximately 1800 yards behind the Red Line. It was sometimes spoken of as "the Haig Line."

line of trench just completed and well wired; behind this there was one more single line, only traced in some parts, but fairly well wired, know as the fourth[1] (Green) system.

The 21st Battery position (Left Group) was *in* the Brown system (C 20 d), where its guns were destroyed by the German bombardment. The 42nd Battery main position (I 17 d) was 2,000 yards behind the Brown Line, and furthest back, being 6000 yards from the nearest enemy or more; it was strongly dug in a widish depression in clay soil; the work was impossible to camouflage without a large amount of material. The 53rd Battery main position (I 5 c) was in a sunken part of the Morchies-Vaulx country road, about 1000 yards behind the Brown Line; it had fair dug-outs. The 87th (Howitzer) Battery main position (I 4 a) was in a small deep depression whose Eastern face was almost perpendicular and contained good dug-outs; the depression was not shown on the map and provided a very good howitzer position; it was close behind the Brown Line. The three forward positions[2] (all of which had dug-outs) were slightly in front of the Brown Line, and were the only ones used for ordinary fire—sniping, calibration, co-operation with air-craft, harassing fire, fire at request of infantry, etc. The O.P's in normal use were unsatisfactory—two in the support trench of the first (or Blue) system and one in the second (or Red) system; they provided however good views and had dug-outs. We shall discuss this point later in the day.

The instructions of January, 1918, were based on the system of centralised control, but this system depends for its very existence on communications. The "bury" will be discussed later in Chapter III; it is enough to say here that the Right Group Headquarters, as taken over in February, were located with its affiliated Infantry Brigade Headquarters practically *in the Brown Line* (C 29 d), and that buried communications thence to batteries were not so very inefficient; it was considered necessary by the authorities to shift these combined headquarters further back; from the new headquarters (I 17 a), occupied only on 16th March, still incomplete and unprotected except for one long unfinished tunnel, there was no single buried line to any gun position, and on the morning of the 21st March the main "bury" was still unconnected to the I.B. Signal Station down in the tunnel; this connection was made during, and in spite of, the enemy bombardment but helped the artillery very little, for it gave only communication to battalion headquarters and flank brigades. Such a condition of communications[3] forbade control of fire and had a vital effect on the support rendered by the Group.

With a remark on the weather this resumé of conditions obtaining at dawn on the 21st March will finish. The weather was unusual; a high barometer; instead of mud there were hard ground, dry trenches

---

[1] Three to four thousand yards back.
[2] 42nd J 7 b, 53rd I 6 b, 87th C 29 a.
[3] Over 2000 yards in a direct line from Group Headquarters to 87th Battery main position.

and *good roads;* instead of cloudy days and dark nights, we had brilliant sun-shine by day, bright and frosty moonlight nights with morning mists till about 10 a.m. The effects of the weather were far-reaching; obstacles usually impassable at this time of the year could be negotiated; air reconnaissance was facilitated; though they made our withdrawal less uncomfortable, such conditions must help the stronger force more in proportion than they assist the weaker; and lastly, the morning mist *could be relied on* by the enemy to conceal the assault.

## CHAPTER II.

### THE DEFENCE SCHEME.

The 6th D.A. used, when a new line was taken over, to issue a Defence Scheme, which was a bulky pamphlet of 12—20 pages of foolscap based on the Divisional Defence Scheme, and attached to it were several tables of which the most important one showed the position of every Headquarters, every gun position, limits of areas of fire, S.O.S. line or points, O.P's and wagon lines, etc.; other tables were attached allotting targets for 'concentration schemes,' targets to assist flank groups on receipt of code calls, inter-group-boundaries, list of O.P's showing areas of observation, a table of information concerning the Heavy Artillery, etc., etc. Unfortunately the writer is not in possession of a copy, and it is doubtful if any copy of the February Defence Scheme still exists. One copy was issued to every group, brigade, and battery, to each infantry brigade, and each neighbouring divisional artillery.

It was necessary to issue from within the Group to each battery, a subsidiary Group Defence Scheme; of the Right Group Subsidiary Scheme one copy[1] exists; it is printed here in full with all its imperfections, exactly as in possession of each battery on the 20th March.

Chapter III contains discussion on various points in the scheme, the numerals (i), (ii), (iii), etc. in the scheme as printed in this Chapter II referring to the various observations on Chapter III.

\* \* \* \* \* \*

*Subsidiary Notes for Morchies (Right) Group to 6th*

*D.A .Defence Scheme.* (i).

### A. General Remarks.

The principal features to notice on the front of the Right Sector are :—

(a). Our forward trench system is on a forward slope.

(b). It is intersected by valleys running roughly at right angles to the opposing lines thus giving the enemy good observation from The Birdcage (D 14) and the heights beyond Pronville over our natural approaches.

---

[1] Still covered with the mud thrown up by shell which burst in Group Headquarters hut on 21st March.

(c). Behind our forward system the ridges and valleys lie more parallel to the opposing lines.

(d). The flanks of our sector lie in depressions while the centre of our front system of trenches lies on a spur (D.20).

(e). We have a Front System, The Red Line (known as the Reserve Line), the Brown Line (or Baumetz—Morchies—Vaulx Line), and the Green Line. All officers must be acquainted with these four systems.

(f). No Man's Land is again very wide, except opposite The Birdcage.

(g). We have little observation over the enemy's front line, but better over his second line.

(h). The area presents no natural tactical obstacles.

### B. Observation, Liaison, and Communications.

*Observation* (ii).

1. (a) Linnet I O.P. is manned by 42nd Battery. Linnet II by 87th Battery, and Sparrow O.P. by 53rd Battery from dawn to dusk.

(b) Bat O.P. D.25.c.O.O. is manned by 53rd from dusk until it is necessary for the F.O.O. to leave so as to reach Sparrow by dawn. It is provided with S.O.S. Signals. 53rd provides rifle.

*Liasion.*

2. 42nd and 87th in turn find *48 hours* (iii) Liaison with the Battalions holding the line.

Headquarters Right Battalion D.26.c.4.1.

Headquarters Left Battalion D.25.d.9.8.

Liaison officer lives with Right Battalion but is to visit Left Battalion every day. (iv).

In case of tactical emergency a liaison officer will be found for both battalions.

*Communications* (v).

3. The 'bury' runs from Vaulx (Headquarters Left and Centre Brigades and Left Group) to Skipton Reserve and to Right Battalion Headquarters through Morchies Copse, whence a branch will eventually run to Right Infantry Brigade and Morchies Group Headquarters at I. 17. a. 6. 8. (vi).

Practically all lines go through exchanges and there is one special O.P. Exchange (O.P.X.), to which the 90th Brigade R.G.A. is connected. Each O.P. has a double line to O.P.X., one of which can be plugged through to the forward section.

Batteries are connected to Group by air-line. (vii).

There is one direct line from Morchies Group Headquarters to 90th Brigade R.G.A. (viii) and also direct lines to both flank groups.

### C. The Defence of the Front System.

. S.O.S. Lines, Concentrations, and Liaison Barrages for the defence of the Front System are given in the 6th D.A. Defence Scheme and its Appendices 'A', 'B', 'C'.

The S.O.S. signal is a rifle grenade bursting into two white and two green stars. Those are kept at Battalion Headquarters and at Bat O.P.

D. *Rearward Defences (Red, Brown, and Green Lines).* (ix).

The system of Reserve and Reinforcing Artillery Positions is given in detail in the "D.A. Rear Defence Scheme" of which all Batteries have a copy. Details as to Position Numbers are also given there.

Appendix I is an extract as regards Right Group.

Responsibility for work has been notified separately.

Hours of work 9 a.m. to 12.30 p.m. and 1.45 p.m. to 4.15 p.m.

E. *Anti-Tank Defences.* (x)

1. (a) 42nd Battery mans a 15-pdr. (Nickel) at D.26.c.2.4. and an 18-pdr. (Leech) in Leech Avenue.
   (b) 53rd Battery has an 18-pdr. (Tiger) at D.25.b.0.5.
   (c) 21st Battery has a gun (Sparrow) at D.25.a.8.8. attached to 53rd.
   (d) 87th Battery mans a 15-pdr. (Shaw's) at D.19.c.20.25.
2. In the event of a Tank attack 42nd Battery sends a gun from J.7.b.10.45. to approx J.1.d.1.4.
   53rd sends a gun from I.4.d.9.7. to approx. I.5.a.5.4.
3. For details see Appendix V.

F. *Miscellaneous.*

1. A set of Standing Orders affecting fire discipline, etc. is given in Appendix II.

2. Wagon-Lines are in H.17.c. In event of emergency, limbers and firing battery wagons will be ordered forward to the valley running from I.13. central to I.7. central. It is to be distinctly understood that, though orders may reach the wagon-lines from higher sources, the real liaison is between the wagon-line and the gun-line of each battery; the Wagon-Line Commander must inform the Battery Commander where the Wagon-Line is. Orders sent to the Wagon-Line from higher sources will always be repeated to batteries. (xi).

3. One gun in each 18-pdr. Battery will be prepared to deal with low-flying aircraft, the shell to be timed to burst 400 feet vertically above our front line trench, using a false angle of sight. (xii).

4. A special form of support exists called 'Counter-preparation' (CPN) designed to interfere with enemy assembly. There are three varieties of it, viz., 'CPN/A', 'CPN/B', 'CPN/C', details of which are shown in the 6th D.A. Defence Scheme. Appendix VI will give further details.

5. A table of harassing schemes is given in Appendix III.

If no orders are received by batteries before 6 p.m. each battery will select its own times and targets keeping well beyond the enemy front line, and firing 12 rounds per active gun. (xv).

6. The Trench Mortar Control Scheme is shown in Appendix IV.

7. Concentrations to meet certain eventualities are given in Appendix VI.

8. Ammunition Orders Appendix VII.

## Appendix I.—Table of Rearward Positions (MORCHIES Group). (xv).

| 1 UNIT. | 2 POSITION. | 3 O.P. | 4 RATE OF PROGRESS. | 5 BRIGADE HEADQRS. |
|---|---|---|---|---|
| **FOR DEFENCE OF RED LINE.** | | | | |
| 42nd Battery<br>87th Battery | 107<br>106 and 118 | C. 30. a. 15. 80. | 107 Complete and occupied.<br>106 occupied; 118, platforms prepared and ammunition stored. | 2nd Brigade at I. 17. a. 6. 8. |
| 53rd Battery | 102 | D. 25. c. 20. 05. | 102 Complete and occupied. | |
| 1st Reinforcing Brigade | 108, 115, 116, 156 | D. 25. c. 20. 05. | 156 still occupied by Left Group. 108-115-116, ammunition stored and rough Bty. Hd.-Qtrs. prepared. | I. 11. a. 7. 0. (ready). |
| 3rd Reinforcing Brigade | 109, 117, 119, 121 | C. 29. c. 9. 6. and I. 5. c. 3. 8. | Ammunition stored. | I. 9. d. 2. 6. (ready). |
| **FOR DEFENCE OF BROWN LINE.** | | | | |
| 21st Battery<br>42nd Battery | 128<br>111 | I. 11. a. 0. 1. | Bty. Hdqrs. 128 prepared, Bty. Hdqrs. 111 ready; (to be shared with H.A. 229); | All three Brigades to be in Bank between Positions 123 and 128 at I. 14. a. 7. 2. |
| 87th Battery<br>53rd Battery | 112<br>110 | I. 5. a. central | Recesses for Ammunition in course of preparation for all positions. | |
| 1st Reinforcing Brigade | 113 (21)<br>114 (87)<br>122 (42)<br>123 (53) | I. 5. c. 6. 6. and I. 11. a. 1. 1. | Recesses prepared or in course of preparation. | |
| 3rd Reinforcing Brigade | 124 - 127<br>(21, 42, 87, 53) | I. 12. b. 1. 5. and I. 5. c. 8. 8. | Ammunition stored; 1500 per 18 pr., and 1200 per 4·5 in. | |
| **FOR DEFENCE OF GREEN LINE.** | | | | |
| 21st Battery<br>42nd Battery<br>87th Battery<br>53rd Battery<br>1st Reinforcing Brigade<br>3rd Reinforcing Brigade | 142<br>140<br>143<br>141<br>144, 145, 194, 195<br>not yet decided | Best sites at<br>I. 14. a. 8. 5.<br>I. 13. a. 5. 8.<br>I. 7. a. 4. 8. | Positions only marked. | Not yet selected. |

O.P.'s (Red and Brown Lines) all ready and labelled—simple pits, trench boarded, sheltered with corrugated tin, and camouflaged.

*MARCH 12th, 1918.*

*APPENDIX II.*

Standing Orders for Positions (2nd Brigade R.F.A.) (xvi).

## 1.  Forward Positions.

1.  An officer will always be with the active section and in possession of a fighting map.

2.  75% of men to have rifles up to a maximum of 12 rifles, with 50 rounds per rifle.

## 11.  Main Positions.

1.  Not to be used except in case of S.O.S. but to be kept in every respect ready as if in daily use.  (xvii).

2.  12 rifles and 100 rounds per rifle to be kept in the gun-pits.

3.  When tactical conditions require it, a mounted orderly with horse, is to be kept at position.

## III.  All Positions.

1.  A good exit to be prepared for every pit.  (xviii).  One gun at every position must be prepared to go out against tanks.

2.  Every position to have a rocket sentry at night and a rocket indicator marked with the flanks of the Battery S.O.S. line, Battalion Headquarters, and Magnetic or True North.  (xix).

3.  Every pit to have a scheme-board signed by an Officer, and a paper showing range, switch, angle of sight to three points in our front line.  (xx).

4.  Not more than 200 rounds per 18-pdr. or 130 rounds per howitzer to be kept in the pit.  Gas shell to be stored separately. 18-pdr. ammunition to be stored not more than three deep.  (xxi).

5.  Two men per gun to sleep in or near the gun-pit.  One officer, one signaller, and two men per gun to 'stand to' from dawn on for one hour.  (xxii).

6.  Every position to have a 'Battle Station Table.'  (xxiii).

## IV.  General.

1.  One gun per Battery to be prepared to engage low-flying aircraft.

2.  Positions to be wired all round.  (xxiv).

3.  Visual communication to be practiced daily.  (xxv).

4.  One hour's drill per week with gas respirators on.  Sights to be checked after a switch.  Officer in charge to wear gas respirator during drill.  All ranks to wear gas respirators at the 'alert', forward of the wagon lines.  Working parties away from position and at night will wear gas respirators at the 'alert' while at work.

5.  Fish-nets not to be used—to be replaced by a rabbit-wire camouflage.

6.  Muzzle velocity to be painted on the piece and on shield. Date of calibration to be painted on off side.  Gun History Sheet to be kept in wallet attached to brake-arm.  (xvia).

7.  Every position to be provided with a grease trap and a lid latrine.

8.  Detachments will be called to 'Detachments Rear' if a General comes to the position.

V. O.P.'s. (xxvi).

1. Every O.P. to be furnished with :—
   (a). Diagram of communication.
   (b). Map showing arcs of fire for all 6" Hows. and
        60-pdrs. firing over our zone. (Batteries must
        keep this map up to date).
   (c). Log Book (marked with name of O.P.)
   (d). Pointer. (e). List of Code Calls.
   (f). Panorama or hand sketch in log-book. (g).
        Beware Notice.
2. Night O.P. to be provided with a rifle and S.O.S. rifle-
   grenades.
3. N.C.O. and personnel to be armed.

*Appendix III to Morchies Group Defence Scheme.* (xxvii).

Group Harassing Shoots will be arranged on the following
scheme and no further orders will be given to batteries than
"Scheme ........................... Time ......................."

*Scheme A.*
                    (In the case of suspected relief.)
42nd Battery Roads from German Front Line to 'Observation'
   Line D. 15. (xxviia).
53rd Battery Trenches from German Front Line to Birdcage
   D. 14.
87th Battery Points where German Front Line crosses above.
*Scheme B.*
                    (In the case of suspected relief).
42nd Battery Melbourne Street N. of D.10. central.
53rd Battery Melbourne Street S. of D.10. central.
87th Battery Points where trenches, river, road, and track cross
   Melbourne Street.
*Scheme C.*
53rd Battery Enfilade streets N.W. half of Pronville.
42nd Battery Enfilade streets S.E. of Pronville.
87th Battery Centres of activity Northern portion of Pronville.
*Scheme D.*
53rd Battery River bank D.3.c.o.o. to D. 9. central.
42nd Battery River bank D.9. central to Melbourne Street.
87th Battery Crossings of the river especially plank bridges.
*Scheme E.*
42nd Battery Road D.4.c.2.3. to D.9. central.
53rd Battery Road D.9.c.0.5. to D.9. central.
87th Battery Selected points on above.
   *Note.* On Code Call 'Transport' all active sections will fire :—
        (a) 3 minutes intense. Scheme D.
   (b) 2 minutes silence.
   (c) 3 minutes intense. Scheme E.
   90th Brigade R.G.A. undertake to co-operate if warned.
*March 12th, 1918.*

*Appendix IV. to Morchies Group Defence Scheme.* (xxviii).

System of Control of Heavy and Medium T.M's.

1. For the battle, the Officer appointed to control T.M's in Right Group area will be located at Right Battalion Headquarters (D.26.c.4.1.).

2. He will have direct lines to an Officer (D.25.a.98.68) i/c Nos. 7 and 8 M.T.M's. and to an officer (D.20.d.90.45) i/c Nos. 9, 10, 11 and to No. 1 H.T.M. (D.26.b.40.45). Communication by runner to Nos. 16, 17, 18 M.T.M's. at J.2.b.3.7.

3. The O.C. Nos. 7 and 8 T.M's will be in the dug-out at Sparrow O.P. which is being prepared accordingly.

4. The O.C. 9, 10, and 11 will be at No. 9 position.

5. S.O.S. Lines are laid down for all Mortars in the 6th D.A. Defence Scheme.

6. Concentration 'A' brings Nos. 10 and 11 on The Strand.
   „          'B' brings Nos. 9, 10 and 11 on The Nest.
   „          'C' brings Nos. 7 and 8 on to Park Lane.

7. Nos. 7 and 8 fire only at the request of the Left Battalion Commander. Nos. 16, 17 and 18 fire only at the request of the Right Battalion Commander.

8. A Table showing S.O.S. Points and Concentrations is to be kept in every Mortar-pit. It will be signed by an Officer.

9. In addition every Mortar is to be provided with range and switch to our own front line at the extremities of its arc of fire.

10. Every Mortar will be kept laid on its S.O.S. Line.

11. Under control of the senior T.M. Officer, rounds will be prepared at 'Stand To' with charges ready to fire.

12. Detachments will invariably 'Stand To' at dawn at the time when the Infantry in their neighbourhood do so.

13.—The N.C.O. i/c of each pit will be given a copy of Standing Orders and Instructions relating to his own weapon.
*March 12th, 1918.*

*Appendix V to Morchies Group Defence Scheme.*

Anti-Tank Defence. (xxix).

1. 42nd Battery mans a 15-pounder at present at D.26.c. 20.35.—Nickel.
   It covers the valley in D.26.c. & b.

2. 53rd Battery mans an 18-pdr. at D.25.b.5.2.—Tiger.
   It covers the valley in D.19.d.

3. 21st Battery (Left Group) has an 18-pdr. attached to 53rd at D.25.a.8.8.—Sparrow. It covers the ground immediately in front of it, and the high ground west of Leech Avenue, and the high ground in D.19.a. & b. It needs Infantry to help to pull it out of its pit.

4. 87th Battery mans a 15 pdr. at D.19.c.20.25.—Shaw's.
   It covers the valley through D.19 central.

5. Another 18-pdr. (42nd) comes in to-night.—Leech.

6.  42nd **Battery** (forward section) sends a gun to J.1.d.1.4.*
7.  53rd **Battery** (main position) sends a gun to I.5. central.*
8.  Standing Orders for all Anti-Tank Guns.
    (i)   Stand To at dawn when the Infantry do and report
          to nearest Infantry Officer.
    (ii)  100 A.X. 'non-delay' for use against tanks.
          100 A. for use against infantry.
    (iii) Nobody to show himself near the gun during good
          visibility.  Practice (including gas-masks) at dawn
          and dusk.
    (iv)  N.C.O. i/c to have a panorama showing ranges.
    (v)   Copy of these standing orders to be up in gun-pit.
    (vi)  Boards showing ranges by hundreds of yards to be
          put out in various required directions.
    (vii) One rifle and 50 rounds per man to be kept in pit.
    (viii) The gun to be silent except in case of actual attack.
          Gun always to be fired 'direct laying' over open
          sights or through the telescopic sights or the
          rocking bar.
          First target Tanks (H.E. non-delay).
          Tanks will be engaged even at the risk of hitting
          our own infantry.
    (ix)  Should it be impossible to continue fighting the gun
          for some such reason as damage to the piece or no
          more ammunition the N.C.O. i/c detachment will
          take breech-block away with him, damage the
          screw head, and smash the buffer with a pick-axe.

*March 12th, 1918.*

*Appendix VI to Morchies Group Defence Scheme.*

1.  In the event of CPN/B (xxx).
    (a)  42nd Battery engage the hollow between The Nest
         and the enemy front line in D.15.b. with 4 guns, and
         the front line in D.15.b. with the remaining two.  The
         four guns will use 106 fuze.  (xxxa).
    (b)  53rd Battery will engage the hollow in D.14.d. as far
         East as the Copse in D. 15. c. with 4 guns.
         Remaining 2 guns enemy front line D.15.a.
    (c)  87th Battery—
         2 guns in hollow D.14.d. (106 fuze of available).
         2 guns search road Nest—D.14.b.5.1.
         2 guns enfilade trench D.14.c.6.6.—D.14.b.5.1.
2.  (xxxb) Should the enemy obtain a footing in our line there
    will be two concentrations :—

*Concentration Lion.*
    42nd Battery D.27.a.28.30—D.27.a.10.56.
    53rd Battery D.27.a.10.56—D.26.b.93.83.

---

* In case of tank attack.

87th Battery Sunken road Lynx-Support inclusive to D.20.d. 85.30. and the trenches about Lion Post (D.21.c.10.17).

Nos. 16, 17, 18 M.T.M's. can join in this concentration.

*Concentration Leopard.*

42nd Battery search valley about D.19.d.9.9.

53rd Battery search low ground about D.19.b.

87th Battery on trenches in neighbourhood according to situation.

Nos. 7 and 8 M.T.M's. can join in this concentration.

*March 12th, 1918.*

*Appendix VII to Morchies Group Defence Scheme*

Ammunition Orders.   (xxxi).

1.  Echelons to be kept full.
2.  Batteries in action :—

    18-pdrs. 200 rounds per gun in pits.
    
    | | 300 | ,, | ,, | in vicinity. |
    |---|---|---|---|---|
    | | 100 | ,, | ,, | A.R.P. |
    | 4·5″ Hows. | 130 | ,, | ,, | in pits. |
    | | 200 | ,, | ,, | in vicinity. |
    | | 70 | ,, | ,, | A.R.P. |
    | | 20 | ,, | ,, | lachrymatory. |
    | | 30 | ,, | ,, | lethal (in small dumps apart). |

3.  Rearward positions :—
    (i)  R 1 and R 3 Brigades (Red) Positions 500 rounds per gun 18-pdr. and 400 rounds per gun 4·5″ H.
    (ii)  R 3 Brigade (Brown Positions 124-127) 250 rounds per gun 18-pdr. and 200 rounds per gun 4·5″ H.
    (iii)  At Positions 106 and 118 ; 400 and 200 rounds smoke shell respectively.
4.  Proportions.
    Guns with range under 4000ˣ 50% shrapnel, 25% H.E. delay, 25% non-delay.
    Guns with over 4000ˣ 40% shrapnel, 110% H.E. non-delay, 50% 106.
    4·5″ 75% 106 (when available) 25% H.E. non-delay.
5.  Empties, clips, fuze-covers to be collected and returned. (Only 10% wastage allowed.)
    Empty cartridge cases to be packed in empty boxes.
    At reserve positions, ammunition to remain boxed.
6.  Heavy T.M's 100 rounds per mortar.
    Medium T.M's active 200 rounds per mortar (9,10,11).
    100 rounds per mortar (7,8,16,17,18).
7.  When light railway is used :—
    Groups notify Staff-Captain, place, time, number, and nature.
    Staff-Captain demands trucks.
    Batteries supply guides at the Dump and unloading parties at battery end.

# MAP No. 3.

See Appendix I, Morchies Group Defence Scheme.

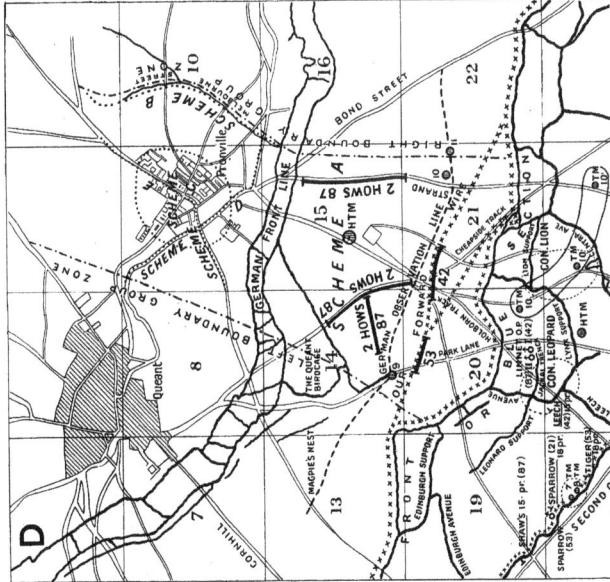

Best O.P.'s
GERMAN POSITIONS.

I.7.a.3/8 looking S.E.
I.18.a.5/9 looking N.E.
I.14.a.6/6 looking N.W.

Suggested Brigade Headquarters 2 and R I in Favreuil.

# MAP No. 1. $\frac{1}{20,000}$

See Appendices III, IV, V, and VI, Morchies Group Defence Scheme.

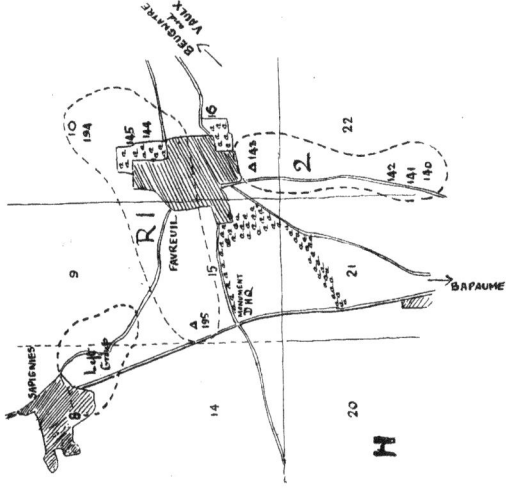

Quick unloading is an essential feature of railway supply.

8. Dump is Harrogate Dump I.l.d. central, or some spot on Decauville Railway in case of shelling.

In the case of withdrawal :—

    (i)   The Corps Dump is in Favreuil Wood.

    (ii)  D.A.C. will establish a dump at H.22.a. central.

    (iii) Dumps will be established on the following roads :—

          Sapnigies—Bihucourt H.7.a.

          Grevillers—Bihucourt G.23.

          Thilloy—Bapaume N.2.a.

    (iv)  D.A.C. will probably be at Thilloy.

*March 12th, 1918.*

## CHAPTER III.

### A Discussion of the Defence Scheme.

(i). *General.* The foregoing Scheme may be interesting to future generations as showing the functions of a Group Commander R.F.A. in 1918; when one considers that it was only subsidiary to a much longer scheme, it will almost certainly be interesting as showing the pitch to which 'control' had got. After all, a Defence Scheme is but a confirmation of verbal instructions; it gathers in a concise form the hundred and one orders which would otherwise be on a hundred and one separate sheets of paper; it is a sort of Standing Orders for Group Area, and it is libellous to suggest that one *raison d'etre* of Defence Scheme is 'against the Court of Enquiry.' But there is the old problem of the horse and the water—one can hand to an individual his very own copy of the scheme, but one cannot make him read it; 'Journalism is unreadable; literature is not read' sayeth the Wit. Anyway we all had defence schemes of one kind or another, and there are many points in this one which afford opportunity for discussion.

(ii). *Observation* Not contained in this early edition of Appendix II, but which appeared in later issues[1], there existed an order that F.O.O's or Liaison Officers who found themselves out of communication with their batteries or brigade, were to make their way back to the nearest point on the 'bury' and report. In practice it seemed never to be realised that a F.O.O. out of communication is an officer wasted. On 21st March both the 'Linnet' F.O.O's were captured in the O.P. after several hours useless waiting in the dug-out; the F.O.O. at 'Sparrow' rightly returned to his battery when he could do no more good where he was. An opinion was not uncommonly held that young officers attending courses should have received more detailed instruction in the combined duties[2] of a F.O.O.; it was not until one had studied Section 5 of the First Army Artillery 'Catechism for R.F.A. Subalterns' that one realised what the full duties of a F.O.O. are; yet this same section (the pamphlet was issued in 1917)

---

[1] See July Scheme, Part II., Chapter VI.

[2] Observation, Ranging, Signalling, Intelligence and Liaison.

B

contemplated an advanced form of a centralised Control and was inapplicable to the war of movement. F.O.O's in trench warfare often sat for 24 hours in one single unsafe, insanitary, and uncomfortable, spot; in a moving battle, where the one great difficulty is to produce *timely* fire, they must move about to collect information; *they should be accompanied by a N.C.O. as deputy F.O.O.*; it is good training for the N.C.O. and gives the officer valuable liberty. The strength of an O.P. party would therefore become one officer, one N.C.O., and two signallers; they need a Lucas Lamp for visual as an alternative to the telephone; they should all be armed, and it has been suggested that on occasions a Lewis Gun would be well employed there.

(iii). *Liaison is an exchange of favours in which each side hopes to gain something for itself.* To perform liaison work efficiently an officer must be known to the people he is liaising with and either personally liked or professionally respected; in 24 hours a strange officer can scarcely make himself felt; 96 hours is better, but the absence of one officer from a battery for 96 hours is often very inconvenient; 48 hours was a compromise.

(iv). The battalions were close together, connected by a good trench, and officers fit to perform liaison were scarce, what with leave, courses, horses, etc. It was a standing Order in the Brigade that no Subaltern did liaison until passed for this duty by the Brigade Commander; to send an insufficiently trained officer does more harm than good; the officer must have *authority*, which is *based* in the first instance *on knowledge*[1]—good artillery knowledge and a smattering of general military knowledge. The system of liaison which grew up with trench warfare had taught the infantry to expect artillery support of a kind impossible in the war of movement, but it taught them also a good deal about artillery, so that in the end it was 'good value.' But the same remark applies to liaison officers as to F.O.O's; once out of communication with the artillery they are useless, and can do better work by personal report to the battery or artillery brigade than by remaining at infantry headquarters. This was not at that time understood; of the two liaison officers on duty on 21st March, one was hit trying to fight an anti-tank gun, and one commanding a company; a liaison officer was captured on 23rd (long after communication was broken) with a battalion headquarters; a liaison officer was wounded on 24th bringing forward a machine gun. None of these four were doing any direct good as a liaison officer.

The period on liaison was often most uncomfortable, accommodation at infantry headquarters being invariably short. A liaison officer generally needs his batman; he may or may not require a couple of signallers with telephones and a lamp, according to circumstances.

(v). *Visual.* No mention is made in this part of the Defence Scheme of Visual, but a visual scheme had been arranged and carefully practised from the February headquarters; the change of headquarters and battery positions in the middle of March, however,

---

[1] Major-General Uniacke, in his address to Young Officers (Journal of the Royal Artillery, May 1919), put great stress on the duty of knowledge.

rendered this scheme null and void; a new scheme was made out, but had not yet been sufficiently practised. Visual needs continual practice, not only general practice of personnel, but detailed practice of the scheme; it often goes well enough on a quiet day, but weather conditions have a great effect—shells even greater; in a prepared visual scheme, the visual stations need the most exact siting, camouflage, *and fortification*; the enemy bombardment was well enough distributed on 21st March to interfere with visual even without a mist; the mist effectively prevented it until well after 09.00.

(vi) & (vii). *Telephonic communication.* It will be seen that 'the Bury' was only in its infancy; a most ambitious scheme existed as a 'pious hope', on the basis of which good artillery communications could later have been organised. It has been said that a man promises according to his hopes but performs according to his fears. It appears to the writer beyond doubt that, to ensure control of fire and thence a proper artillery defence, the importance of buried communications was not appreciated in high places. It is contended that the labour used on the construction of rearward positions, some of which were really worse than useless (see para. xv), would have been better employed on 'buries'—an opinion stoutly put forward at the time; presumably it was not beyond hope to beat off the enemy without any withdrawal? There was hardly any communication on 21st, except by runners, who had a rough passage and much exercise.

(viii). *Heavy Artillery.* We come to the controversial question of co-operation between the Heavy and Field Artillery. In the Third Army, the Heavy Artillery was decentralised and liaison existed between the two branches; there was a direct line from Right Group Headquarters to 90th Brigade, R.G.A., and fire arrangements to meet circumstances were commonly made with the Infantry Brigadier by the Right Group Commander for both branches. In addition, all sorts of minor liaison was put into force with various batteries of 90th Brigade, R.G.A., whose commanders placed themselves at the disposal of Right Group Commander after communications gave out on 21st March. All this was the result of personal, not official, arrangements. Later on, in another Army, a different state of affairs existed; it was actually necessary for the Infantry Brigadier to deal with two Artillery Commanders—an unsatisfactory condition of things. To *prevent* that condition seems to point to amalgamation of the branches, or training together in peace, or the inclusion of a larger F.A. group of a few such weapons as 60-pdrs. and 6″ Hows.

(ix). *Rearward Positions.* See para. (xv) where question is fully discussed.

(x) *Anti-Tank Defence.* See para. (xxix).

(xi). *Wagon-Lines.* In peace time, we had been trained for open warfare, and to regard the battery as an indivisible entity, but the long range of the German guns had necessitated the horses being accommodated many miles behind the gun position, and it gradually became a habit of mind to consider an artillery unit as consisting of two echelons—the 'gun-line' and the 'wagon-line.' The latter was generally run by the Captain, B.S.M. and B.Q.M.S.; many batteries located their 'offices' there; they were often used as rest houses. This was well enough for trench warfare, but it proved necessary to modify the custom for a war of movement. An artillery brigade generally had an air-line to one office in the wagon-lines, otherwise communication was entirely by orderly; to save time, D.A. often sent orders to the wagon lines direct, which orders were not always repeated to the gun-line; it happened more than once that the B.C. found his wagon-line gone 'into the blue.' Gun-lines in a war of movement shift as tactics demand and the wagon-lines might not know of the move for some time, unless careful arrangements are made. In a war of position the guns get their ammunition from a dump beside the guns which is replenished by its wagon-line or by rail[1] from the Divisional Dump which was run by the D.A.C. or from even further back; in a war of movement there can be no dumping and the supply in the battle area is mobile, which means that the batteries must have their firing battery wagons close to, or with, them. The wagon-lines supply also rations, stores, etc. Already at Cambrai, mistakes had been made—hence this note in the Defence Scheme; but no amount of foresight can prevent things sometimes going wrong, especially when there is heavy shelling about, and it is not too much to say that the efficiency of a whole group (three or more Brigades, R.F.A.) was impaired by the failure of a brigade-staff wagon line to keep touch with Group Headquarters during the later stages of the March fighting. A brigade commander in a moving battle really needs a special brigade representative[2] at the wagon-lines, but it is not desirable to arrogate or to centralise too much.

(xii) *Enemy Aircraft.* The order to detail one gun per battery to deal with low-flying aeroplanes came from above; it was once practised, not without success; it necessitated certain alterations to the gun-pits.

(xiii). *Counter-preparation.* 'Counter-preparation A' was a sort of S.O.S. the target being the enemy's front trenches instead of on No Man's Land. 'Counter-preparation B' was the commonest form of 'C.P.N', the targets being selected portions of the enemy's forward area, on a regular fire-time-table. 'Counter-preparation C' was against the enemy's rearward area. 'CPN' was designed of course, to catch the enemy during or after assembly, but before the assault; it had become a recognised form of bombardment, having been initiated on our side during 1917, so far as the writer knows. 'Silent' (as well as 'active') positions were used for this; of course, if the alarm was false, there was a danger that the 'silent position' would be given away, and for that reason Counter-preparation was not to be put in force without orders from higher authority, *so long as the communications were holding.* It appears to afford great opportunity for the use of gas-shells.

---

[1] The supply of ammunition by light railway is a tricky thing; it needs good staff arrangements, a thorough understanding of the rules by the troops, and often considerable determination on the part of the railway personnel.

[2] Consider March 23—withdrawal of transport behind the railway—Chapter VII.

(xiv). *Harassing fire.* Night firing had not in March 1918 reached the pitch of organisation that succeeded the German offensive; after the capture of Mount Kemmel in April, it is supposed to have been the constant harassing in the salient created by the enemy for himself between Bethune, Hazebrouck, and Dickebusch, which eventually influenced Prince Rupprecht of Bavaria against a renewed offensive, until the enemy failure about Rheims made such a move impossible.

(xv). *Rearward Positions.* We come to the question of Rear-ward Positions :—

(a) It will be noticed that two reinforcing brigades were allowed for in this scheme; roughly, therefore, there were 12 positions to be prepared for the defence of each of the 4 systems, or a total of 48, including the three actually occupied by 42nd, 53rd, and 87th batteries.

(b). As regards the positions for the defence of the First (Blue) System, it was believed to be understood that forward sections would join the main positions in case of necessity,[1] but most people had realised that, unless the move was completed *before the assault started*, these forward sections might not be able to get away—in any case they would probably join up with their batteries at the positions for the defence of the Second (Red) System, if not still further back. We shall see what happened; the Defence Scheme was not too clear on this point.

(c). It will be seen that the positions had been grouped on a linear basis, as if at a given moment the whole infantry line would withdraw from any one line to the next. This was obviously wrong and so it turned out; on the evening of the 22nd we held the Brown Line in some parts and the Green Line in others; the Artillery were chiefly in the Green Line positions (by order from superior authority) and too far away to meet the tactical situation. The solution is that rearward artillery positions must be sited *in depth*[2] if it is to meet whatever tactical conditions obtain at the time. In 'the Salient' in April and May this was done; an immense amount of reconnaissance[3] had to be carried out, and automatically *all responsible people became acquainted with the rearward areas, which is the one essential.* It must be added that, owing to insufficient liaison between Heavy and Field Artillery, cases frequently occurred of heavy and field batteries selecting the same positions unbeknownst to one another. Care must be taken not to site rearward positions with obstacles behind them.

(d). The January instructions were particular about the pre-paration of O.P's in depth, and, obediently to orders, all the O.P's mentioned in Appendix I were prepared, but of course without com-munications.

---

[1] Except that the 87th Howitzer Battery, which was to go to Position 118 (behind the main battery position).

[2] See figure, sub-para (e) below.

[3] A custom exists in the French Artillery by which officers who have recon-noited Artillery Positions fill in a printed "Carnet de tir" for that position, which is filed for future reference.

(e)  For rearward positions what digging is necessary?  A position can be over-dug—difficult to enter and still more difficult to vacate. A battery commander forced to withdraw will almost certainly make for a rearward position which he has dug, even if this position is not well suited to the new tactical situation which had arisen; and the tactical situation is seldom understood before midnight.  The order of priority of work was constantly being changed, but whatever it was at the moment, the authorities expected to *see* 'work' and therefore stress was laid on artillery entrenchments.  For every rearward position a fighting map was prepared, but did ever a map reach a battery in time to be used?  It was at last decided to fill these positions with ammunition, see Appendix VII, para. 3 of the Defence Scheme and this was done.

On the 20th March work, the progress was as follows :—

    Red Line

    Blue Line     Positions occupied or ready.

Brown Line positions—rough shelter for brigade or battery head-quarters, gun-platforms sited, with ammunition stacked in shallow pits.

Green line positions marked only.

O.P.'s all constructed for use by F.O.O. and telephonist; no communications.

Ammunition placed in accordance with orders

Fighting Maps still in possession of Survey Company.

The preparation was not complete, but we were certainly approaching the condition of 'having a splendid future behind us.'

It is contended that the following is a better order of priority :—

(1)  Positions sited, Brigades distributed in depth :—

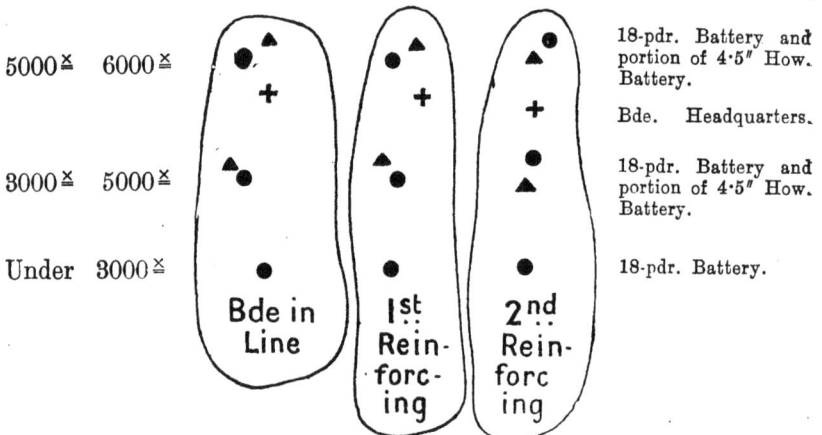

| | | | |
|---|---|---|---|
| 5000 ✕   6000 ✕ | Bde in Line | 1st Reinforcing | 2nd Reinforcing |

18-pdr. Battery and portion of 4·5″ How. Battery.

Bde. Headquarters.

18-pdr. Battery and portion of 4·5″ How. Battery.

18-pdr. Battery.

3000 ✕   5000 ✕

Under   3000 ✕

Group Headquarters wherever Infantry Brigade is.

With Group Positions (Brown, Green, etc.) behind one another at 1000 ✕—3000 ✕ distance there would be positions to suit *any* tactical situation.

Positions *must* be known to both gun and *wagon-line* personnel.

(2). O.P's sited, not too far from positions, capable for use not only for defence but *for support of possible counter-attack.* Visual station (fortified) from O.P. to some place near Brigade Head-quarters. One O.P. per Brigade, with simple trench and covered approach.

(3) Group Headquarters fixed[1] and communications prepared beginning from top downwards. Plan of communications, at any rate, worked out in detail and known to all; *telephone wire stored* at Group, Brigade, and Battery Headquarters—it is always short in a moving battle.

(4). A rough shelter in which a Commander can lay out his maps at once; stored in this shelter a fighting map; brigade head-quarters to be in a more advanced state of preparation than battery ditto, as there is no labour available after occupation.

(5). The question of ammunition depends on circumstances; by far the larger portion of that stored was never touched and some was to be found there on our return in the Autumn! Where good liaison exists between gun-line and wagon-lines, storage of ammunition is not absolutely necessary.

(6) Hardly any construction of gun positions is necessary and is indeed inadvisable, unless it can be properly camouflaged.

(7). A 'Rearward Area Bury' in the II Army area was of inestimable value, but a F.A. Group cannot initiate so big a task.

(f). The question of labour is difficult; the battery has two sources of supply—gun-line and wagon-line; the claims upon battery labour are endless, much of it unfortunately connected with things of no material importance in a time of stress. Decentralisation of responsibility for work is valuable to a point; possibly it may be best to go as far down as batteries, but where the matter is urgent as in February and March and decisions as to priority[2] are necessary, the best arrangement is probably brigade working parties under an officer specially told off and free from other duties; the question is one of circumstances, but labour will certainly be hard to find what with leave, hospital, and courses, and assistance must be given by the D.A.C. In a war of movement the B.A.C. is preferable to a D.A.C., one of the advantages being that the Brigade Commander has a reserve of labour which otherwise is non-existent. The work on hand in March included the re-distribution of the forward positions, the construction of rearward positions, and the protection of the wagon-lines against bombing![3]

(xvi). *Standing Orders.* Gun-pit Standing Orders were unknown to our pre-war artillery. In imitation of the gallant Cavalier,

---

[1] For this we must depend on the Infantry.

[2] Decisions of importance such as between communications (affecting the fight in the battle zone) and rearward excavations (in expectation of withdrawal) must originate from the general staff.

[3] Quite a different set of authorities threatened the unfortunate regimental officer over this last mentioned question. We had actually been ordered to provide a *six-foot wall* round standings.

we 'fired and drove away'; every individual was a professional artillery-man. At the period here under discussion, we were auctioneers, acrobats, or policemen interested in polo or philately perhaps, but seldom in ballistics; yet the sorting of ammunition was a life-study in itself! A man's reputation depended on his knowledge of the meteor and the latest modification to the outpost line. In each different Corps or Army, some special fancy of a Chieftain entailed some special rule within the gun-pit; the unpardonable sin varied from being seen without a steel helmet to growing oats within the limber boxes; officers and men changed nearly every day. The later stages of Cambrai had taught us that even in a war of movement there is still a S.O.S. Line, there are still concentration schemes, aiming posts still blow down, sights still need daily checking, the meteor to be considered, rocket indicators to be put up, ammunition to be sorted, etc. Appendix II was the first time that a set of standing orders were attached to a defence scheme in 2nd Bde. R.F.A.; later in the year it was much elaborated. The more widely these standing orders are known and drilled into the detach-ments, the more rapidly a battery becomes efficient after change of position. The next Field Artillery Manual may contain a chapter on Trench Warfare, under which it is to be hoped there will be grouped a set of simple gun-pit rules; for purposes of gunnery and efficient support of the infantry, there is no difference whatever between the elaborately emplaced gun and the weapon dumped during a moving battle among the ruins of a roadside cottage.

(xvia). *Gun History Sheets.* The procedure as regards gun history sheets was not well carried out; in most cases there existed no such sheets; where they existed they were often kept with the office papers instead of with the guns. If the case on the gun can be made waterproof, it is obviously the place for the sheet.

(xvii). *Silent Positions.* The question of 'silent positions' has been already discussed at some length in Chapter I. The essence of their existence is that they are not known to the enemy. They must not therefore be registered from, nor used[1] except during a general bombardment; nor must they be recognisable on an air-photograph. Unless they fulfil these conditions they are useless and should be 'active' or unoccupied in which case the personnel could rest and train. It is to be feared that a large number of positions sur-named 'silent' in February and March failed to fulfil these conditions. Where camouflage is easy such as in a 'close' country, the permanent occupation of silent positions may do no harm; where it is practically impossible, some other device for concealing artillery must be dis-covered. Immediately before an *offensive* the time is short and the enemy has not time to note much more than that artillery reinforce-ments have made their appearance; but on the *defensive*, one may have

---

[1] Never firing from a position tends to make detachments slack and lends itself to "showing-off." Change of detachments is the remedy for the former, within limits there are advantages in the latter.

to wait weeks or months, and the solution appears to be a series of alternative positions into which one can move if the defenders have the luck to get warning of an attack (as at Rheims in July). Alternative positions can be occupied from the wagon-lines as well as from other positions, and personnel might be better employed at rest and training than in occupying gun-pits which they dare not use.

The desiderata of a 'silent' defensive gun-position, if otherwise tactically and technically suitable are :—

(a). Its *not* being *known to the enemy* : subject to this proviso, it should be as strong as possible.

(b). First-class communications.

(c). Gas-proof shelter in the neighbourhood.

(d). Facility of exit.

(xviii). *Exit from positions.* The importance of facility of exit varies with circumstances dependent on the special task of the battery, but a gun should not take more than a very few minutes to pull out. This was unavoidable on the Passchendaele Ridge, owing to the broken nature of the ground. Normally batteries get some time to move; in a very rapid withdrawal a gun fought up to the moment of its capture probably performs a duty of the highest importance, even if the incident finds no recognition in the Honours List

(xix). *Rockets and Rocket Indicator.* Battalion Headquarters was the place where S.O.S. rockets were to be looked for; rockets[1] had recently been much improved and were now easily distinguished. The rocket-indicator was the night sentry's post—it is necessary to fix some such post, as a F.G.C.M. refused to convict a man as absent from his post when found dozing in a dug-out.

(xx). *Registration within our own lines.* The Germans used to register their front line intentionally, as well as occasionally dropping a 'short' there. Just previous to the March offensive, the Right Group registered all its T.M's with dummy rounds on points within our own lines.

(xxi). *Storing of Ammunition.* A selection from orders by various higher authorities.

(xxii). *Dawn and alarm arrangements.* 'Dawn' was determined by the Infantry Brigade in the Line. If the alarm arrangements are good, two men per gun is enough; men thus accommodated have to be very much on the alert as regards gas. The dug-outs were often some distance from the position, a condition which offers advantages.

---

[1] It was commonly thought that light signals might have been more freely employed than they were for co-operation between infantry and artillery in the war of movement; the French wrote much about them and certainly the German artillery seemed able to co-ordinate its fire with its infantry "Here-we-are-again" white-lights. But rockets are apt to be unsatisfactory; as a raid commander once reported, "this rocket was an exception, it actually did go off, but along the trench instead of up in the air". The man carrying light signals in an attack seems always to get hit.

(xxiii). *Battle-stations.* The 'battle-station'' table dealt with Lewis guns, rifles, the duties of cooks, officer's servants, etc., it included a scheme for the close defence of the actual position.

'Battle-stations' was the code word used as a warning of attack.

(xxiv). *Wiring-in gun-positions.* The question of wiring in positions was a very controversial one and arose after the German break-through near Lagnicourt in April 1917. The authorities wanted wire round every gun position to help the close defence. It can be fairly argued that an attacking force which has broken through the bigger wire obstacles will not be stopped by a few strands round a gun position; but later an idea grew up which contemplated gun-positions as independent strong-points and even provided special troops for their defence; this is quite another matter. Some battery commanders[1] liked wire round their positions to keep intruders off, but one photo appeared showing a 6″ gun position within a sea of tracks—an example of the mask telling more than the face. The Germans, faced with this same problem, solved it by having one special belt of wire in front of which artillery was not to be emplaced; it was known as the Artillery Protective Line. Now-a-days such a line must be tank proof.

(xxv). *Visual.* See para. (v).

(xxvi). *Furniture of O.P.* This list of stores with which O.P's were to be furnished was copied from an order by higher authority. It gives some idea of the multifarious duties of a F.O.O., see para. (ii); but in practice it was almost impossible to get this order carried out, however correct in theory. A 'Beware Notice' was simply a printed notice 'Beware! the enemy can hear you.' Particularly difficult was it to make officers realise the difference between a diary (which is not mentioned here, as it was considered the property of the officer who has to write the daily report) and the so-called 'log-book' (which belongs to the O.P., and contains only items of permanent interest). In one Army the O.P. stores ordered to be maintained were so numerous that they required a good-sized inventory board! It is very uncertain whether the ordinary F.O.O. observed any better for all this regulation.

Still some furniture is necessary, and once the order is marked up by a commander 'This is an order to be obeyed,' battery O.P's are not difficult to administer. When, however, it is a case of a Group O.P. or Brigade O.P., the question is different; the Group or Brigade can provide the furniture, but no power on earth can prevent its disappearance and see to the proper handing over of stores to succeeding F.O.O's. This question again crops up when it becomes a question of fortifying O.P's; the process is often a dangerous one only to be done at night; one cannot keep a Brigade Staff officer at it continually, while work handed over to a different officer every night usually ends in nothing being done.

---

[1] Another battery commander hoped to hide the work on his gun-pits by directing a public track right across his position.

The Pointer was to report lateral angles from True North of flashes, etc., for the benefit of the Heavy Artillery.

It must be remembered that every battery had a forward or active position, whence the F.O.O. obtained his normal fire, and a main or silent position, his main fire-power in battle—different ranges, angles, etc.

(xxvii). *Harassing-fire Schemes.* One has to vary these prepared schemes from time to time, the advantage of them being that one has time to reason out the selection of targets; also they save an immense amount of trouble in the nightly harassing-fire wire, but of course it means more defence papers in the battery defence-file.

(xxviia). *German foremost trench.* The German 'observation line' lay at varying distances in front of their Front Line; it was usually manned only at night—by a few picquets which frequently changed stations.

(xxviii). *Trench Mortars.* No Man's Land was so wide that trench mortars could not fire on the enemy's front line; in the Right Group area they were divided into 4 groups :—

(a). One Heavy T.M. (9·45″) with a S.O.S. point in No Man's Land.

(b). Three 6″ T.M.'s. (Nos. 9, 10, 11) ditto.

(c). Two ditto (Nos. 7 and 8) emplaced to meet a break through in the Right Battalion area.

(d). Three ditto 16, 17, 18 ditto Left Battalion area.

Nos. 7, 8, 16, 17, 18 had been registered (in foggy weather) by means of dummy rounds.

The range of T.M's had been much increased during 1917 with the arrival of the new 9·45″ and 6″ (Newton pattern) but the equipment left something to desire. One could not trust the 6″, for after a few rounds the stays connecting the mortar to its bed were apt to break away. The T.M. took a considerable time, over a minute at least, to prepare for firing; one could not keep it ready to fire because the charge if exposed to the air deteriorated—hence para. 11 of Appendix IV. These were the most important defects, but the equipment was 'rough.'

It is not necessary here to review the history of T.M's, but it was well on in 1915 before they became standardised. The first D.T.M.O. was appointed early in 1916. The H.T.M. appeared rather later, but before the Somme, as did also the light (3″) Stokes Mortar. Perhaps it might be said of the 9.45″ *in defence*, as of a certain statesman, that his dignity lay in his ruff rather than his reason. The Stokes Mortar was manned by infantry; the Medium by infantry and artillery, but by this time they had practically become Field Artillery[1] weapons; the H.T.M. was usually manned by Heavy Artillery per-

---

[1] The provision of F.A. personnel seemed to present difficulty to the higher authorities; it proved rather a drain on the batteries and the T.M. batteries were apt to suffer from the system adopted.

sonnel, and in February, 1918, H.T.M's had become part of the Corps Heavy Artillery.

Controversy reigned for some time as to who should 'run' the Heavy and Medium T.M's. One school said it should be done by the Divisional General Staff, the basis of their argument being that they were emplaced in the trenches amongst the infantry, that they were employed exclusively against the enemy infantry area, and that infantry had practically always to carry up the ammunition. The other school said that much of the modern artillery bombardment was done by heavy and medium T.M's, and that therefore they should be under the C.R.A.; also that the methods of the T.M. were of an artillery nature. What decided the matter seems to have been that unless the C.R.A. ran them, they were never employed at all, because they induced 'retaliation' by the enemy, to which the infantry were naturally averse. However that may be, in 1918, while a light 3″ was run entirely by the Infantry Brigade, the Heavy and Medium was run by the Field Artillery Group Commander; this took the Group Commander out of his area for at least two whole days every week, for he had to arrange details of every kind with the battalion; one cannot but add that such an arrangement automatically brought the Group Commander more than ever in touch with the Infantry.

Appendix IV of the Defence Scheme gives a good idea of the stage of development in March, 1918; but centralised control of T.M's means as in all other cases a careful system of communications, which was very far from being obtained, as higher authority was obstinate regarding provision of telephones and wire for T.M's, probably owing to lack of telephone material.

The idea of mobile T.M's was still but a 'pious hope'; the enemy gave us a lesson in March which we began to develop in the '100 Days' Battle.'

One H.T.M. (manned by Heavy Artillery) was attached to the Right Group. Nos. 7, 8, 9, 10 and 11, were manned by Y/6 T.M. Battery; Nos. 16, 17 and 18 were manned by the personnel[1] of the 25th Divisional T.M's and attached to the Right Group. O.C. Y/6 T.M.B. acted as controller of T.M's in Right Group, though he was not the officer mentioned in para. 1, Appendix IV on the night before the battle. The D.T.M.O. (an infantry officer) lived with C.R.A.

The mortars were well accommodated, with good dug-outs, and their emplacements were (it is believed) quite unknown to the enemy, as they were 'silent' *and had never been given away*; Nos. 16, 17, and 18 were newly emplaced and were only just ready.

(xxix). *Anti-Tank Defence.* The Divisional Defence Scheme contemplated three echelons of Anti-Tank Defence—(a) guns sited to meet the first appearance of enemy tanks (b)[2] guns detailed and prepared for dragging out of their pits should the tanks get through,

---

[1] And very gallant work did they do, see Chapter V.
[2] In practice, there is not the time to do this.

(c) a battery of the Reserve Divisional Artillery detailed to move out of its billets against tanks. The argument was that our wire was so good that we could stop any *sudden* assault unless supported by enemy tanks.

The siting of the guns emplaced to meet the first appearance of enemy tanks was most difficult. To begin with, there was absolutely no natural cover, so that one had to hide them in the trench system; secondly, in order to meet the tanks early, one had to place them very far forward, owing to the shape of the ground. As a consequence of these conditions, the 'anti-tanks' were almost certain to be caught by an enemy preliminary bombardment.

It will be noticed from Appendix V that there were five guns so emplaced :—

No. 1 deprived 42nd Battery of a detachment.

No. 2 deprived 42nd Battery of a detachment.

No. 3 deprived 53rd Battery of an 18-pr. and a detachment.

No. 4 deprived 21st Battery (Left Group) of an 18-pr. and detachment.

No. 5 deprived 87th Battery of a detachment.

An already slight artillery support was therefore weakened by the separation of one 18-pdr. and 4 detachments. It will be seen that all the guns were either destroyed by the enemy's fire or eventually captured; only a very few of the men got back to their batteries. *But*, the enemy used no tanks; another time he may and probably will; the problem of how to deal with them is a very real one and must be mastered.

(xxx). *Counter-preparation.* See para (xiii).

(xxxa). Batteries sited at over 5000$^{\underline{x}}$ from their S.O.S. Barrage Line had some of the new 106-fuzed 18-pr.

(xxxb). *'Concentrations' against a break through.* Owing to the failure of communications during the battle, it was never possible to put these (or any other) concentrations into force in the Right Group Area.

(xxxi). *Ammunition.* Appendix VII was an attempt to summarise in a convenient form a variety of orders by a variety of authorities; different ideas obtained in different areas.

It may be remarked that very little gas was available.

The supply by rail was not a success (in this area).

(xxxii). *Maps.* Map No. 1 attached to the Defence Scheme illustrated Appendices III (Harassing fire), IV (T.M's), V (Anti-Tank Defence), and VI (CPN). Maps Nos. 2 and 3 illustrated the organisation of Rearward Positions. No. 2 is not forthcoming, but No. 3 is given and No. 2 was very similar—No. 3 shows very well the *linear* grouping as opposed to the grouping in depth, as suggested in para. (xv, c, d, e) of this chapter.

A word about such sketch-maps; they are labour-saving, and indeed in the later stages of the war the 'barrage map' was the essential part of the orders for a battery commander. To make these maps, units need draughtsmen, at least 1 per artillery brigade, as well as any allowed to D.A. Headquarters.[1]

(xxxiii). *Lewis Guns.* A Lewis Gun had just been issued to each battery, originally for anti-aircraft work. No mention of them occurs in the Defence Scheme, but their employment was considered in the 'Battle Station Table.' Later, each battery got 4 and the 'standing orders' included a ruling as to their distribution, of which mention is made in Part II, Chapter VI.

(xxxiv). *Width of Front.* It will be seen that, excluding anti-tank guns, a group of (at the most) 11 18-pdrs. and 6 4·5″ Hows. were supporting an infantry brigade of three battalions. Say, 17 field guns to 2,400 bayonets.

The actual S.O.S. barrage contemplated 11 18-pdrs. over a front of 2400 yards, i.e., 220 yards per gun; in an offensive an 18-pdr. generally had a barrage front of 20-25 yards.[2]

In addition it must be mentioned that the lateral effect of the new 106 fuze had been over-estimated; a 6″ howitzer (of which there were a good many) covered 200 yards, whereas 50 yards would have been a more correct allotment.

(xxxv). *S.O.S. Policy.* The defence schemes of the time ordered, so far as can be remembered, 10 minutes 'intense' in case of S.O.S.; there may have been certain extra instructions—but the optimism of the authorities contemplated ability to act according to circumstances, without however taking the necessary steps to ensure communication. Of one thing one may be certain—and that is that communication in the forward area during the hours following an enemy assault will be, at the best, trying to the impatient; unless lines are buried, there will be no communication except by runner. Owing to casualties and to the stress of the moment, there are no proper records of what targets were engaged by batteries on March 21st after the S.O.S. period was completed and in the absence of orders from Group Headquarters (owing to break down of communication). In the mist not a soul knew what had happened, and no amount of personal reconnaissance could have led to brilliant independent action until the day was well advanced; that is to say, 'action according to circumstances' was out of the question.

That this particular lesson reached home is evident from the fact that in July a new S.O.S. policy was initiated from above. Units were to remain firing on their own S.O.S. lines until otherwise ordered, and it was (normally) only a very high authority who could 'otherwise order.' The idea was, of course, that even if your S.O.S. has failed to stop the enemy advanced troops, the latter cannot get on without their support, who will be unable or unwilling to pass the continued S.O.S. barrage. It seems curious that we were not better

---

[1] *A battery should mobilize* with a proportion of tradesmen—tailor, shoemaker, clerk, draughtsman, a few miners.

[2] Ludendorff says that on March 21st the Germans had more than one gun to every ten yards.

guided in this matter, for the complaint in so many of our own offensives had been that our leading infantry waves got through but that later waves were caught by the enemy barrage and that the leaders being unsupported failed to make good.   Just as, in the offensive, artillery sub-commanders had the right to take certain batteries out of the barrage for special purposes, so, according to these July instructions, certain artillery units were told off as 'swingers,' whose fire could reinforce the S.O.S. barrage wherever the enemy's advanced troops had effected successful penetration. But in March, 1918, we had 'not got so far'—at least most of us; our energy was absorbed in making somewhat flashy excavations in the rearward area; very little labour we had to do it with, too!

Some authorities were very keen on lines of fire being parallel (within each battery) on the S.O.S. Barrage Line,[1] their argument being based on the unsoundness of trying to be strong everywhere. This is a controversial point; distributed fire can be brought parallel by a single word of command.   On March 20th lines were distributed, by sections, within the battery; but the writer never happened on a formed body of infantry officers who did not rest assured that at the word S.O.S. the Field Artillery,[2] if it was efficient, would open an overwhelming fire opposite each bay of every trench-length in the front line.

## CHAPTER IV.

### MARCH 21ST UP TO 10.00.   THE PREPARATION.

On the afternoon of March 20th the relief of the 6th Division was postponed for the n[th] time in view of expected attack.   A considerable amount of work attendant on this decision kept everyone at 18th Infantry Brigade and Right Group Headquarters up till after midnight.

Some time later the Group Commander was awakened by the Acting Adjutant[3] with news that an aeroplane had reported masses of German Infantry marching into Pronville or Queant.   In the light of after-events it seems surprising that more detailed steps were not taken; he was however sleepy and what influenced him was that Counter-preparation was *not* ordered.   Now this was the 5th day since March 10th selected for the German attack, and on all previous occasions 'CPN' had been ordered—it will be remembered that 'CPN' was not to be put into force even by Infantry Brigadiers unless out of communication with Divisional Headquarters.   The fact remains that the impression of immediate attack did not convey itself to the Group Commander's mind; however, 'Battle Stations' was ordered—the extra liaison officer[4] summoned—all O.P's to be manned by 04.00—wagon-lines to 'stand to' at 05.00—mounted orderlies to be sent to Group and Battery Headquarters—and harassing fire was increased.

---

[1] As distinguished from the S.O.S. Line of a gun which is perhaps better named "night-line."

[2] 11 18-prs. to 2,400 yards.

[3] The Adjutant had been selected as "Learner" for Staff Captain.

[4] See Defence Scheme, Chapter II.

At approximately 04.50 the enemy opened a violent bombardment on 18 I.B. and Right Group Headquarters, with gas, which
left no doubt in our minds that 'Der Tag' had arrived; there was
also some low-flying enemy aircraft. Within a few minutes the
combined-headquarters office was established in the unfinished tunnel;
followed the complete destruction of the Group Commander's above-
ground residence by a shell or a bomb with nearly all defence schemes,
etc.

It now came to light that the new 'bury,' though laid last night
(and trench filled in), was not connected with the office in the tunnel;
18 I.B. Signals achieved the connection in spite of the bombardment,
a fine performance.  The sergeant in charge of the 2nd Brigade
Signal Sub-section was wounded almost immediately afterwards.

The Group Commander had a few minutes conversation with
O.C. 42nd Battery, and a word or two with an officer of 53rd Battery
before the cables gave. To attempt to repair them and keep them
going was out of the question and attention centred on visual, but
there was a very thick mist, mixed with the smoke of bursting
shells.  It was some time before visual was started with 42nd Battery,
and considerably longer as regards 53rd Battery. There was never
any connection with 87th Battery, except by 'runner'.[1]

Under instructions from the Brigadier, 18 I.B., Counter-preparation was ordered at 05.30.

At 07.05 Group Commander informed 6th D.A. that our front
line was intact but that it looked like trouble on either flank; that
the enemy bombardment was rather less in rearward areas but
increasing in front.

By 07.45 written acknowledgement of the CPN order had been
received from all three batteries.

At the same time news was received from 53rd Battery that the
body of Major Charles Stuart Lyon, M.C. (Comdg. 53rd Battery)
had been found. The death of this most able and gallant officer was
a great blow. The Captain of the 42nd Battery was sent for to
take command of the 53rd Battery. (He arrived there about 10.30.)

At 08.40 Group Commander spoke (on the infantry line) to one
liaison officer, the burden of the information given being that both
liaison officers were 'in position' and that there was no news from
the front.

At 09.35 he spoke to the Left Group Commander who said that
the Germans had made an attack on his front but had been repulsed,
and also announced that the O.C. 21st Battery had been wounded.[2]

At 09.40 a conversation with the Group Commander next on our
right who had little news, but said that, so far as he knew, nothing
was amiss.

At 09.00 42nd Battery had heard from its forward section where
a few casualties had occurred.  The main position had been, and was

---

[1] 87th visual apparatus had been destroyed.

[2] Battery Headquarters completely wrecked, including a valuable Battery Diary
kept since August, 1914.

still being, heavily bombarded, and a subaltern who had but made his bow last night, had been killed.

At 09.15 87th Battery had reported 'O.K.' but did not know for certain about their forward section.

At 09.20 it was reported from several sources that the enemy were using gas projectors from the Birdcage (D14).

At 09.40 the battalions reported that the enemy barrage seemed to be creeping towards them, but that no attack had taken place on our front.

The situation at 10.00 might therefore be described as 'awaiting developments.' It might have been advisable to visit 53rd Battery on the news of the B.C. being killed; it was much quieter after 08.00; on the other hand it seemed better to remain at headquarters for the present in view of what might occur—and it must be remembered that the acting-adjutant had but just taken up duty and was still then inexperienced. Had the Group Commander been able to visit the 53rd and 87th Batteries, and to discuss the question with B.C's personally, action might have been taken with regard to their forward sections.

In real fact, much was happening. The O.P. parties at 'Linnet' I and II were captured complete. With one officer the writer has never been able to gain touch; the other one appears to have given S.O.S. to 87th at 05.00, which was answered; questioned at to why he did not return to the head of the 'bury' (Battalion Headquarters) when communications 'went,' he denied acquaintance with the order to that effect and further said that he kept up communication with 87th for a considerable time.

According to his account, the bombardment lasted with great severity for about 2 hours, gas being sent for over $1\frac{1}{2}$ hours. After that he was constantly in and out of the dug-out, peering through the mist, but could not see much more than 20 yards. Once he heard machine guns close behind him, and when going to see what was afoot was immediately captured by German infantry coming from the flank along the trench; the machine guns were German. He does not remember the time, but it "may have been 09.00 or soon after." The signallers were used to carry wounded, he and his brother F.O.O. being taken to Pronville or Queant, where he saw large concentration of German field guns firing about a round a minute; our guns were not then doing much, but did damage later. From Queant he saw much enemy infantry (with trench mortars) on both flanks. The officers appear to have been fairly well treated—at first they were not even searched, and he managed to dispose of his map.

The German bombardment is worth notice. It was at its height for only about 2 hours, but its distribution was remarkable; it opened simultaneously on every battery position, on I.B. and Group Headquarters, on the wagon-lines, on Bapaume, and St. Pol to the writer's knowledge—aiming at our communications as its principle objective. The gas part of it appears to have created moral effect in the trench system, but there may have been more H.E. in the rearward area than on the trenches until the enemy infantry advanced; it is hard to say. There was a very heavy fire along the track from Mariecourt Wood to the X tracks in C.29.a., which made the passage of our runners to the 87th perilous.[1] They must have had an immense number of guns[2] firing. Previously, in the various Counter preparations, etc., we had exploded a great number of ammunition dumps and our planes were always notifying new enemy gun-positions.

## CHAPTER V.[3]

March 21st, from 10.00 until 22.00. The First Assault.

### A.—The Day at Group Headquarters.

*10.05.* Right Battalion telephoned S.O.S. to 18 I.B. Passed on 10.07 by visual and orderlies to batteries.

*10.15.* Infantry report enemy reached our support line (First or Blue system) on right, and request that barrage be brought back. (i)[3]

*10.20.* Infantry report enemy lying outside our wire in front of our Reserve Line (Red System).

Gave 42nd and 53rd Batteries targets accordingly (by orderly), and asked 299th Siege Battery to engage Area D.26.b.

*10.55.* 42nd Battery report two guns (main position) received direct hits. (ii). Shortly afterwards told 42nd Battery to get ther forward section (three guns) back in order to strengthen their barrage and facilitate control. (iii.)

*10.57.* Reported situation by mounted orderly to 6th D.A.; repeated report that we had lost but regained Skipton Reserve Trench (71st I.B. on our left); also that Germans had a gun at the end of Central Avenue, which may have been a British anti-tank gun.

Wagon-lines told to send up more mounted orderlies.

*11.07.* Received a message from 87th, timed 10.30 a.m., announcing the unloading of 12 wagon-loads of ammunition at the main position, and enclosing an untimed message from their forward section saying, "short of ammunition, because ammunition train[4] cleared off directly enemy barrage started before it could be unloaded. Otherwise O.K. Infantry say enemy concentrating Cornhill Valley." (iv.)

*11.20.* 299th Siege Battery say they are firing on Lynx (D.26.b.).

---

[1] As a matter of fact not a single Group orderly was hit on 21st March, and not a single message failed to arrive.

[2] See Colonel Bethell's article in July 1918 number of "The Journal of the Royal Artillery."—Not more than 18 yards to a field artillery weapon, at a moderate estimate. Since then Ludendorff's book has been published and he says, the attack was to be prepared by artillery on a basis of 100 guns to 1000 yards!

[3] Numerals (i) (ii) etc., refer to paragraphs in comments.

[4] The forward section got its ammunition always by light railway.

*11.25.* Infantry report Posts 27 and 28 on right of our Reserve (Red) Line lost.

*11.35.* Left Group report enemy advancing in fours over the ridge in D.20.

*11.45* Enemy said to be in J.2.b. Officers of 95th Siege Battery and 299th Siege Battery came in for information and were given situation as we knew it.

*11.55.* 42nd report (time unknown) forward section has only one gun capable of firing and several casualties.

*11.59.* Infantry say enemy advancing in masses through Louverval.

*12.35.* News from 6th D.A. of two batteries 110th Bde., R.F.A., coming in to reinforce Right Group.

*12.45.* Believe all Batteries now engaging enemy in front of the wire of the Reserve Line. A message from 90th Bde. R.G.A., says enemy through our Reserve (Red) Line on Right, and a German battery in action at D.13.d.9.0. (v.).

*About 13.15.* Received a message from 87th Battery (timed 12.45) "with main position am covering our Reserve Line in D.25.b., and am laying forward guns on Leopard Support (D.20.c.). Have ordered up six loads to section, but doubt if they will arrive for some time. Forward Section O.K., and no casualties; 5 casualties at main position." This was an important message, in that it presented no hint of trouble on our left. (vi.)

*13.45.* 42nd Battery report (13.40) "Still firing from D.26.c.; teams not yet back with guns from forward position; sergeant in charge of No. 2 anti-tank gun (Leech) had returned."

*13.47.* S.O.S., Barrage Line to Batteries; D.27.c.9/0—D.26.d.7/5, thence along wire of Reserve Line; 87th, various trenches.

*14.00.* 67th report[1] (12.10 p.m.) (vii) "so far as can be seen, enemy through Lagnicourt and advancing under fire from 18-pounders."

*14.05.* Orderly Officer went to 299th Siege Battery with situation.

*14.25.* 53rd report (time not given) "Enemy in Lagnicourt, we are engaging them. Ten casualties, of which two at forward section —one gun of forward section out of action."

*14.45.* 42nd report (2.40 p.m.) "guns not back yet, but forward section was still firing at 1.30 p.m."

*15.20.* Officers Commanding A/110 and C/110 reported in person. Situation explained, and they were given orders as follows:

"A/110. W 334. 21. Take your battery to 127. My O.O. will guide. Our line runs approx. J 2 b 8/8—D 26 c 5/2—D 25 b 7/0

---

[1] Compare time with last message from 87th.

—D/25 central—C 29 central—and probably C 29 a 0/8. Intention is to occupy Brown Line to-night withdrawing troops now in Red Line. Your S.O.S. 150$^x$ in front of brown Line in squares C 29 d, I 5 b, and I 6 a. O.P's I 11 a and I 5 c. Position No. 127 co-ordinates I 8 d 0/8."

A similar message to C/110, which was to go to position 125. State of affairs as regards ammunition stored there was explained, and warning given to be prepared to use open sights.

*15.25.* Orders for employment of "A" and "C"/110 were received from 6th D.A. These orders did not agree with those just given to Battery Commanders who had already left. D.A. Orderly took back at about 16.00 a note giving reason for non-compliance, which was that positions 109 and 121 (ordered by D.A.) would be rather close for supporting Brown Line. The latest news from 87th was also given.

*15.38.* 87th report (untimed) "guns at main position withdrawn to Position 118 in order to facilitate ammunition supply. No sign of forward section, and enemy have reached sunken road.[1] Captain killed, self hit." The report was initialled by the B.C. in a very shaky hand.

On receipt of this, orders were issued for the captain of the 42nd, now commanding 53rd, to go and command 87th, who could have few officers left.[2]

*15.42.* 42nd report (3.40 p.m.) "Forward guns back at main position. One gun knocked to pieces left at forward position."

*16.05.* Gave situation in J.2.b. valley to 299th Siege Battery.

*16.15.* 18 I.B. situation report :—"71st I.B. holding (left) flank from D.25. central (in Red system) to C.29.c. of 7 (Brown system); Battalions 18 I.B. from D.25. central to D.26.c.8.2. (Red system) to J.1.b.7.5. (flank refused to meet 51st Division on right). If no counter-attack being launched, 18 I.B. will withdraw at dusk . . . to Morchies Line (Brown System) . . ." Batteries were ordered to prepare to withdraw at dusk. The following guns now in action :—42nd, 2 (main position); 53rd, 4 (1 forward); 87th, 3 (position 118).

*16.35.* 53rd report, "Infantry say Germans already in Brown Line, C.27 and 28."

Whether some Germans did or did not get into this portion of the Brown Line has not, to the writer's knowledge, been decided; something uncertain occurred here, for a battery commander of the Left Group went into this trench line to see for himself, and was shot at close quarters. A D.A. message, timed 7.10 p.m., speaks of enemy holding a small loop in the Brown Line at C.29.c. 53rd was told to

---

[1] In a part of which the forward section was emplaced.

[2] In real fact all 9 officers were now casualties and the battery gun-line was under command of a wounded corporal.

verify this information. If correct, 53rd and 87th were to withdraw at once. The situation as thus reported could not be verified.

*17.00.* O. C. 87th Battery arrived and was "dressed" at Group Headquarters. From him it was learned that his forward section must have been captured, and that the main portion of the battery (3 guns) was in position 118 (on Morchies—Vaulx road) under Corporal Martin. See Section D of this chapter.

Orderly Officer returned from guiding A and C/110 into position, and reports C/110 actually in position at 125.

*17.15.* Situation, intentions and useful targets sent to 299th Siege Battery.

*17.50.* On reports of congested enemy transport J.2.b. valley, 42nd and 299th Siege Battery (viii) to concentrate on the tracks in this area.

*18.20.* Sent Orderly to 6th D.A. giving whole situation as conjectured. In this message the number of guns still in action was slightly over-estimated.

*19.25.* An officer from 53rd arrived, by whom orders were sent to 53rd and 87th to withdraw to position 110 and 112 (I.15.c.).

The state of affairs in the Brown Line C.27, 28, and 29.c. was still uncertain. South of that it was known we held the whole line.[1] An order was therefore sent to all batteries detailing a S.O.S. Barrage Line to cover the Brown Line, giving each Battery (42nd, 53rd, A and C/110, 87th) its task.

Two guns of 42nd were to go to position 111 (I.15.c.) forthwith. Later the remainder of the battery was ordered back.

*19.45.* Saw O.C. Y/6 T.M.B., who brought what personnel he could collect and asked for orders. He was able to give some rough information as to what had happened to the T.M's (see Section F of this chapter).

*21.00.* B.S.M. 21st Battery reported, and about this time a message arrived from 6th D.A. saying 21st Battery would join the Right Group at Position 128.

Pending decision as to what troops were to be responsible for defence, and who would command, and where he would have his headquarters, it was not possible to leave Group Headquarters. The last battery to withdraw was 87th, which left position 118 at 21.20.

*The war of movement had begun.*

---

[1] A few Germans got into this part of the Brown Line during the night 21/22, about J.7., but were ejected.

## COMMENTS.

(i) *Infantry Demands.* It seems that the infantry had expected our fire to fall concentrated on the particular spot on the extreme right, where the danger lay, when S.O.S. was sent; the bringing back of the barrage, at all times difficult, *especially on the defensive*, is impossible to achieve without notice when no artillery communications exist.   It is for us to get as near as possible to meeting whatever demands the Infantry make, but we must realise that these demands are sometimes high, and in the mean (peace-) time the more we can tell them what we can, and what we cannot easily do, the better. It might have been better to have a pre-arranged Brown Line Barrage with a code-call; such a barrage had been arranged elsewhere.

(ii.) *Fitters' duties in action.* The 42nd Battery fitter did good work on damaged guns during the day, and the battery armament (less broken gun left at the forward position) was nearly complete by 22nd.

(iii.) *Reason for withdrawal.* The situation of the 42nd Battery was unsatisfactory with one gun in action at the main position, and three (by now, dangerously) far forward and out of communication. The 53rd, with only two forward and with flanks protected, was not so badly placed.

(iv.) *Writing of Messages.* The meaning of the last sentence of this message is obscure, "Enemy *concentrating* Cornhill Valley"; it might mean "massing" or it might mean, in the language of the day, "concentrating fire." The use of the expression "concentrate" meaning "concentrate fire" is loose and has, in the writer's experience, led to considerable misunderstanding. The drill of writing messages must be persistently inculcated; during the operations under discussion at least three important messages were received whose usefulness was discounted by the neglect to time them. A similar source of error has been the expression "heavy artillery bombardment"—did "heavy" refer to "artillery" or to "bombardment"?

(v.) *Flank Communication.* News from our right-hand neighbours was much needed all through this and subsequent days.

(vi.) *Flank Patrols.* The two 87th Battery positions lay on the Southern slope of a ridge running N.E. and S.W.   A flank patrol a couple of hundred yards to left would have kept the battery commander aware of events on his left; this is a singular instance of the illusive security resulting from trench warfare and the continual offensive; the exposed right flank could be (and was) better watched from the 42nd position on 25th (Chapter VIII); after our experiences in March we used flank patrols frequently, standing patrols, or officers or N.C.O's mounted on horses or bicycles; and most valuable was the information they brought in, both on the defensive in April and later in the "100 Days' Battle."

(vii.) *Error of Timing Messages.* This was the first hint of trouble on our left flank, hitherto thought safe. A message timed 12.45 had reached Group Headquarters about 13.15—about the time it would take a runner. The message to which this note refers was timed 12.10, and got to Group Headquarters at 14.00 hrs.; either the 12.10 or the 12.45 message must have been wrongly timed—it looks as if the 12.10 message should have been timed 1.10 p.m.

(viii.) *Liaison with Heavy Artillery.* It will be noticed that there was effective liaison all day with 299th Siege Battery, and the Group Commander ventured to give *an order* to the latter at 5.50 p.m. There had been liaison once during the day with 90th Brigade R.G.A., and with 95th Siege Battery by an officer coming from that unit. It is contended that if Heavy Artillery units defending the line were more closely connected with the F.A. Group, whose Commanders are, quite simply, representatives of the G.O.C., R.A. Corps, the defence would be more efficient.

(ix.) *Fire Records.* It is a pity that batteries did not keep better records of targets engaged. Military history is the basis of training, but it is absolutely dependent on the accuracy of records. At 1 p.m. there was some alleged short-shooting on the Red Line and one cannot tell at all whence it came.

(x.) *Wagon-lines.* The wagon lines had to shift about a great deal during the day owing to shell-fire, as they did to even a greater extent during the April operations about Kemmel (see Part II). The insistence on proper liaison came from our experiences during some parlous days opposite Cambrai at the end of November, 1917—a most valuable lesson; unfortunately Group Headquarters (with R.S.M. on leave) had not learned it so thoroughly.

(xi.) *Visiting.* It may be taken as an axiom that, no matter how much it adds to work and physical fatigue, it is absolutely essential for a commander to obtain touch with events in battle by personal visits. Every soldier knows it. It is no case of "small profits and quick returns"—sometimes the time so spent seems wasted; it is rather a case of increase of capital at (a high rate of) compound interest, for not only will the knowledge thus gained be of inestimable value to the wanderer when studying the map at his headquarters for a later situation, but also the presence of seniors on the field is a thing highly valued by the troops, of which in public little, but *in private a great deal, is said.* Position warfare creates the illusion that one can do one's work at home, but the surprises which greet one when on the tramp tear away even quite comfortable veils; *Malheureuse est l'ignorance et plus malheureux le Savoir.* The writer has never ceased to regret not visiting his batteries during this day; even now it is hard to select the time when such a visit might have been made. Had he gone between 08.00 and 10.00 and discussed the situation personally, it seems to him not unlikely that the forward sections of the 33rd and 87th batteries would have been withdrawn during the morning; but at that time it seemed possible that no attack on our front was impending. Later, there seemed to be always a time just ahead when it would be not only advisable but necessary to go to the batteries.

The conclusion appears to be that, so long as communications hold, and a commander can speak to subordinates, he is well placed at headquarters—even one may say best-placed;[1] we all met the gentleman who could never be found at home to do business. When communications are gone, his principle task (that of command) has become most difficult, and he is well advised to beg leave to go visiting, so be he is not too long absent at one time.

(xii.) *Business at Headquarters.* The summary of events given in this chapter gives no idea of the "business" which went on at Group Headquarters during the 12 hours—the rumours, the conflicting reports, the uncertainty. One felt it was all only the beginning, and a small part, of a much bigger series of events; if blame be given for not ordering this movement or that, it must be remembered that in trench warfare battles move very slowly; and that, over and over again, a few remnants of units hanging on where they were had held up large bodies of attacking troops and brought to nought all sorts of ambitious schemes concocted in the quiet of some distant office. Again, the mental attitude of a man accustomed to a rifle, when suddenly handed a gun and shown driven grouse, gives an idea of the impression created by the first day's moving battle after years of position warfare—that is to say when it is at the enemy's will that it moves. It was a most anxious and tiring day, but "Be the day short or be the day long, at last it reacheth to evensong."

### B.—THE DAY WITH 42ND BATTERY.

The day was an exciting one. Both positions were under heavy fire from the very start. The main portion of the battery had only just settled in its new position, which was still incomplete; it was strong enough, but the advantage of its strength was discounted by the impossibility of concealing (in such surroundings) the work done. Two guns at the main position, and one of the three at the forward position, received direct hits early in the day. One of those at the main position was mended by the fitter under fire; the other had to go to the I.O.M. The one at the forward position was destroyed in its pit. The battery had thus four guns in action that night.

The captain of the battery was taken away early to command the 53rd Battery; one subaltern (just joined) was killed at the main position, one subaltern (borrowed from 87th) was captured with the O.P. party at 'Linnet,' and one subaltern was on leave. Four subalterns remained, one at the forward position, one at the main position, and two at the wagon-lines.

When the order came to withdraw the forward section, 2nd Lieut. X. reconnoitred the task. The enemy were already on the

---

[1] Unless of course there is some particular thing he considers it his duty personally to see

heights W. of Louverval, and quite close to the forward section in its immediate front. This officer thought the task could not be achieved, but asked to be allowed to try; volunteers to drive were at once forthcoming; the officer personally led the limbers forward through the wire of the Brown Line one by one; and one by one the two guns returned; a wheel horse of the last team got his foot entangled in the wire, and the team had to stop while the wheel-driver dismounted and disentangled the horse's foot. In the meantime the officer at the forward position was organising fire with small arms, after having prepared the guns for withdrawal. It was a gallant performance, and those concerned were deservedly decorated; it shows what can be done.

A fine instance of infantry co-operation occurred here (i.); the 51st Divisional Infantry in the Brown Line[1] noticed the attempt, and at each critical moment developed a heavy rifle and machine-gun fire on the Louverval heights, without which the task could never have been accomplished.

On arrival at the main position the two guns were sent back (by order from Group Headquarters) to the Brown position allotted to 42nd Battery—No. 111 (ii.).

The battery wagon lines suffered considerable casualties in horses during the day, and like all others had to shift.

### COMMENTS.

(i.) *Infantry Co-operation.* In another part of the battlefield some limbers coming up to withdraw guns had a very different experience at the hands of the neighbouring infantry. Intent on a stout defence, the infantry had blocked up a certain gap in the wire; the team drivers had to unwire the gap, but, to their disgust, on returning with the gun they found their gap re-wired!

(ii.) *Method of Withdrawal.* It is a moot point whether a withdrawal is best conducted by sending a whole battery back at a time to cover other batteries' retirement, or by each battery sending one section to cover its own. This last method divides every battery into two portions, making control difficult for the B.C.; and the section sent back first is very short of orders and information until the main battery arrives. On the other hand the battery is the fire unit; the more preparations made at the new position the earlier will efficiency be reached; observation and communication have to be arranged there; angles must be calculated for the new S.O.S. line. Still further, each battery has a certain task as a fire unit—maybe a zone to cover; if a whole battery is taken away, it means constant alteration of tasks, at an already difficult time. Throughout the March and April withdrawals the writer adopted the section method —with success.

In the advance it is quite another matter. A section sent forward for close support of the infantry has so much to do with obser-

---

[1] The 42nd forward position was in the 51st Divisional area.

vation, liaison, flank reconnaissance, and fire-command, that it has to borrow officers from the main battery in order to carry out its task. Instead of sending a section forward it was our custom to send forward a complete 4-gun battery under its own Commander with his full staff, and to treat the remaining two guns as a reserve of personnel and equipment.

The question is rather a controversial one.

### C.—The Day with the 53rd Battery.

It is no reflection on the 53rd Battery to say that the death of its Commander during the first moments of the battle had a serious effect on its efficiency. The B.C. in question was a born leader of men, and the very life and soul of the whole unit.

On the news of his death the captain of the 42nd was placed in command, and arrived at 10.30, but in the afternoon, the 87th being left without a single officer, the captain of 42nd went on to the 87th, which he happened to know well. The captain of 53rd was on leave; there were five subalterns, one at the forward position, one at 'Sparrow' O.P., three at the main position, of whom but one had experience. Except during the short time mentioned, the battery was commanded throughout the March operations by its senior subaltern; it had an excellent B.S.M.

The forward section could have been withdrawn without undue trouble up to the sudden and unexpected capture of Lagnicourt by the enemy; after that, the machine-gun fire from the Lagnicourt and Louverval heights rendered withdrawal practically out of the question, for the ground behind was on a forward slope and devoid of cover; the Group Commander gave no order for such withdrawal.

The forward section was bombarded like all others, and one gun destroyed by enemy fire at an early hour. The remaining gun was most gallantly fought by the officer in command; when the enemy appeared at Lagnicourt it was brought into the open against them with success. Between dark on the 20th and the late afternoon of 21st it fired over 1,700 rounds, in fact every round within reach of the position. The section commander having fired his last round, destroyed the gun and withdrew what remained of his detachments.

The O.P. party, being out of communication, and therefore of no use, the F.O.O. rightly rejoined the main portion of the battery.

At the main position also, guns were taken out of their pits, and the enemy at Lagnicourt effectively engaged.

The battery withdrew at dusk to its Brown Position (110); it had lost its two forward guns and the anti-tank gun; one of the remaining guns was temporarily out of action.

There seem to be no special comments; one can say that the battery put up an effective defence under difficult circumstances.

### D.—THE DAY WITH THE 87TH BATTERY.

If it was exciting with 42nd, it was perhaps more so with 87th. The visual station was hit in the first few minutes. Previously noted messages show that early in the day the forward section was in trouble as regards ammunition, owing to the sudden departure of the light railway truck which was bringing up the daily supply. Unfortunately 12 wagon-loads[1] had just been dumped at the main position, and, by the time more could arrive, the forward section no longer needed supply. It is possible that the Battery Commander was too occupied with fighting the main portion of the battery to give all the attention due to the other half of his command; he was singularly badly placed as regards communication with Group Headquarters, and it can justly be said that he did not get all the help and advice which might normally be expected. It must also be remembered that chance rendered him very short of officers; he had his captain with him until the latter was killed; pure chance dictated the fact that the 87th were finding *both* liaison officers that morning; being so rich in subalterns, the battery had lent one to 42nd, and that lent subaltern was doing a tour of O.P. duty for 42nd at Linnet I on his way back to his own battery, so that *both* the captured Linnet F.O.O's were 87th officers; two subalterns were with the forward section (one for instruction), a seventh subaltern was on leave, an eighth had been just seconded for services with the T.M's (where he was wounded early in the day). When the Battery Commander was wounded there was, therefore,*not one officer left out of the ten*, for both liaison officers had been wounded by the early afternoon.

No order was given to withdraw the forward section by the Group Commander; it has already been suggested that the defence scheme should have been clearer on this point. The section was badly placed for such a battle, more particularly as steps were not taken to keep the northern side of the ridge under observation.

It has never been decided at what time the forward section was captured, for the last message from them was untimed. Reference has already been made to the difficulty of determining whether a mistake was not made in the timing of the 12.10 or 12.45 messages to Group. By 14.30, in any case, our fire from the forward position had stopped, and a German machine-gun opened from further South (to the right) along the same roadway in which lay the forward section—in fact from what had on 16th March been I.B. Headquarters and still was a dressing-station (C.29.a.6/0). That the Germans came along the sunken road from the left (North) over the crest of the ridge, is obvious; this movement probably took place *after* they occupied Lagnicourt (a useful pivot).

An untimed message from the wounded B.C. arrived at Group Headquarters at 15.38. The battery was getting short of ammunition; there was plenty stored at Position 118 (the position allotted to

---

[1] Ordered early in the morning by Group Headquarters.

the forward section for the defence of the Red or Second Line); further, ammunition had by now arrived at 118, intended to refill the forward section, but unable to get there because the ground East of 118 had become completely swept by German machine-guns from the above-mentioned dressing station. The B.C. therefore determined to move his three howitzers back from the main position to 118 instead of bringing the ammunition up to the main position—an important decision which brought about one of the most stirring episodes of the day. The wagon-limbers unhitched their wagon-bodies and drove forward over the open to withdraw the three howitzers from the main position. They got there all right, but the withdrawal took place under heavy machine-gun fire at about $1,000^{\times}$—$1,400^{\times}$. Scarcely a single horse escaped being wounded, and in two of the three teams there was an empty saddle. The whole incident was exciting and most creditable to the battery, but the Captain was killed and the Major wounded in the process.

Up to this withdrawal the B.C. had gallantly fought the battery by voice from an exposed position on the hill behind; he described his method of getting his 'line' unorthodox, but the fire was considered effective by those at hand. The wireless mast had long been hit, but the operator succeeded in saving all the instruments.

On arrival at 118, the battery was fought for some hours by a corporal, himself wounded. At night it withdrew without great difficulty to its Brown position (112), where it found itself with one (borrowed) officer and three howitzers, of which one was temporarily out of action.

The wagon-lines had had a bad time, but this battery also possessed a first-class B.S.M.

### E.—THE ANTI-TANK GUNS.

No. 1 Gun (15-pdr.—42nd Battery) "Nickel" was hit almost at once. The sergeant in charge got back with two men in the evening after fighting all day with their rifles.

No. 2 Gun (18-pdr.—42nd Battery) "Leech" was caught by the enemy barrage. A gallant effort was made by a liaison officer to get it into the open, but its detachment was practically wiped out, and the Germans were in possession of that area about 10.00. (i.)

No. 3 Gun (18-pdr.—53rd Battery) "Tiger" fired two successful bursts early in the day when good targets presented themselves. While sitting on the layer's seat trying to open fire later in the day, one of the liaison officers was hit by a splinter in the eye from a rifle bullet which struck the rocking bar sight; the enemy was quite close, and it proved impossible to go on manning the gun. The detachment retired with the infantry at dusk, but only the N.C.O. (wounded) and one man got back.

No. 4 Gun (18-pdr.—53rd Battery) "Sparrow" appears to have

done good work; it was run out of its hiding place soon after 08.30, and was firing at 500$\times$ when the infantry officer on the spot told the detachment to give it up and rejoin their battery.  The N.C.O. and one man got back.

No. 5 Gun (18-pdr.—87th Battery) "Shaws" was in the centre of one of the main depressions.  It had fired 25 rounds when the infantry officer told the N.C.O. to stop firing as the gun was drawing the fire of the enemy on to his men (ii).  The N.C.O. and two men rejoined their battery forthwith.

It is believed that every gun, if not already destroyed by enemy fire, was rendered useless by the detachment before withdrawal, except (possibly) No. 2 Gun, "Leech."

### COMMENTS.

(i.) *Siting.*  Siting of the anti-tank guns in the trenches was not a success, but too much stress was perhaps laid on their being able to cover ground *at short range,* and there was nowhere else but trenches to hide them.  One frequently comes across good sites in a forward area for an anti-tank gun, with a covered approach for its detachment, good camouflage, and well away from trenches; nothing like such a site existed on this front.

(ii.) *Artillery in the Infantry Zone.*  One of the great objections to placing artillery weapons in the infantry zone is that pressure is exerted to keep quiet, so as to avoid retaliation.  An officer can withstand such pressure; a N.C.O. scarcely has the position.  Had the medium T.M's remained entirely under infantry control, it is not unlikely that the natural objection to enemy retaliation would have tended to make them too inoffensive; it was this that weighed so heavily towards the decision to make them part and parcel of the F.A. Group.

(iii.) *Loss of Power—Anti-Tank Guns.*  It has proved almost impossible to get accurate information as to what happened in each of the five anti-tank gun cases; the infantry were too busy to notice, and returning members of the detachment naturally made out the best possible accounts for themselves.  The anti-tank guns cannot be said to have done much for the defence; but then, no enemy tanks appeared on the scene.  Had the tanks come there would have been less enemy barrage (after the preliminary bombardment was over) and doubtless the carefully selected detachments would have rendered good account of themselves; they could ill be spared by their batteries, and their absence was felt on the 21st.

### F.—THE TRENCH MORTARS ON 21ST.[1]

As regards the Heavy T.M. nothing is known except that it fired from 05.30 until captured.  By the middle of the day the dug-out was holding a large collection of German infantry.

---

[1] The writer is indebted to several people for information given after repatriation.

As regards Nos. 9, 10 and 11, it is believed that Nos. 9 and 10 fired; the officer in charge was captured, it is understood, between Infantry Company Headquarters (D.21.c.0/0) and his guns. An officer in charge of No 11 was killed—if rumour is to be believed— while most gallantly directing an infantry fight on the top of the parapet after his gun was captured.

Nos. 7 and 8 were fired at the request of the Left Battalion Commander. One received a direct hit. The Officer in charge was wounded early in the day.

The history as regards Nos. 16, 17 and 18 is better known. Lieut. C. was acting T.M. Control Officer (see Appendix IV. to Defence Scheme) on the evening of the 20th. At 05.15 it was only just possible to see the wire in front of each trench, and such telephone wire as it had been possible to steal (in order to allow of control) was already cut, so that three of the T.M. Groups had to act on their own responsibility. The Right Battalion Commander very naturally refused to allow Lieut. C. to go forward himself, as his group of T.M's might be wanted at any moment. Every fifteen minutes reports were coming in the front line, but only bombardment was taking place.

At 09.25[1] a company runner reported the enemy in possesion of our support line (First or Blue system)—the first intimation of actual attack. About this time the F.O.O's at 'Linnet' must have been captured, as well as the group of Nos. 9, 10 and 11 T.M's. About 09.40 enemy infantry were observed outside the wire of the Reserve (Red) line, in which Battalion Headquarters were situated.[2]

It was now that the Right Battalion Commander gave permission to put Nos. 16, 17 and 18 into action. Lieut. C. reached his guns (not without difficulty) and fired them on their registrations.

Going up to the Red (or Reserve) system, which was close in front, he obtained touch with a post of the Division on our right and, seeing a party of 75 Germans cutting our wire by hand, he changed his target on to the enemy party at the shortest possible range. The fire was successful, and that party 'evaporated.' Going back after this episode to his guns he found three of his men dead or wounded; Lieut. C., the N.C.O., and the remaining man each took one gun.

At 11.00 rifle and machine-gun fire was received from the right (Southern) flank, and the N.C.O. was hit; the party was, however, reinforced by a man who had escaped from the Heavy T.M. detachment. About 11.30, while working his gun, Lieut. C. received a blow on the head; when he came to a German was standing over him calling him "Good English comrade." He and two men were sent towards Queant, but crossing the support line of the Front or Blue system they found a British post under a sergeant-major still holding out; they escaped and joined the garrison; the sergeant-major was expecting a British counter-attack and refused to surrender; ammunition gave out later, and after an unsuccessful attempt to get away,

---

[1] This is valuable as deciding the time of the enemy success.
[2] Group Headquarters knew this at 10.05.

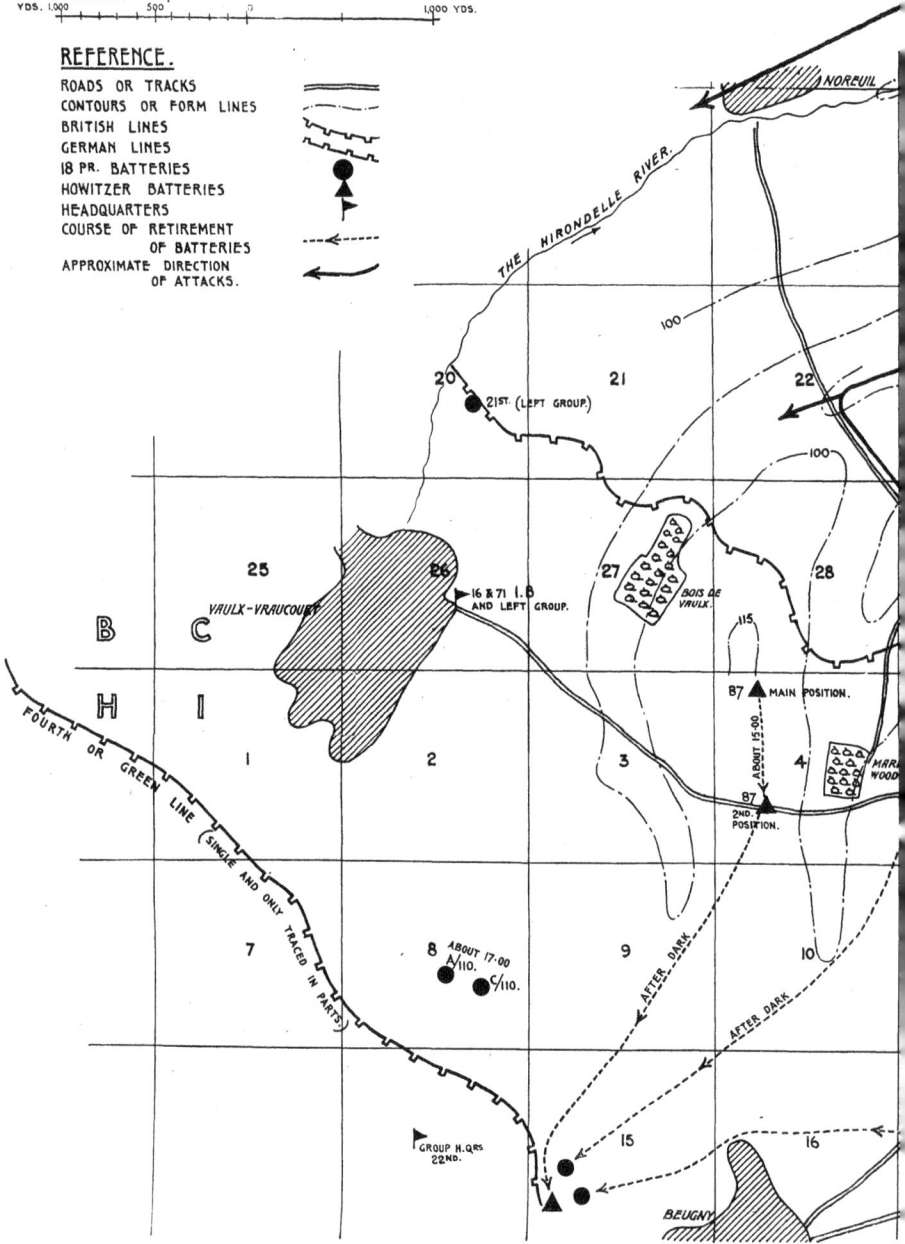

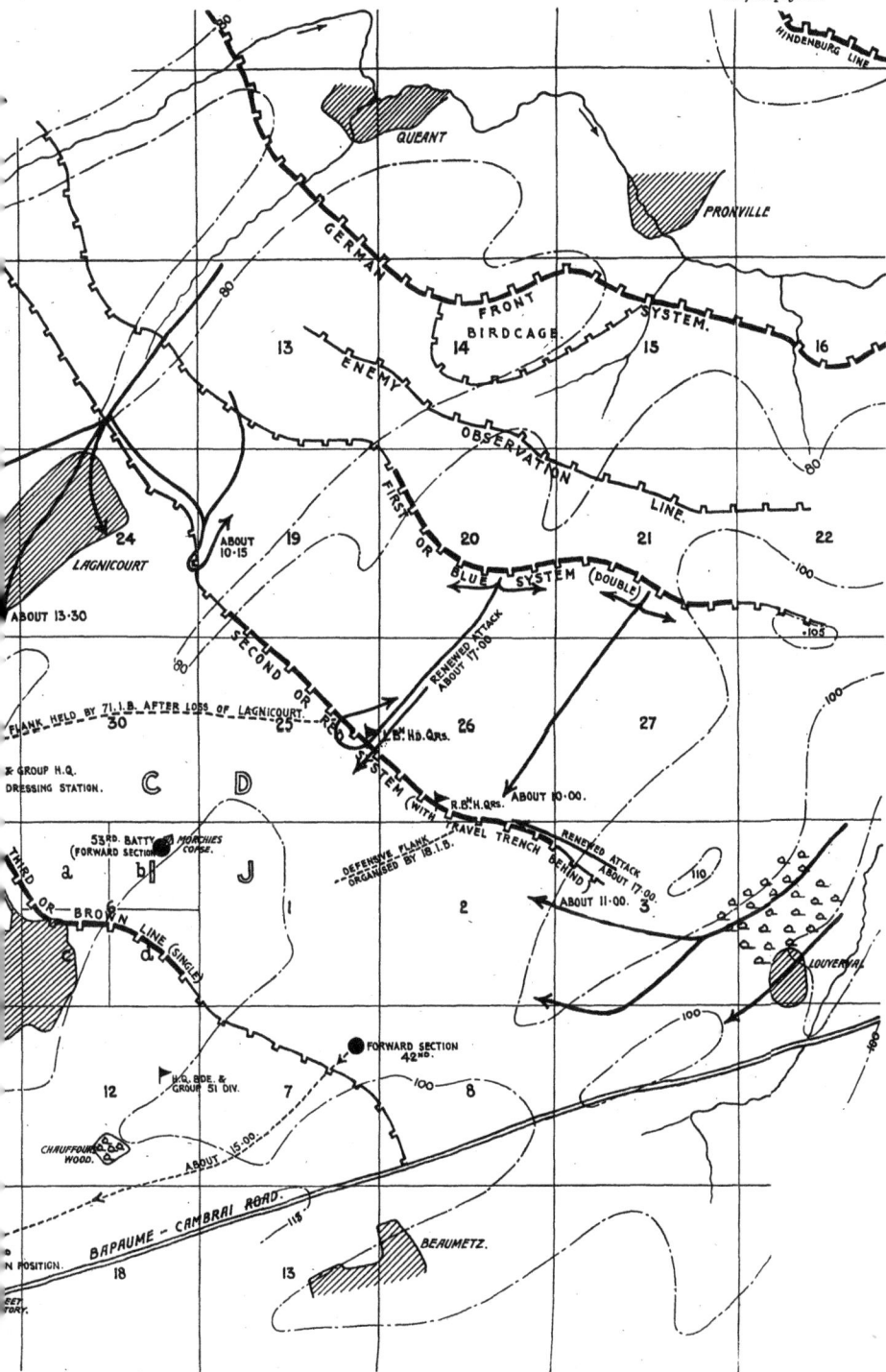

HINDENBURG LINE

QUÉANT

PRONVILLE

GERMAN

FRONT SYSTEM.

BIRDCAGE.

13    14    15    16

ENEMY

OBSERVATION LINE.

80

FIRST OR

24

ABOUT 10·15

LAGNICOURT

19    20    21    22

100

BLUE SYSTEM (DOUBLE)

·105

ABOUT 13·30

SECOND OR RED

80

RENEWED ATTACK ABOUT 17·00

FLANK HELD BY 7⊥ I.B. AFTER LOSS OF LAGNICOURT.

30    25    26    27    100

& GROUP H.Q. DRESSING STATION.

L.Bⁿ.Hᴅ.Qᴿˢ.

SYSTEM (WITH

R.Bⁿ.Hᴅ.Qᴿˢ.

ABOUT 10·00.

C    D

RENEWED ATTACK ABOUT 17·00.

53ᴿᴰ BATTY. MORCHIES COPSE. (FORWARD SECTION)

GRAVEL TRENCH BEHIND

110

a    b    J

DEFENSIVE FLANK ORGANISED BY 18.I.B.

1    2    3

THIRD OR BROWN LINE (SINGLE)

ABOUT 11·00.

LOUVERVAL

c    d

100

100

FORWARD SECTION 42ᴺᴰ.

100

H.Q. BDE. & GROUP 51 DIV.

12    7    8

CHAUFFOUR WOOD.

ABOUT 15·00.

115

N POSITION.

BAPAUME – CAMBRAI ROAD.

18    13    BEAUMETZ.

EET TORY.

the party had to surrender. They had a bad time, and indeed Lieut. C. tasted nothing between dinner on 20th and the end of a 70-kilo. march! It was apparently not salubrious to "fall out" during this march.

Lieut. C.'s impression of the German method of attack was that it was not made in line, but in very deep columns at intervals along the front—this is an interesting point and might account for the dis-jointed nature of reports. The carnage inflicted on the enemy between our support line (Front or Blue System) and the Reserve (Red) Line was a credit to the close defence—it is to be feared that the field artillery did not pull its full weight as regards infliction of casualties on this occasion.

### Comments.

(i.) It is claimed that the Heavy and Medium Trench Mortars put up a fine defence.

(ii.) *T.M's in the Defence.* The employment of T.M's in the defence is difficult; T.M's are primarily a material-destroying, not a man-killing, class of weapon, and best suited to preliminary bombard-ment before an offensive. For purely trench warfare they are well enough sited in the front-system; but they are not good for S.O.S. against an assault, and would seem better placed, when on the defen-sive, in some reserve trench ready to assist a counter-attack. Nos. 16, 17 and 18 (and perhaps 7 and 8) did better work than Nos. 9, 10 and 11.

(iii.) *Control of T.M's.* Trench Mortars cannot be treated like another battery in the Group, but rather as a sub-group, for they form another echelon of the artillery defence; they need as careful arrangements for control as the batteries of a brigade, R.F.A., which form the second echelon of the group. For actual gunnery they need telephone equipment, and much more of the same for tactical control; the reluctance of the authorities to provide this telephone equipment was never understood, unless it was that the equipment did not exist to be issued.

### G.—The 18th I.B. Fight on 21st.

The 18th I.B. had the 1/West Yorkshire Regiment on the right and 2nd D.L.I. on the left; 11th Essex Regiment in Reserve.

The Left Battalion Liaison Officer was the one ordered up during the night (see Defence Scheme); the German bombardment had begun before he had reached his post. The Left Battalion was not on the "bury"; the only communication was therefore from Right Battalion Headquarters; both battalion headquarters were in the Reserve (Red) Line. At 10.00[1] the sentries reported German infantry advancing; they captured our Front Line (Blue) system, but were held up by the wire of the Reserve (Red) Line; however they managed to get up Leech Avenue (the main C.T. which left or joined the Reserve Line near where the two battalions joined hands), and the Left Battalion

---

[1] T.M. account (written from the right) gives capture of front system at 09.25.

was obliged to vacate the Reserve Line and occupy the "Travel Trench" in rear; however, a counter-attack was made, and the Reserve Line re-occupied, and two German machine-guns captured.

Up to now this Liaison Officer had been fighting with rifle and bayonet, bomb and revolver. He then tried to reach No. 2 Anti-Tank Gun, but found it already in enemy hands; he also tried to work No. 3 Anti-Tank Gun, but was wounded in the attempt without however leaving the fight, for he again took a rifle. *An attempt to effect liaison* was now made, for he sent an orderly from No. 7 T.M. to tell his *battery* commander the situation. Many S.O.S. signals were put up, he says, by the infantry after 11.30, but "no answer came."[1] Enemy aeroplanes were circling overhead. A detachment of 11th Essex Regiment arrived by 14.00. The enemy had now captured Lagnicourt, and were obviously getting round the right also; the two battalion commanders decided to fight on where they were; Leech avenue was "blocked," and all papers were destroyed. At 18.45 the Germans by bombing up Leech Avenue had again reached the Reserve Line, while practically all our ammunition was expended. The withdrawal took place under heavy rifle and machine-gun fire from both flanks. Both the battalion commander and the liaison officer got back; the latter rejoined his battery at once, was sent to be "dressed," and was shipped by the doctors, under protest, to England.

The Right Battalion Liaison Officer spoke on the 'phone to the Group Commanders about 09.00—an effort to effect liaison. At 12.00 danger became imminent from the right flank. At 12.15 he manned a rifle and a trench. At 13.00, just after three companies of 11th Essex had arrived, he went to help form a defensive flank on the right, at right angles to our line, and in rear of battalion headquarters. At 13.30 the infantry officer was hit and our *liaison* officer found himself in command of the defensive flank; the troops to our right had withdrawn, and the Germans were trying to bomb up the Reserve or Red Line from the South; they were stopped about 60 yards from battalion headquarters. At 14.00 he was hit, and sent back with an orderly; he only succeeded in reaching the dressing station at Beugny after a perilous journey.

From the accounts of the T.M. Controlling Officer and these two liaison officers, the story of our own front becomes fairly clear. What had happened on the right is borne out by the 42nd Battery account (Section B). We know that on the left the Germans suddenly appeared at Lagnicourt, and that the 71st I.B. were forming a defensive flank South of Lagnicourt, running from the Reserve (Red) to the Brown Line. One can only wonder that anyone got back alive to the Brown Line from the 18th I.B. front, of which the O.C. 1/West Yorkshire had been deputed to take command.[2] Returning artillery

---

[1] The Gunners had their own troubles by now.

[2] He was hit on the way back and after certain exciting episodes became a prisoner of war, where he enjoyed further excitement in the form of the German doctor's efforts to keep his wounded leg straight.

personnel speak with great enthusiasm of the fight put up by these two grand old battalions.

An endeavour has been made to depict graphically in the map attached to this chapter the general course of events from the point of view of the infantry.

### COMMENT.

*Liaison Duties.* It is obvious that the two liaison officers, finding communication difficult, abrogated their liaison duties and fought as infantry so long as it was possible. One admires their spirit, but what they did was *not* liaison between the infantry and artillery. Whether, had they reported personally to Group Headquarters, the artillery could have done anything, is nothing to do with the case. On the 23rd, and again on the 24th, the Group lost valuable officers in the same way.

### H.—THE DAY WITH THE 21ST BATTERY (ATTACHED TO LEFT GROUP).

On the morning of 21st March, the 21st Battery had one gun attached to Right Group as an anti-tank gun (see Section E); it had one gun in a forward or "active" position, of which nothing is known; it had an O.P. party which was captured, including the F.O.O.; it had three guns[1] in a "silent" position sited *in* the Brown Line for the specific purpose of covering the Hirondelle Valley. Several officers were on leave or courses; one was at liaison and returned safely; the captain was at the wagon-lines; at the main position were the B.C. and one subaltern. Two of the guns at the main position were completely knocked out with their detachments early in the day, and the subaltern wounded. Battery Headquarters was destroyed within the first minute or two, and the B.C. seriously wounded. The captain came forward, and with two sergeants and a few men with rifles, one 18-pdr. and a Lewis gun, put up a first class resistance[2] for the rest of the day. The one remaining 18-pdr. was brought out into the open and escaped damage for several hours, during which time it did sterling service, until eventually it also got hit. The Lewis gun, however, remained in action to do effective damage to the Germans about Lagnicourt, and, with two undamaged rifles, was carried out in triumph at dusk.

The 21st Battery rejoined the Right Group, in accordance with orders, for the defence of the Brown Line at position 128; it consisted at midnight of a captain, perhaps a dozen men, and the wagon-line.

It was withdrawn on 22nd, re-armed, and attached to the Left Group, when the latter was reconstituted from 25th Divisional Artillery. It did not rejoin 2nd Brigade until March 27th, so appears no more in Part I., but we shall hear of it again in Part II.

---

[1] One gun at I.O.M.

[2] Probably the only defenders of this part of the Brown Line until late in the afternoon.

## CHAPTER VI.

### 22.00 March 21 to 02.30 March 23rd.

#### THE RENEWED ASSAULT.

In the hope of hearing something definite from the infantry as to the morrow's doings, the Group Commander waited several hours at Headquarters; in the meantime there was established at position 128 (I 14 a) a signal-distributing station to the battery-positions, and a line was commenced to 128 from Group Headquarters with what wire could be collected on the spot.[1] At 03.00 hours on 22nd nothing having transpired, he left in moonlight and quiet to visit the batteries in their new positions; he found 42nd, 53rd and 87th batteries (or what remained of them) in position and engaged according to orders in harassing fire; the distributing station was in working order, but as yet the line from Group Headquarters was not "through." He lost his way to A & C/110 and, wishing not to be absent too long, returned to Group Headquarters in time to attend an informal conference of B.G.C. 18th I.B., B.G.C. 14th I.B. (25th Div.), and B.G.C. of the neighbouring brigade on our right (51st Div.) with his group commander. B.G.C. 18 I.B. was still in charge but only relics of his brigade existed any longer and, in practice, B.G.C. 74 I.B. (25th Div.) directed operations on the 22nd. The Group Commander considered it advisable under the circumstances to be with his batteries rather than with the infantry (i). At 06.00 hours, it being still quiet (but as misty as it had been 24 hours previously), he visited A & C/110 and found them efficient. The efforts of the previous day had not increased the efficiency of the 42nd, 53rd and 87th Batteries and there was much to be done there (ii). At position 128 he found the promised 21st Battery, but, as it consisted of only one officer and a handful of men, conditions were not improved by their arrival. The line was now "through" to Infantry Brigade Headquarters and information was received that the two Brigadiers would be at Fremicourt. With their concurrence, the writer stopped at 128 and sent as liaison his own Adjutant who had just received permission to rejoin from D.A.

An enemy barrage, which had commenced soon after 06.00 hrs. on the Brown (now our front) Line, gradually extended westwards until the Green Line became unhealthy; it interfered with digging which had been going on all night. It was already obvious that the five battery positions (42, 53, 87, A/110, C/110) were sited with an obstacle (the Green Line wire) behind them (iii). Two F.O.O's and battalion liaison were established, the F.O.O's being particularly instructed to watch the flanks. At 10.40 there was a report that the enemy were in Mariecourt Wood (I 4 b and d) on our side of the Brown Line and at 11.31 the Left Group could be seen withdrawing guns; on the right it was quiet. Orders were therefore sent to A and C/110 on the threatened flank to withdraw behind the

---

[1] Shortage of wire is more felt during a withdrawal than during an advance because the enemy captures so much. The provision of spare wire is a necessary part of preparation for withdrawal.

Green Line when necessary, an operation which was well carried out[1] at the psychological moments selected by the battery commanders concerned. At 11.40 74 I.B. protested against this withdrawal saying that the enemy had been driven back, but the Group order only anticipated a definite order from 6th D.A. to this effect which was received at 12 noon having been written at 10.40. The D.A. order gave liberty as regards withdrawing 42nd, 53rd and 87th batteries; these batteries moved successively back through the wire into position along the bank in which lay position 128 (now Group Headquarters). During the morning Lieut.-Colonel B. arrived (preceding a written order) to command a sub-group consisting of C/236,D/236 (his own brigade) and A and C/110. The Right Group now consisted of 7 batteries (5 18-pdr. and 2 4.5″ totalling 29 guns in action) all within easy distance and in view of Group Headquarters; the line laid to the infantry at Fremicourt was working well; the sun was shining brilliantly, casualties were few, and conditions were actually pleasant. Information, however, came in very badly, and a succession of S.O.S. calls for fire along the Morchies—Mariecourt Wood road[2] told its tale. (iv).

During the afternoon the enemy captured Vaulx and the Left Group was heavily engaged. Right Group offered its assistance, but the enemy's efforts to debouch from Vaulx had already failed with loss. The Favreuil area was reconnoitred by all batteries in case of withdrawal. Consultation with 74 I.B. as to an S.O.S. line showed that whereas the enemy was close enough to the Green Line on the left, on the right he had not yet reached the Brown Line beyond Beugny—in fact had not advanced at all along the north side of the Bapaume-Cambrai road.

At 20.30 the D.R. brought from 6th D.A. a set of orders timed 18.05. As these orders were subsequently modified in certain details, and so as to avoid confusion, it will be sufficient to state that they arranged for the withdrawal, and reconstitution after withdrawal, of the 2nd Bde, R.F.A., by embodiment therein of the 24th Bde. R.F.A. (which had previously formed the nucleus of the Left Group). They allotted the Green Line Positions (see Defence Scheme, Chapter II) to various brigades, ordering the reconstituted 2nd Bde. to occupy positions 141-143.[3] Lieut.-Col. B's sub-group was to reconnoitre others. The Right Group, consisting of 2nd Brigade R.F.A. and Lieut.-Col. B's sub-group (A/110, C/110, C/236, D/236), was to continue under the same command.

This operation order was accompanied by a message timed 18.30 which announced that the infantry to hold the new line would be 123 I.B. of 41st Div. and that all Infantry and Artillery Headquarters would be in certain dug-outs near Favreuil "where ample accommodation exists."

---

[1] Under machine gun fire. But see Maj.-Genl. Uniacke's article in this incident on page 186 of Vol. I., No. 4 of "The Gunner," July, 1919.

[2] By telephone from 74.I.B (25th Div.).

[3] See map No. 3, attached to Defence Scheme, Chapter II.

At 21.45 a conference was held at Right Group Headquarters attended by Lieut.-Col. B. and all B.C's. It was explained how our line now ran with a marked salient round Beugny; the 2nd Brigade from its new positions 141-143 could only just cover the left or northern portion; Lieut.-Col. B's Brigade must therefore find positions about I. 19. d. or H. 23. c. whence it would be possible to cover the right or Southern portion of our line. (v.)

Immediately after the conference Lieut.-Col. B. started to conduct a reconnaissance of the areas selected—probably A & C/110 in I. 19. d. and C & D/236 in H. 23. c.—Sub-group Headquarters at Favreuil. The batteries of 2nd Brigade moved off without delay, as they had to reconstitute. The withdrawal was covered by Lieut.-Col. B's Batteries, of which A and C/110 moved back at 23.30 and C & D/236 were not to move until 00.30 on 23rd. Group Headquarters remained in position until 23.30 then withdrew, leaving the senior officer of 236 at position 128. All batteries were given their new S.O.S. lines before starting.

On the way to Favreuil the Group Commander visited positions 141-143 and found the reconstituted 2nd Brigade R.F.A. getting into position (42nd reinforced to 6 guns, 53rd reinforced to 6 guns, 87th 3. 4·5″ Hows. and 112th 6 guns). It was another moonlight night and fairly quiet.

On arrival at Favreuil dug-outs, there were lines to lay out, group headquarters to accommodate, and people to locate. It was found that there were trying to "squeeze" into the dug-outs 3 Infantry Brigade Headquarters, 2 Group Headquarters and 6 Field Artillery Brigade Headquarters—it was excruciatingly cold. It was 02.30 on 23rd before the writer located 123 Infantry Brigade (41st Div.) where he learned that the battalions of this Brigade were in the act of relieving 7th I.B. of 25th Div. The relics of the 6th Div. infantry were to pull out as best they could.

As Major-General Sir Thomas (then Colonel) Capper had said in a lecture at Camberley "It looks, gentlemen, as if in future wars. the night would be a period, not of rest, but of increased activity."

## COMMENTS.

(i). *Location of Headquarters.* In such a state of affairs Infantry Brigade Headquarters was likely to get but poor information, while the group commander had every reason for wishing to be near his batteries. As it was thought (and actually proved) possible to get communication by telephone between Group and I.B., the group commander decided[1] to separate himself from the Infantry Brigadier. The value of the two commanders being together is as a rule inestimable, and it was commonly felt by the artillery that in choosing headquarters, the importance of artillery communications was not always realised by the infantry. In one division, the

---

[1] (With permission from the Infantry).

divisional operation orders usually contained a paragraph to the effect that infantry and artillery headquarters would be at such and such a place; it is the surest road by which the General Staff can initiate co-operation.

(ii). *Change of Position.* It is said that the best way to obtain good work is to issue clear orders; this is based on experience that, in the absence of clear orders, good work is *not* obtained. Give a battery a clear order to move to such and such a position and the move is well enough done; but it is what the battery does after getting into the new position that makes it a factor in the battle. The procedure to be adopted should be drilled into all ranks until it is a habit; it is for that reason that some sort of standing orders for positions and emplacements are valuable. Efficiency is not always achieved at the earliest possible moment after change of position, and this is more so in a withdrawal than in an advance; in an advance the spirits are elated—in a withdrawal there is present the sense that one has escaped a danger and can rest awhile. Even *potential* power does not exist until certain procedure has been carried out. Immediately on arrival each gun must be emplaced, ammunition sorted, aiming point selected, camouflage erected; the B.C. must work out his lines, see to communications, arrange observation, and 'shoot himself in'—some of which requires daylight. If a battery has been fighting all day and moving all night, to obtain efficiency in the early hours of the morning requires an unusually fine B.C.; to order heavy counter preparation at dawn is to *ask for* short shooting, especially in cold weather with salved ammunition—a thing which a man fighting by a map has a tendency to forget.

(iii). Here was an instance of siting rearward positions with a defile behind them. Vide remarks, Chapter III (xv).

(iv). All ranks were still suffering from the settled habits induced by trench warfare; observation has to be improvised; information can often be obtained only by violent methods, and *is even then of no use unless communicated.* Officers were still slow to obtain the information, and the group not yet insistent enough on getting it, getting it accurate, and getting it early. It is useless to expect it to fall like manna—a commander must obtain it with means at his disposal. Much of the trouble here was due to lack of wire.

(v). The Green Line positions were only suitable for covering the Green Line; on the right our infantry were still in the Brown Line; here is a typical example of the advantages of grouping rearward positions in depth instead of on a linear basis. Even 141-143 was not perfectly suitable, being at a very long range; Lieut.-Col. B's batteries had to be obliquely advanced. Vide Chapter III (xv).

(vi). March 22nd was perhaps the most interesting day in this period of fighting—for the artillery; for once one could see what was happening. The tactical problem presented by the forcing of the Brown Line in the morning and the evening's loss of Vaulx had to be dealt with by those on the spot at once. For the mixed-up infantry of the 6th and 25th Divisions the day must have been terribly trying; on the right it seemed easier. Wagon-lines as usual spent the day moving and the 42nd Battery was again unlucky.

## CHAPTER VII.

### From 02.30 on 23rd until 02.00 on 25th.

#### THE TURNING MOVEMENT.

In the very early hours of daylight, the enemy forced the Green Line away to our left and captured the village of Mory which increased the salient nature of our Beugny position; for a time the state of affairs was critical, but he did not improve his advantage; he also made an effort to force the Green Line on our own front but completely failed.

As the C.R.A. 6th Division remained in charge, the command of the Right Group was unchanged and the group was later increased by another sub-group—the 187th Brigade, R.F.A. of 41st D.A., in position N. of Favreuil.

The Group S.O.S. line had been arranged from a point just N. of Chauffour's Wood (I 12a 5/4), where it met the S.O.S. line of 51 D.A., via Morchies along the Vaulx Road to I 2 c 4/5, where it met Left Group.

The relief of the troops holding the Green Line by the 123rd I.B. of 41st Division was not successful; two battalions of 123 I.B. took over the front line on the right as far north as I 9 central, but the third battalion failed to relieve 7th I.B. (25th Div.) whose right was in the Green Line at I 15 a o/o. Between I 9 central and I 15 a o/o there was a gap; the effect of this gap as with all such gaps[1] was very serious; further than this, it was not for a considerable time understood that the Right Group was covering two Infantry Brigades *both* of which retained responsibility for holding the line.

Liaison was maintained by the Group at Headquarters 7th I.B. (presumed to be under the Brigadier of 123) and with two battalions in the front line, but was far from successful in so much as concerned information. Each sub-group maintained its own observation; the 2nd Brigade had out two F.O.O's. A report from one (I 14 c, timed 11.40) received at 12.45, stated that our fire at 11.05 was most successful. The reports of F.O.O. No. 2 merit study later.

Throughout the day attention was being directed to enemy movement about Vaulx; S.O.S. on the line I 8 a 6/6—I 9 a 6/6 was asked for at 10.50, 13.30 and 15.45. The Left Group was constantly shooting on the southern exits from Vaulx and batteries of the Right Group joined in as required; so pressing was the attention

---

[1] A French divisional commander on the Somme had cried to writer "I hate gaps."

directed to this area that the quieter right was less considered; the
F.O.O. (No. 2) specially detailed to watch this flank was himself
drawn to the left where the principle fighting was apparently taking
place.

At 14.45 a Group message was issued which announced capture
by the enemy of Lebucquiere, our right being thus threatened; it
became necessary to withdraw Lieut.-Col. B's batteries in I 19 to the
area H 23; successful repulse of the enemy efforts about Vaulx was
also announced in this message. At 15.05 an untimed message from
F.O.O. No. 2 was received reporting that our infantry were retiring
in I 14; this was thought by 123 I.B. to be part of the relief of 7th
I.B.; it may have been so,[1] for a later message timed 3 p.m. and
received via 53rd Battery at 15.10 reported our line in I 7, 8 and 14
as "still holding." A written report from the same F.O.O. reached
Group Headquarters at 18.05 saying our line in I 7 and 8 was correct,
but not otherwise optimistic; this officer visited Group Headquarters
about 22.00—his attention had been entirely taken up by events on
the left. About 21.00 a report from quite another officer (2nd Bde.
R.F.A.) announced that Beugny was in enemy hands but that we held
the Green line west of it. It was not until much later that a wounded
infantry officer reported personally that the two infantry battalions of
123 I.B. which had completed their relief last night had been captured
almost en masse, a condition of affairs entirely unsuspected at I.B.
Headquarters and which accounted for the silence of our liaison officer
with those battalions. It appears[2] that the enemy got in during the
early afternoon from the Beet factory in I 17 and through the gap
between the 123 and 7 Infantry Brigade; by this concentric advance
they cut off the salient holding the two battalions of the 123 I.B.

At Group Headquarters there was much to attend to as well as
this. A section of one of Lieut.-Col. B's advanced batteries which
had got into position by moonlight found themselves in the morning
in full view and had to shift under heavy fire. On news being received
of the capture of Beugny the advanced batteries had to be withdrawn—the whole sub-group being collected into the area H 29—
H 35 by 21.10.

6th D.A. ordered 187th Brigade R.F.A. out of its positions N. of
Favreuil in the morning into positions about the Monument (H 15) to
cover a possible retirement; once there, they came (about 19.00) into
the Right Group.

Rearward positions had to be allotted and reconnoitred by
everyone; as regards 2nd Brigade R.F.A. the area G 18a, E. of
Bihucourt, was reconnoitred by the Brigade Orderly Officer.

An officer of rank arrived during the morning at Favreuil with
instructions to arrange for all transport to get west of the defile
formed by the Achiet le Grand—Bapaume railway. It was desired

---

[1] More likely, it was connected with the capture of the two battalions of 123
I.B., see below.

[2] From a letter written after the armistice by that liaison officer who was captured about 15.00 in the original (March 21) 18 I.B. Headquarters.

by him to move *all* battery wagons, but the Group Commander declined to part with his firing-battery wagons, for rearward positions stocked with ammunition no longer existed. An officer was detailed to conduct the reconnaissance and guide all the wagon-lines back; fortunately the wagon-lines (except 2nd Brigade R.F.A. Headquarters Staff) kept liaison with their gun-lines.

The batteries of the reconstituted 2nd Brigade R.F.A. along the Bapaume-Favreuil had suffered fairly severely from shell fire directed against that road, especially 112th. Communications were difficult to maintain in consequence. Some "short shooting" S. of Vaulx occasioned worry during the day.

Orders had to be issued for observation and liaison for the 24th; a new S.O.S. line had to be traced to meet the altered situation on our right. It was past midnight before the Group Commander was able to leave his Headquarters and visit his batteries.

At dawn on the 24th our infantry, consisting of 123 I.B. reinforced by sundry units of 41st Division to make up for the two battalions lost on the 23rd, were holding the Green Line from north-west of Beugny to near Vaulx (as before). By order of higher authority counter-preparation was fired at 05.00 and 06.15; as short shooting still took place, all batteries were ordered to register their lines at stated times; the result was reported as satisfactory; the origin of the short fire was not traced—salved ammunition and intense cold was the most probable cause, but the co-ordinates of the Green Line were perhaps still inaccurate, though an official tracing had been sent round late on 23rd. Liaison was working satisfactorily on the right; there was also an experienced artillery officer at Headquarters 7th I.B., for the Adjutant of the 2nd Bde. R.F.A., available again on return from Fremicourt, went at 11.00 to 7 I.B. (and thence to a battalion in the front line where he was dangerously wounded while assisting to bring up machine guns).

At 10.40, the C.R.A. 41st Division having taken over the artillery defence, the Right Group passed to Lieut.-Col. L. commanding 187th Brigade, the writer remaining with 2nd Brigade R.F.A. as a sub-group.

The same officer who had sent in the good information on 23rd[1] was again doing F.O.O. He verified S.O.S. fire at 11.00. At 11.55 a message came from him asking for fire on enemy infantry in I 2d and I 3c. At 15.25 he reported line in I 7 and 8 holding well; I 14 was not so saisfactory. He visited a battalion commander at I 14a 1/6, and was on his way to the right about 16.00 when he saw our infantry retiring there; a heavy hostile bombardment was in progress; moving back north towards the left he was hit by a German machine gun firing from the battalion headquarters he had left about 15.00. After lying in the open for 24 hours he was picked up by the enemy (and was well enough treated during captivity).[2]

---

[1] Spoken of about as F.O.O., No. 2.

[2] For his excellent work with the forward section of 53rd on 21st and for his work on 23rd and 24th, he received notice.

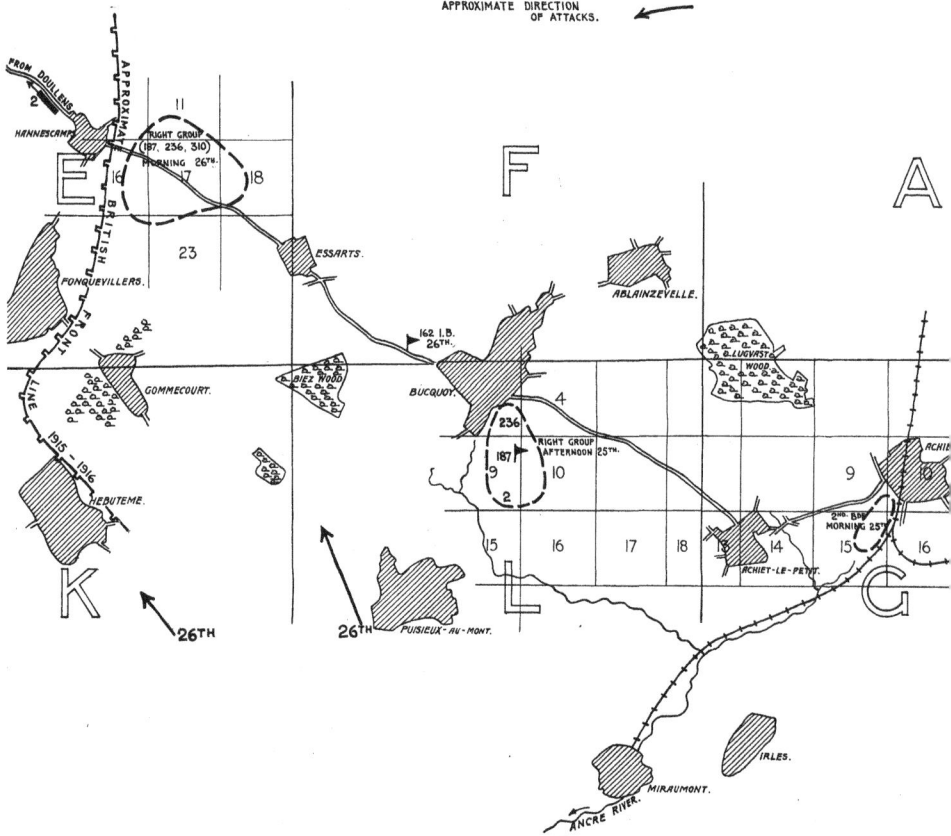

B
23RD

MORY.

13

19    20    21

VRAUCOURT.    22ND.    3RD.

25    26    BROWN SYSTEM    BOIS DE VRAUX.    ORIGINAL POSITION    LAGNICOURT.

27    28    29

4TH OR GREEN SYSTEM.    1    VRULX-VRAUCOURT.    2    3    22ND.    MARICOURT WOOD.    4    5    6    22ND.    C D / I J    2ND BDE. (RIGHT GROUP)    MARCHIES.

BÉHAGNIES.

SAPIGNIES.    H    BEUGNÂTRE.    7    8    9    LINE RIGHT GROUP NIGHT 22/23.    12
MORNING    24TH (AFTERNOON)    2ND. BN. 123.I.B. CUT OFF AFTERNOON 23RD.    23RD.

FAVREUIL.    15    123 I.B. & 17    18    13    14    15    16    17    18    23RD.
RIGHT    GROUPS 23 & 24.    R.G. 22.    REST FACTORY.    TO CAMBRAI.
2    GROUP EVENING 22ND    MORNING 23RD.    21    22&36    23    24    19    20    BEUGNY.    23RD.    LEHUCQUIÈRE.
BIEFVILLERS.    EVENING 23RD TILL EVENING 24TH.    FREMICOURT    24TH    74 AND 181. B. 22ND

13    14    28    29    30    25    26

FROM ALBERT.    BAPAUME.    35    BANCOURT.

NOREUIL    RIVER HIRONDELLE    BRITISH FRONT LINE MARCH 21.

C

In the meantime bad news was coming in from another F.O.O. further right; it was reported at 12.40 that hostile infantry were massing in I 21 and 22; at 15.05 we had a report of our Infantry retiring "wholesale in I 14b and d and I 21c, with the enemy close behind"; the last message from this front asked for a barrage all over I 21, I 27b and I 28. The 2nd Brigade R.F.A. was chiefly engaged in helping the Left Group in the area I 2d and I 3d.

From other sources news came in of the breaking of the Green Line south of Beugny and of enemy occupation of Fremicourt, and by 15.00 Lieut.-Col. B's Brigade in H 23 and H 35 had been withdrawn and moved back towards G 14a and G 23b. There was no liaison whatever with tne troops on our right and it is obvious that the enemy, having got in S. of Beugny and captured Fremicourt, was sweeping north.

During the morning a representative party from all batteries, led by the Brigade Orderly Officer, had reconnoitred the G.18a position in detail.

The difficulty was now to extricate the 2nd Brigade R.F.A. without stopping fire too suddenly. Orders were sent (by telephone) to batteries to withdraw one section each to the G 18a position directly Colonel B's Brigade had passed. (It was not then known at Group Headquarters that several guns were out of action; the B.C's all decided to send two *useful* guns back and to send as well all guns temporarily out of action.[1])

At 17.30 123 I.B. Headquarters with the (new) Group Commander withdrew to Bihucourt. Just after the last battery had received the order to send back a section, the telephone lines broke; it was no longer of any use to remain in Favreuil and the Sub-group Commander, 2nd Brigade R.F.A., considering it his place to remain in action with his brigade, proceeded thither at 18.30 (under threat of revolver fire from an agitated infantry officer).

He took up his post with the 87th (Howitzer) Battery and saw the last of the leading sections go by; he then ordered away the remaining gun of the 87th as unsuitable to the close combat, after which he went along, well behind the gun-line to avoid the road, to order back the rest of the 42nd Battery as being on the dangerous flank. Coming *back* along the gun-line to 53rd, where he expected to find four guns, he discovered an error had occurred in one message —53rd was not to be seen, having already withdrawn complete (instead of only sending one section); expecting to find four guns of 112th, he found only two (owing to guns out of action); of these one got hit soon after; instructions were given to the officer commanding to withdraw this last gun at 19.30 if nothing further transpired, which order was well carried out at the time stated, under rifle fire but no severe pressure. The brigade commander then walked towards Bihucourt and at G 18a the 2nd Brigade R.F.A. was duly found

---

[1] It looked as if casualties to certain guns occurred through trying to fire the guns with the "safety catch" on—orders as to use of this safety catch were issued later by higher authority.

getting into action; the batteries had by his order avoided Bapaume during the withdrawal, as being too near the point of danger and, until quite recently, too much shelled; they had reached G 18a unmolested.

Preparations were being made to achieve efficiency, but at 21.30 the Group Commander arrived with orders to withdraw still further. The new position was reconnoitred by moonlight and the 2nd Brigade R.F.A. got into action west of the railway and south of Achiet le Grand at about 02.00 hours on the 25th.

Many things needful for comfort were by now missing, but there was ample whisky in this neighbourhood. This was the sixth brigade-position taken up since the morning of the 21st. That something had "gone" on the right was obvious to all, but the retreat of the Fifth Army was not known except to a few. Behind us were some very active 60-pdrs., welcome company for all their noise.

### COMMENTS.

(i). *Artillery protects its own front.* The general lesson of these two days fighting seems to be a verification in a new form of Prince Kraft's conclusion that *Artillery can only protect its own front.* In spite of troops inexperienced in the war of movement, in spite of heart-breaking failure in communications, in spite of increased gunnery difficulties and consequent short shells, the Right and Left Groups did materially assist in a successful defence of our front within their own zones of responsibility; but they could not seriously affect enemy action coming from a flank. What happened to the artillery covering the troops south of the Bapaume-Cambrai road the writer does not know; the last touch he had with his neighbouring Group Commander was in settling the junction point of the S.O.S. Line on the evening of the 22nd; by wire through D.A., and by orderly, and through the infantry, efforts were made to get liaison on 23rd but without success; doubtless the neighbour made similar efforts.

(ii). *The troubles of a salient.* The capture of the battalions in the Beugny salient was a minor disaster which it does not appear that the supporting artillery could have prevented. The enemy's points of entry were (a) from beyond our extreme flank, (b) through a gap known to exist, but which could not be properly barraged because the left of 123 I.B .was beyond the gap and the right of 7 I.B. was this side of the gap; machine guns are the weapons to meet such an eventuality. The incident illustrates the objectionable points of there being a gap at all and the disadvantages of a salient in a withdrawal. Further, the existence of a salient renders the distribution of artillery very difficult.

(iii). *Flank patrols.* More, and earlier information might have been obtained by employing flank patrols, but at that moment horses were hard to get at, casualties had lessened the number of men available, and above all some of us had half forgotten (and still more had never known) the war of movement.

(iv). *Groups*. The habit had arisen of forming large groups of artillery under the senior Brigade Commander without consideration for the means of "running" such a group. Such a thing can be done with impunity in position warfare where there is little movement and all ranks get warning of each event; even then, three brigades are about as much as one brigade staff can manage. In an advancing battle, it can be done, because mistakes made have a less serious result with a beaten enemy in front; the writer had five complete brigades under him on October 17th, 1918. But in a battle of withdrawal, the command of a big group is most difficult. Either one has to steal the Brigade-Staff to run the Group and leave the Brigade to improvise a staff, or one has to command several Sub-groups and several batteries as well. Groups must be formed, to give each infantry brigadier his local artillery commander, but they need special organization of a staff to meet the purpose[1]; it is a point that wants consideration at the time that they come into existence. The alternative of keeping group-staffs going in quieter times has obvious disadvantages, but, so far as work goes, the group-commander's time would be well occupied in doing liaison, co-operating with the heavy artillery, visiting neighbours, and supervising T.M's. If the F.A. Brigade Commander does all these he has little enough time for wagon-lines and administration.

## CHAPTER VIII.

### From 02.00 25th until 12.00 26th.

#### The Pursuit.

It was difficult to "get going" on the morning of the 25th, no one had much sleep since midnight 20/21. Two officers were out by 07.00 for observation and liaison. A succession of orders were received, the first affair being trouble near Sapignies said to have been caused by an enemy agent within our lines; the real trouble lay, as before, to our right (South). At 09.15 a set of orders (based on a message from the Group Commander) was issued to batteries which gave our front line as from Grevillers to Sapignies, and a provisional S.O.S. line was traced. Ammunition supply was now according to F.A.T. 1914; the position of 41st D.A.C. was known, but not yet that of the 6th D.A.C. Wagon-lines had split on 23rd into two echelons—the firing battery and the rest; the firing battery wagon-lines were maintained henceforth as close as possible to the guns.[2] The enemy artillery was still quiet, but our batteries had begun registration when at 10.00 an abrupt order was received to "clear out at once owing to a break-through on our right," a rendezvous with the 41st D.A. Staff being appointed to L 11 b.

---

[1] A Group certainly needs at least one D.R.

[2] Nobody yet knew where the Brigade Staff wagon-lines were.

As it was not known how pressing the need might be, the guns were withdrawn directly horses could be procured, some wagon-bodies being left on the position; all these "bodies" were fetched later, however[1] The only road lay through Achiet Le Petit and was blocked; later, but not until the brigade had passed, this road was shelled by the enemy with all too good effect.

Between Achiet Le Petit and Bucquoy the block was worse; no touch could be obtained with 41st D.A.; the countryside was, however, dry and the Brigade Commander formed up the 2nd Bde. R.F.A. off the road, fell out the battery staffs, and reconnoitred a position as in pre-war days. An almost ideal 'half-covered' position was found; its left lay not far from Bucquoy and it ran nearly due N. and S.; in front lay a well-wired (old German) trench containing quite a number of filthy but well-constructed dug-outs; this trench had been for the Germans on the reverse slope and was therefore for us on the forward slope and provided excellent O.P's almost within sound of voice of the guns. The whole country from Logeast Wood to Achiet Le Grand and Le Petit was in full view. The "half-covered" position seems to be the secret of support in a running fight. The danger was to the south, but from the right hand gun of the right hand (42nd) battery there was a grand view of the low ground towards the Butte de Warlancourt, High Wood, and Martinpuich; though flank patrols were not sent out, the nature of the ground permitted us to watch this danger area—empty of troops, British and German, so far as could be seen, but with the dry grass burning in a hundred places. We were now off the last 1/20,000 map and felt lucky to get a few copies of the 1/40,000.

During the critical moments previous to taking up this position there arrived a low-flying German plane, which was successfully brought down by the Lewis gun of the 42nd Battery.

At 14.30 the O.C. 2nd Brigade R.F.A. was again put in charge of the Right Group and told to obtain touch at once at a certain place with the Brigadier of the 186 I.B. of 62nd Division—the fourth division which we had had to support since 21st March. The Brigadier was not there and it was 17.00 before he was found but a few hundred yards away from Group Headquarters. There was now considerable shelling, and the journey in search of 186 I.B. was both wearisome and depressing. The infantry were manning a line round Achiet Le Petit with detachments of unknown strength and composition some distance in front; it was still impossible therefore for us to shoot— or indeed to make any definite arrangement, for it had not yet been decided whether we were to hold on to Achiet Le Grand. The loss of our vehicles[2] was becoming something of an incubus; our very last one (the telephone wagon) had but just escaped destruction from a chance shell, leaving Achiet Le Grand; and our dinner this night consisted of a tin of pork and beans from an abandoned dump, eaten off an envelope with a penknife.

---

[1] Enemy artillery already active and enemy machine-guns not far off at the time.
[2] Brigade Staff wagon lines.

Returning to Group Headquarters at 18.00 hours, the writer gained touch with 62nd D.A. and issued such orders as were possible to 2nd, 187th, and Lieut.-Col. B's Sub-group. A small visual party was left at Headquarters 186 I.B. and visual kept up until nearly midnight; the Group Commander himself intended to reach 186 I.B. again by 03.00 on 26th. The two officers sent out at 07.00 rejoined in the evening with a considerable amount of information as to the day's doings and after fairly exciting experiences.

At approximately 02.00 on 26th, an order was received from 62nd D.A. that 2nd Bde. R.F.A. was to move at once out of the battle to Souastre; that the O.C. 2nd Bde. was to retain charge of the Group; that 187 and Lieut.-Col. B's brigades were to withdraw and come into action in certain named squares east of Hannescamps (our old front line of 1915) where we should find 310 Brigade R.F.A. of 62 D.A. already in position. Again luck was with us and the improvised telephone-lines 'held' to the two other artillery brigades; it was even possible to talk through the 62 D.A. to 186 I.B., but unfortunately not possible to get out of the latter where 186 I.B. would have its headquarters next morning; this was a misfortune. The visual station left at 186 I.B. had suddenly ceased to function— indeed we never saw the men again but heard of them months later as prisoners of war in Germany.

At 04.30 on 26th every battery had gone and Group Headquarters moved (walked—no touch with wagon-lines yet obtained) through Essarts to Hannescamps. 310 Brigade was found and its position generally inspected; 187 and Lieut.-Col. B. were also found, positions inspected, and orders issued verbally as regards liaison, observation, etc. so far as could be done. A group signal-distributing station was established in a convenient place. A personal inspection of his position is an absolute *sine qua non* for an Artillery Commander (i). The impression gained by this tour was that either the artillery position had been chosen in connection with some definite purpose strategic plan[1]; or else the batteries had been sent unduly far back. The position was at least 8,000 behind the infantry line.

It was a mistake not to borrow horses at this point, but one had little idea where to find 186 I.B. and the country was cut up and wired over by the old German trench system. A new but not less weary journey commenced at 08.00 and took us through strange sights and places[2]; in at least one place it was necessary to retire with more speed than dignity, but a little before 10.00 the Brigadier was found just west of Bucquoy. The problem was now how to control fire; there was no wire to be got until some could be picked up from the countryside; visual was impossible; for a time one could rely only on mounted orderlies. (ii).

The news at 186 I.B. was not too satisfactory; machine gun fire

[1] The imagination flew to Austerlitz and Bull Run. A pre-arranged counter-attack?
[2] Including a meeting with part of a machine-gun battalion which claimed to have been captured by the enemy and to be still in his charge!

was already being directed on these headquarters; there was a rumour that the enemy had reached Hebuterne, the neighbourhood of which was visibly being shelled by British guns; a huge snake of men of unknown nationality[1] was trailing about the hilltops to the south like the 'useless months' of the Green Curve; there was no communication with anyone and S.O.S. calls were already beginning.

About 12 noon the writer was relieved of the command of the Group and allowed to pursue his own brigade. It was past dark by the time he had reached a place called Gaudiempre and extracted his batteries from the since famous battle of Souastre.[2]

Next day after gathering the 21st Battery into the fold, we marched north towards Part II of this little history.

The 2nd Brigade R.F.A. had lost 18 Officers (including three B.C's and the Adutant), 106 men and 106 horses—the last named as usual came first in the animal-loving acting-adjutant's lists.

### COMMENTS.

(i). *Personal acquaintance with terrain.* An Artillery Commander fighting his batteries without having seen them in position will be putting himself to a great disadvantage; what would one think of a man trying to arrange a day's cover shoot off a map without visiting the woods? The only time to carry out this tour in a withdrawal is after the batteries have reached their new position but before the new battle has begun. A motor-bicycle with a side-car combined with (not instead of) his horses would enable a commander to do this. The writer has enough doubts in his mind as to some of his conclusions—but on the question of personal acquaintance with the gun-positions he is as confident as he is on the question of frequent visits to personnel.

(ii). *Infantry Brigade Headquarters, and the best method of maintaining co-operation in the retreat.* Here is an example of the difficulty of combining the functions of command with the functions of liaison. Command without communications is practically impossible; liaison without knowledge of the capability of the gun position is equally so; the combination of communications and presence at infantry headquarters was not possible in this case unless the brigadier so placed himself as to meet the needs of the artillery. The writer does not forget his sense of depression when after extricating a big group from the clutches of battle, seeing them in their new position with his own eyes, and at last finding infantry headquarters in a position singularly unsuitable to the artillery, a senior officer of fresh appearance addressed him as follows "You Group Commanders must keep touch with your batteries."

---

[1] Proved to be stragglers of many divisions.

[2] Caused by a rumour spread by a strange individual (said to be wearing general's badges) that the German cavalry had passed Hebuterne. This battle boast of many varied and stirring incidents, including a ride to Doullens by a modern (Gallic) John Gilpin in search of eggs.

The question is—in a very rapid withdrawal such as this had become, is it not better to establish the bulk of the guns well back, thus gaining time to organise an efficient artillery defence, and to entrust to a detachment the duty of providing immediate support to the rearmost infantry? An account of an action of this nature, fought by a French battery detailed for the purpose, appeared in the February 1916 number of the R.A. Journal.[1]

In this case the retiring infantry stopped (for many months) where they were at 06.00 on 26th, and the guns had to advance from the position to which they had been ordered.

(iii). This phase of the withdrawal is negligible as regards fighting lessons, but full of instructive situations affecting the art of extricating artillery while still retaining its power to support the infantry—though doubtless not to compare with 1914 experiences?

The movements and experiences of the wagon-lines since March 21st would take more space to describe than can be granted here.

Though guns, men and horses had been lost and though no one had had rest, there existed in the batteries a certain sense of elation. Someone meeting them remarked contemplatively "You ought to be feeling 'down' after a retreat!" The answer lies perhaps in Rudyard Kipling's conditional "If you can meet with Triumph and Disaster, and treat these two *Impostors* just the same."

With regard to our German criticism,[2] there can, one hopes, be little doubt as to the British Artillery's "splendid service." As to its "bad direction"? After the 21st March there was nothing for the Directorate to do but punctuate the withdrawal and leave the rest to the gods and the men on the spot; the criticism affects therefore only the pre-battle ordinances. 'Direction' includes the issue *and application* of instructions. There was little enough fault to find with the January Instructions (see Chapter I) except perhaps as regards not laying down an S.O.S. policy; it is when one gets nearer the fighting man that troubles begin—in other words, it is the carrying into effect of changes in policy, which calls for so much training and character, knowledge of the soldier, sacrifice of advertisement, and concentration on essentials; in this difficulty of application all formations have their share, from even the very formation-commander who has issued instructions to the No. 1 in charge of the gun. The student must judge for himself how far 'direction' had shown itself at fault; it is easier to be wise now.

---

[1] An abridged translation from the German by Brig.-Genl. H. A. Bethell.
[2] See Heading, Part I.

# PART II.

## A SALIENT IN DANGER.

---

### CHAPTER I.—PRELIMINARY.

ON the 4th and 5th April, after a hasty reconnaissance conducted during the last part of our march north, the 2nd Bde. R.F.A. entered the Line in support of the 71st I.B on the front J. 16. c. 8 9 —J. 5. d. 9. 7, taking over guns *in situ* and forming the nucleus of the Right Group 6th D.A., which was composed as follows :—

        2nd Brigade R.F.A.
        110th Battery, 24th Brigade, R.F.A.
        A detachment of 113th Brigade, R.F.A.
        Headquarters at Westhoek.

The outgoing group, themselves strangers, could hand over only their predecessor's defence scheme, which already needed numerous amendments.[1] Within the next few days a revised scheme was issued; it is not reproduced here, as, owing to our withdrawal from the Passchendaele salient, it was never put into effect; nevertheless its existence assisted the outposts to put up an effective delaying action between 15th and 26th. Roughly, the scheme, recognising the need of deeper defence, provided five lines (Front system, Divisional Support and Reserve systems, Corps Support and Reserve systems), for each of which the artillery had positions, O.P.'s, and zones of responsibility; the artillery had detached active, and silent, main positions; there were various stages of alarm, of which the first was 'Precautionary Measures' and the second 'Battle Stations.'

It must be remembered that at this time we held the Wytschaete —Messines ridge[2] away to the right (south), but the enemy held Houlthurst Forest (which the great Duke of Marlborough is alleged to have christened the 'Key of Flanders') on our left; this flank appeared to be the more exposed one, but a salient still existed.

It is not within the powers of the writer properly to describe the surroundings. The surface of the ground was like that of an Alpine glacier; no vestige of vegetation had as yet appeared to relieve the brownish tints of the tortured earth; the woodlands were but groups of blackened stumps standing or lying at every conceivable angle. In each crevasse lay some relic of the terrible autumn struggle—most

---

[1] These constant modifications of frontage are no doubt unavoidable, but involve an enormous amount of extra work and a temporary loss of efficiency; in the infantry area they sometimes affected the whole plan of the trenches and occasioned demand for a definite trench authority—an officer permanently in charge of a certain length of forward area. But one should not think too much in terms of trench warfare.

   [2] The geography is sufficiently known to dispense with description.

were half-full of a crimson brown oily liquid which our M.O. described
as containing 'organic matter'; wherever one looked, it was to see
broken ordnance, derelict tanks, huge dumps of abandoned stores,
piles upon piles of gun ammunition; sprinkled freely over the country
were human relics, British or German[1]; and dotted about this ugliest
of landscapes were the famous pill-boxes which had cost so much
human life to attack and defend and which now occasioned bitter
strife at each relief[2] as to who should shelter in them from shell,
gas, and weather.   Under each knoll, wherever its height above water-
level was sufficient, were dug-outs, which afforded indifferent head-
cover against heavy shells and were only kept dry underfoot by frequent pumping.   All accommodation was crowded to the last degree
and work had to be done under conditions which might have disturbed
the mental balance of (say) 'Mr. Britling' when 'seeing it through'
(at home).   The gun-positions were under cover from direct observation, but the tracks necessary for supply must have made them
obvious to airman.   Communications were of two kinds only—the
log road and the duck-board track; along either side of each
log-road lay a profusion of broken vehicles, damaged harness, and
skeletons of animals, souvenirs of some Boche "road-strafe."   No
lunatic in his mania could have imagined such hideous desolation,
rendered doubly trying by the distant view of green fields and church-
towers peeping from foliage in those parts of a once prosperous
Flanders still held by the enemy.   The truth was forced upon us of
the German version of the autumn fighting "we have left the crater
area to the enemy."

The conditions of fighting, so different from those of Picardy,
necessitated, for Field Artillery at any rate, quite different procedure.
Whereas a few trenches and some belts of wire had formed the only
obstacles on the Somme, here, by Ypres, movement off the roads was
impossible[3]; the single rider being thus confined to the roads, the
bicycle was preferable to the horse; in general one's own feet were
safer than either.   There camouflage had been almost impossible
without a heap of material which was not vailable, while here[4] in
old gardens, along ditches, amongst ruins, it was easy to conceal a
battery so long as the flashes were not exposed to Hill 60, Wytschaete
or Kemmel.   Alternative observation was usually to be found in the
Bapaume district—the difficulty lay in the maintenance of long air-
lines; between Ypres and Popperinghe it was limited to a few well-
known spots which were frequently shelled, but there existed a good
'bury.'   The undulations of Picardy could screen large formed bodies
of troops from ground observation; when Kemmel was in enemy hands
it was difficult to hide a dozen horses, and, until Summer in its
mercy brought foliage, wagon-lines were hard put to find a home

[1] 42nd Battery had a weathercock of a most remarkable description.
[2] It was a common plaint in the infantry the gunners gained a pill-box every time
a relief took place.
[3] At any rate in April.
[4] Speaking now of the less damaged country West of Ypres.

E

and were always, even in July, 6—10 miles away. The highly populated Flanders provided innumerable good cellars for accommodation of personnel, which were few and far between further south. What with poor observation, good maps, and a minimum of movement by day on either side, no wonder that the artillery turned to the map rather than to its field-glasses.

One condition at any rate was in our favour; the Second Army policy must have laid stress on buried communications in the past; from the neighbourhood of Vlamertinghe right forward to our autumn-gained ground, there existed an elaborate buried system which seldom failed when the exchanges were properly handled and which proved invaluable as regards artillery support during the critical period in 1918. Compare the value gained from labour so expended with that of elaborately dug rearward gun-positions!

## CHAPTER II.

### April 5th to 07.00 April 15th.

#### The Creation of the Bailleul Salient.

On April 7th, B/113 left the Right Group which was, however, increased by the emplacement of two anti-tank guns by C/113. On April 8th a section of B/113 rejoined the group.

On April 9th, the new Right Group Defence Scheme was issued, but was never used, for the enemy attacked the same day between Fleurbaix and Bethune and preparations had to be made for firing at the shortest ranges S. and S.E.

April 10th was a most anxious day. At 03.30 there was counter preparation and 'Precautionary Measures' was ordered. At 03.45 we were examining a frightened prisoner who brought intelligence of a forthcoming attack. At 06.10 and again 07.20, counter-preparation; at 09.32 a Group Concentration on a report of enemy massing on the Menin Road. At 09.45 came an order to withdraw the most advanced section (42nd). Soon after, as nothing occurred, it was possible to visit O.P.'s, battalion headquarters, and trench mortar positions to discuss the situation. At 16.15 orders were received to withdraw three 18-pdr. sections to First Reserve positions; to avoid difficulty of control, the *detached* sections of 21st, 110th, and 42nd batteries (the latter had but just completed its first move) were selected, which selection made the main positions 'active' instead of 'silent'; these three sections on getting into position were ordered simply to reinforce the barrage on their battery frontages, but certain readjustments of S.O.S. became necessary. At 17.00 counter-preparation, and again at 18.00, when 'Battle Stations' was ordered. At 23.15, 18th I.B. had relieved 71st I.B. and it had been confidentially explained that, though both the Wytschaete ridge and the Bluff were solidly held by us, parties of the enemy had penetrated the interval and that there was a shortage of troops available to clear the area.

We 'stood to' at 03.00 on April 11th and got rid of all possible kit; C.P.N.[1] at 05.00, 06.00, 17.15, and 21.15. The items of principle interest during the day were the news of the evacuation of our old friends 'Ahmentears' and 'Plugstreet' Wood, and considerable gas-shelling of 42nd Battery, whose officers' mess staff suffered. At 23.00 an order was received to withdraw the whole 110th Battery (which subsequently left the group), a second section of 21st and 42nd batteries, and one section of 53rd, to First Reserve positions; what with carting of ammunition (500 rounds per gun), this move extended into daylight on 12th, and left 10 18-pdrs. and 6 4·5″ hows. (whole 87th Battery) to support the Front System.

It is possible the enemy observed the move, for on the 12th the First Reserve positions were shelled; the 21st and 42nd had to shift after dusk, while one more section of each of 21st and 42nd and 53rd batteries was withdrawn, and B/113 left the group for good, leaving 2 18-pdrs. (53rd) and 87th for the defence of the Front System. During the day the withdrawal of all wagon-lines complicated matters, but a quiet 13th gave opportunity for settling in, inspection, organisation of O.P's, and registration.

April 14th provided occupation to pass the time. After the usual C.P.N., Group Commander met C.R.A. and was taken by him to reconnoitre the rearward area, west of Ypres, to which we might have to withdraw to-night. The four Captains were collected from the wagon-lines to assist. After the reconnaissance Group Commander returned through Ypres, met B.C's by arrangement, and explained procedure. During this conference, a message was received to come at once to D.A. with battery representatives; with one set of officers doing observation and another studying routes of withdrawal, it was difficult to complete a third set, but at last we reached D.A. and found ourselves with $\frac{3}{4}$ hour of daylight to chose quite a different brigade position which was to be occupied that night. Orders were dictated to representatives at 21.00, and were taken by them personally to their batteries, a special D.R. taking copies to group headquarters (still at Westhoek) and O.C. 87th; these orders were (a) for the immediate withdrawal to the area west of Ypres of Group Headquarters and Batteries, less 1 section each, (b) allotment of routes for withdrawal, (c) a rough statement of infantry dispositions, (d) orders for concentration of wagon-lines about Busseboom, (e) appointment of O.C. 87th Battery to control the four sections[2] left behind and making him responsible for liaison as regards this detachment with 18 I.B.

At 06.30 on 15th April, Brigade Commander (the Right Group now consisted of only 2nd Brigade, R.F.A.) visited the new position

---

[1] Counter-preparation.

[2] These four sections were distributed more or less in depth, with their limbers close by them (E. of Ypres).

along the Grünen Jäger (H.16.d.)—Café Belge (H.29.b.) road and found the four batteries settling in. Having reported progress to D.A. (H.22.a.) he met his headquarters at their wagon-lines (in the immediate neighbourhood) in time for a welcome breakfast.

### COMMENTS.

It was obvious from the first that the importance of increased depth had been realised, both for infantry and artillery; as regards tactical lessons, divisions coming in from the South brought their own lessons and applied them without asking. The emplacement of artillery in the salient, which had been the source of many an argument in the Ypres area in 1915 and 1916, had again become a question of the first importance; the problem had now been solved by the decision to withdraw the bulk of the guns while there was still time, so as to afford them opportunity to arrange good support of the line it was intended permanently to hold—leaving, the while, a detachment to support infantry which remained in the salient. The composition of such a rearguard artillery detachment merits further discussion, but the solution is similar to that suggested in Part I, Chapter VIII.[1]

### CHAPTER III.—April 15th/26th.

#### OUTPOSTS DELAYING ACTION.

The initiation of the Outpost Artillery has been noted; we will trace its development from four detached sections controlled by a senior liaison officer into a detachment commanded by an Outpost Artillery Commander acting as C.R.A. to the Outpost Commander and composed of what was practically one complete (his own) 18-pdr. battery reinforced by a section or two of 4.5″ hows.

On the 15th, attack from the East was still daily expected. The sections of 53rd and 87th were withdrawn and it was necessary to arrange for a possible rear-guard action by the sections of 21st and 42nd. The controlling-and-liaison officer had much trouble with his communications due to the hurried nature of the arrangements made by the signal service to man some test-boxes E. of Ypres while destroying others; it took some time to organise these communications on to a satisfactory basis. During the night 15/16 our Infantry evacuated the Front (1st) System and occupied the Corps Support (4th) System.

On the 16th, the enemy crossed our old front line but met with an effective check, suffering considerably; he withdrew to the Divisional Reserve (3rd) System, where he was bombarded by all available guns. On this day O.C. 87th Battery became "Rearguard Artillery Commander" instead of "Controlling and Liaison Officer."

---

[1] It will be remembered that the whole group of 3 brigades was withdrawn several miles on the night 24/25 March; that it found itself at least 8,000 yds. from behind the infantry next morning; and that Group Commander was expected to be able to fight his group from alongside the Infantry Brigadier who was close behind his front line.

On the 17th April Divisional Headquarters went further back being replaced in H.22.a. by Headquarters 18th I.B., while a special officer was nominated to command the Rearguard; by this time it seemed doubtful if the enemy meant to occupy the "crater area" at all and the talk was of re-occupying it in force ourselves.

On the 18th April a section of 87th (Howitzer) Battery was ordered forward to reinforce the Rearguard Artillery.

On the 21st April the "Rearguard" was re-organised into "Outposts"; its headquarters moved from Westhoek to Hooge Craters. The re-organised force consisted of the whole battalion 2/D.L.I. plus one company 11/Essex Regt., supported by whole 21st Battery (minus one section, but reinforced by one section 42nd[1]), one section 87th and one extra section of 4·5″ Howitzers from elsewhere; the Outpost Artillery was to be commanded by O.C. 21st Battery.

It needed pressure on 22nd to get Outpost Artillery Headquarters properly housed at Hooge Craters, where there was the usual scramble for accommodation; it had not been properly realised by either the Outpost, or the Outpost Artillery, Commander, that the latter was a local C.R.A. with a scattered command, requiring a clerical staff and good communications—for which purpose a detachment had to be made from the 2nd Brigade Signal Subsection.

Very little occurred on 23rd and 24th; even the fighting of the 25th and 26th scarcely affected the quiet, but with the decision to evacuate Hill 60, the outpost position became untenable. Towards dusk on 26th the outpost artillery was very quietly withdrawn and occupied the positions into which the 2nd Brigade was about to move and where they would therefore be reunited into the normal organisation. They had a most disagreeable time passing through Ypres, the enemy doubtless guessing what would happen as the result of the fighting on the Kemmel—Bluff front, but they got back with few casualties.

### COMMENTS.

It is curious how slow people were to realise that we had formed an Outpost Force; the very word had become forgotten; yet the moment they were called 'outposts,' the mind went back to Aldershot, and all pre-war soldiers were quite clear as to the functions of this detachment.

The composition of the artillery detachment merits study; it is an integral part of the Outposts and not of its own formation; it needs a separate commander and staff, and should be composed as far as possible of complete units. A battery reinforced by a howitzer section seems to be a suitable force for Outposts consisting of the greater part of an infantry brigade.

If the Heavy Artillery is so disposed as still to be able to lend assistance, an officer must represent them at the Outpost Artillery

---

[1] The object of this was to equalise work between batteries, for it was expected that the outpost artillery would get all the work.

Headquarters. In this case a Heavy Artillery F.O.O. observed from alongside one of the F.A. F.O.O's, but communications were difficult for him to make use of the guns at his disposal.

Great disappointment was expressed on all sides at our failure to 'booby-trap' the enemy; we had had a liberal experience of such methods of warfare when the enemy retired through Bapaume early in 1917; his methods were not only ingenious and humorous, but extremely effective—and never more so than in the early autumn of 1918. Of course, at the last moment, we were tied by the need to conceal our withdrawal, but, the fact is, such methods were rather foreign to our pre-war training and need the most careful preparation. Nevertheless, taking the fine dug-outs at Hooge Craters as an example, one felt it was not necessary to have rebuilt them and pumped them out for his benefit—to leave him our best pump with printed directions how to use it!

## CHAPTER IV.—07.00 April 15 to 00.01 April 25th.

### The Enemy widens his Salient and the Allies prepare to
#### defend theirs.

2nd Bde. R.F.A. was now in action[1] about where the Grünen Jäger—Café Belge Road crosses the Vijverbeek with headquarters close by Divisional Headquarters at H.22.a.2/5[2], where was also located the commencement of the 'bury.' At 10.00 a conference of B.C's was held at which arrangements were made regarding ammunition, alternative and reserve positions, observation, camouflage, wagon-lines, etc. After that, the day was spent by all hands in reconnaissance, the Brigade Commander himself doing the "Segard Ridge," from which the whole country lying North-West of a line drawn from the Northern end of the Wytschaete Ridge to The Bluff and thence to Hill 60 can be viewed. Another conference was held at 17.00 after the reconnaissance, as a result of which an operation order was issued at 21.15. In this O.O. a German attack about Bailleul was prognosticated for the morrow; the 18th I.B. line was given as I.21.d.5/0—S.W. corner of Zillebeke Lake—along the Western edge of the lake—I.15.d.6/0—I.15.d.9/3 on the Warrington Road; the lake was treated as an impassable obstacle; observation was to be from Ypres Ramparts and Kruisstraat, relying on convenient test-boxes; registration would be impossible with our outposts still on Hill 60; Wytschaete believed still in our hands. Beyond an unfortunate shell in the 42nd wagon-lines, the day was uneventful; at night rear wagon-lines moved back towards Popperinghe.

Divisional Headquarters moving back on 16th, 2nd Bde. R.F.A. occupied D.A. accommodation; there was heavy firing towards Wytschaete.

---

[1] 21st Battery H.23 c 2/8    53rd Battery H.23 d 2/1
42nd Battery H.23 c 9/4    87th Battery H.23 C 0/5
[2] Known as "Pioneer Farm."

It is now advisable briefly to describe the future theatre of operations. A single ridge[1] runs from Ridge Wood through Scottish Wood, Chateau Segard, Swan Chateau, and comes down to the Ypres-Comines Canal near Doll's House in I.19.d. *On our right* in prolongation of the line Segard Ridge—Scottish Wood—Ridge Wood, approximately three miles S.W. of Dickebusch Lake, towered Mount Kemmel from which the country in every direction is in full view; flanking Mount Kemmel in the low ground lay the villages of Dranoutre (S.W.) and Kemmel (N.E.). *On our left*, in the angle formed by the Ypre-Comines Canal and the Ypres-Menin Road the ground was quite flat and swampy until one got to the line of heights from the Bluff (I.34.c.) through the famous Hill 60 (I.29.c.) to Observatory Ridge (I.24.c.); the lowest part of these swamps forms Zillebeke Lake, so that from the ramparts of Ypres an excellent view can be obtained from South to East. *In front* (S.E. of the Segard Ridge) there was low ground in which was situated Voormezeele; beyond this low ground lay a row of heights from the northern end of the Wytschaete Ridge to the Bluff; this row of heights apparently joining the Wytschaetre crest to Hill 60 is broken by the Ypres-Comines Canal, but the break is not easy to see, and the canal lies north of a feature called Spoil Bank in I 33.a., but south of the Bluff. *On our side* (N.W.) of Ridge and Scottish Woods lay Dickebusch Lake, still an impassable obstacle dividing up either attack or defence, should the enemy penetrate our front line.

The Segard Ridge was of the utmost importance; for, though one could never afford to forget them as regards flashes, it screened the whole Vlamertinghe plain from Hill 60 and the Wytschaete Heights. But from Mount Kemmel was nothing hid—or so at least it seemed to us crouching for months in the plain.

On April 17th the firing on our right grew so heavy after 05.30 that an officer's patrol (an officer and orderly on horses) was sent out and returned with information collected from Headquarters 9th Division.[2] The day ended in the fixing of the First Reserve positions and the establishment of forward and rear wagon-lines; O.P.'s were located at Ypres Ramparts (53), looking south, at Swan Chateau (42, looking S.E.) and at Segard Chateau (87, looking S.) while another one was reconnoitred in the Ecole (I.9.c.) E. of Ypres; 'visual' was initiated from every O.P., but we were suffering from a pronounced shortage of Lucas Lamps, by far the best visual equipment. A provisional S.O.S. Line was fixed in consultation with 18 I.B., who joined us at H.22.a. Headquarters Left Group also arrived, though only for a few days; there was good 'speaking' to Outpost Headquarters.

---

[1] This will in future be spoken of as the "Segard Ridge."

[2] These patrols would have given us early warning of need to move, even if as a rule they brought back only negative information. Their news was often most valuable to us and the infantry, and arrived many hours before the fragments doled out from official sources.

The 18th and 19th brought nothing more than the now constant noise away to our right; the official news from the French, from the First Army on the south, and from the Belgians up north, was good —indeed of strategic importance; it began to be doubtful if we had been wise in evacuating the Passchendaele Ridge. Second and Third Reserve positions were reconnoitred and allotted to meet immediate attack, forward 'sniping' positions were found, and liaison effected with our right-hand neighbours (49th D.A. supporting 21st Division Infantry). Further experience led to a decision to occupy permanently only Ramparts and Segard O.P's, and a particularly good one on the top of a test-box in the western bank of Zillebeke Lake when occasions demanded; this decision took into account neighbourhood of test-boxes, available dug-outs, enemy-shelling, facilities for visual, the economy of officers, as well as providing observation along our immediate front and over the ground where we knew the trouble would soon come—i.e. the Voormezeele area could be well seen from Segard.

On the 20th, although our provisional S.O.S. Line remained the same, the greater part of 2nd Brigade was allotted night-lines in support of 21st Division—i.e. firing south; on our own lines we were to shoot next to one group 49th D.A., on our night-lines next the other group. We were closer the British front line on the south than to our own 'front line' to the east, and although our true task lay in the latter direction all our daily and nightly work and all the danger came from the south. This was the most interesting tactical situation that has occurred within the writer's limited military experience; there were actually no less than *nine* possible, even probable operations for which preparation had to be made. They were:—

(i). Permanent re-occupation of the Rearguard (later called Outpost) Positions.

(ii). Withdrawal under pressure through Ypres of the Rearguard; withdrawal occurred on 26th, but fortunately not under pressure.

(iii). Support of our proposed front line along the Western edge of Zillebeke Lake; we held this line all through the summer.

(iv). Support of another front line, should it be decided to include Hill 60; this actually occurred on the 26th.

(v). Support of 21st Division Infantry on our southern lines; an S.O.S. occurred nearly every morning and evening just about now.

(vi). Participation in a possible operation to recapture the Wytschaete Ridge.

(vii). Action should the enemy attack Mount Kemmel, which occurred on 25th.

(viii). Withdrawal under pressure should the enemy capture Mount Kemmel; he did not press his advantage on the 25th, so we hung on.

(ix). Defence of the next line after such withdrawal.

On 21st April the Rearguard was definitely organised as an
Outpost Force, see Chapter III. At night the whole 18th I.B.
side-slipped nearly a brigade front to the right, entailing a change
of the S.O.S. Line, but not necessitating any material change of
position. The main body of the Brigade was now 10 18 pdrs. and 4
4·5″ Howitzers strong, the Outpost Artillery totalling 6 18-pdrs. and
4 4·5″ hows.

The 22nd April was much like its predecessors. Some good
registration was carried out to the south, which proved valuable on the
25th. The Reserve positions were by now fairly clearly defined,
though, had it come to withdrawal under pressure, there would have
been *some* hustle'; for the salient was pronounced and all roads led
to Popperinghe! We had arranged :—

(a). To support the front line of the battle-zone from our
present or alternative positions.

(b). To support the rear line of the battle-zone from First
Reserve positions.

(c). For 'intermediate positions' should it come to a running
fight between the battle-zone and the (at that time so-
called) Vlam Line.

(d). For positions to support this Vlam Line.

(e). For positions to support the G.H.Q. Line—these positions
were west of Popperinghe.

On April 23rd a change of policy was announced. It was
decided to include Hill 60 in our Front system, which entailed considerable advance on the part of the whole 18th I.B. (less the Outposts) and therefore on 2nd Brigade. R.F.A supporting it. Reconnaissance took place at once and on April 24th single guns from each
battery moved forward to 'warm' the new positions; a conference was
held to discuss the usual questions of observation, communications,
etc. The move was decidedly unpopular—and not without good
reason, as will be seen in the next chapter.

It should be remembered that all this time the outposts were
well forward and from the east we got few worries and fewer shells;
everybody's mind was occupied with the situation growing hourly
more alarming about Kemmel—Dranoutre—Bailleul. We were all
delighted to know that a French division was well established on
Mount Kemmel.

### COMMENTS.

It is not only that one gets more than one's fair share of shells
in a salient, but that work is so much harder on the occupant artillery;
it is called upon to fire in several different directions entailing a
proportionately increased amount of observation and frequent change
of positions hard to find. It is obvious that the more guns there are
in it, the harder it is to supply them or to get them away. The list

of possibilities to be contemplated on 20th April, as given in this Chapter, fairly illustrates the point; they arose from the configuration of our front line at the moment and the 2nd Bde. R.F.A. happened to be at the busy corner.

## CHAPTER V.—00.01 25th to midday 29th April.

THE ENEMY ATTACKS OUR RE-ENTRANT FROM THE FLANKS OF HIS SALIENT
WIDENED BY THE CAPTURE OF THE WYTSCHAETE RIDGE.

Hostile bombardment began at 02.40 on 25th; at 03.15 a prisoner stated enemy intention to attack at 05.00 after gas shelling; at 05.00 there was undoubtedly much gas about. The enemy shelling went no further east than roughly a line from Swan Chateau to Grünen Jäger—evidently a flank barrage to include the Vlamertinghe Grünen Jäger—Café Belge Road; it was severe. The noise on our right was very heavy and at 09.30 one of our aeroplanes had reported being fired at from the lower slopes of Mount Kemmel; at 10.30, 18th I.B. had news that the enemy held Vierstraat, upon which the single guns sent forward yesterday were withdrawn to rejoin their batteries; at 11.15 came official news that the enemy held Mount Kemmel and Kemmel Village. This was the limit of his advance for the day; firing died down without ever stopping, all roads being barraged by the enemy, especially after dark.

Information had come in better to Brigade Headquarters, officers being sent to neighbouring groups and the neighbouring Infantry Brigade, while Ramparts and Segard[1] O.P.'s gave valuable news from time to time; an officer's patrol was out a long time towards Ouderdom with orders to gather all possible information, but to return at once if there was anything to indicate the necessity of withdrawal; in addition one of the batteries waylaid and questioned a Corps Mounted Troops patrol, whose officer had been killed; from so many and varied sources can news be gleaned *if troops are trained to glean.*

It was a surprise when, at 16.35, in spite of the loss of Mount Kemmel, the order was received *to advance* in consequence of a decision still to include Hill 60 in our front system in view of the French intention to retake Mount Kemmel. Troops had been busying themselves rather in preparing for a withdrawal! A brigade position to meet all conditions had by now become much harder to select. The batteries had worked hard all day to assist 49th D.A. on its southern front—with good effect, one hopes, for they had had an unpleasant time; everything pointed to our principal task being still in that direction and the only area which admitted of this task (while still being able to put up a good S.O.S. in support of the Zillebeke—Hill 60 line) had already been, and *was still being,* "crumped to blazes." However, it had, like a lot of other things in

---

[1] The F.O.O. was unfortunately hit.

peace as well as in war, to be done. By 23.00 on 25th most of the guns were "in" and Brigade Commander had met B.C's on the new position and discussed the situation. Brigade Headquarters remained with 18th I.B. in H.22.a.

42nd Battery (inclusive of section 21st) was at H.24.b.2/4. 53rd and 87th Batteries were about H.24.b.6/7.

26th April was still more exciting. Early in the morning there was an S.O.S. at the Bluff. Before long we heard that the enemy had captured Voormezeele and the Brasserie (N.6a), but it is doubtful if the enemy ever occupied Voormezeele solidly; the Brasserie was recaptured by our neighbours. Information was again coming in well—through stragglers collected by an artillery officer and guided to Infantry headquarters, by batteries questioning wounded men, by two officers' patrols, and from Segard O.P.

At 13.00 batteries of 49 D.A. had been somewhat withdrawn and some were in action close round 18th I.B. Headquarters (H.22a). At 13.15 the first intimation was received that the Outposts were to be withdrawn.

At 14.20 a 6th D.A. order timed 13.25 corroborated this news, adding that ammunition left on positions was to be rendered unfit for use[1], that 18-pdr. primers and 4·5″ cartridges were to be brought back, and that no fires or explosions were to be caused—so that the withdrawal should be concealed from the enemy. The 14.20 order also announced that the Hill 60 line was to be abandoned in favour of the line along the Western edge of Zillebeke Lake, but doubts were cast upon this decision by a second message timed 13.30; it was an order timed 20.00 (received 23.45) which announced the "line of resistance" would run through Doll's House (I.19.b.) and Ypres (Ramparts) while the line through Bedford House along the western edge of Zillebeke Lake would be the Outpost Line.

At 14.50 a 2nd Bde. R.F.A. Order was issued for the reoccupation of the H.23 positions (April 15-25)—'forthwith' by the Outpost Artillery—'on receipt of orders (probably after dusk)' by the main body of the Brigade; but the situation must have appeared threatening at Divisional Headquarters, for at 15.05 an order was received that the new positions must be further north—i.e. further away from the exposed southern flank of the salient; the previous orders to batteries had therefore to be amended.

Between 15.40 and 17.15 information from our officer's patrol and a message from our Infantry Company commander combined to clear up the situation and established our line as from Hallebast—Ridge Wood—Brasserie—Voormezeele—Lock 8—Spoilbank—Ravine Wood to Hill 60.[2]

---

[1] It is to be feared that there were difficulties in the way of meticulous obedience to this order.

[2] The moment at which The Bluff fell into enemy hands was never ascertained by the writer.

The difficulty now was to find a set of positions complying with the 15.05 order from D.A. (see above), but at 17.45 it was ascertained that the Left Group was shifting further north, which made their area (H.17) available—the range was suitable both east and south, while it was screened by trees from Mount Kemmel[1] The following order was therefore issued (cancelling previous orders) and the four Captains, whom Brigade Commander had summoned to Brigade Headquarters, were sent to take over and prepare the new positions :

21st Battery[2] to drop 42nd Section at H.23.c.2/8 and to take over a main 4-gun position from 111th Battery at H.17.d.5/1.

42nd Battery to send 21st Section to H.15.d.3/3 and to take over a main 4-gun position from 112th Battery at H.17.d.5/5.

53rd Battery to go complete to H.16.c.2/6.

87th Battery (outpost section) H.15.b.6/0.

87th Battery (main portion) to take over position from 43rd Battery at H.17.d.5/3.

The object of detaching sections from 21st, 42nd, and 87th Batteries was to avoid too many eggs in one rather shaky basket; the design of the whole scheme was the treatment of the H.17.d. group (3 batteries, less 1 section each) as the main body of the brigade, with the 53rd battery rather drawn back so as to be able to cover a withdrawal, from whatever direction danger came. The positions were considerably modified during the month of May, but the general design remained; the reason of this modification was that the area H.15.b. and d. and H.16.c. proved 'unhealthy.'

At this juncture the situation became complicated by the enemy concentrating a violent fire on the H.24 area where our (and other) batteries were; it broke all lines joining the batteries to the test-boxes and threatened to destroy every gun; of course it interfered with the arrangements for the move. It was calculated that the fire of 3 h.v. guns, 1 battery 77$^{m/m}$, 2 105$^{m/m}$ batteries, with some 5·9's and even perhaps 8″, had been concentrated on this unfortunate area, to which was added an attack by low-flying aircraft; it seemed for a time as if nothing could escape; however, our fire in a southerly direction went steadily on in spite of some casualties, and by 19.45 the trouble was over. Our pessimism of yesterday as to the warmth of this area had not remained unjustified.

At 20.00 the Outpost Artillery was back, a little breathless after the passage through Ypres, the western exits from which were receiving attention which reminded one of April 1915, Second Battle of Ypres.

At 21.30 the 53rd was in its new position; the 42nd was still in H.24.b. keeping up fire as necessary during the change.

---

[1] In later days, the danger of ground observation was from Hill 60 and Observatory Ridge.

[2] It will be remembered 21st battery (including 1 section 42nd) formed part of the Outpost Artillery.

At 23.00 an operation order had been issued giving infantry lines, S.O.S., etc. for the morrow; at 02.55 on 27th the Brigade Commander was able to inform the C.R.A. that he had visited the whole brigade in its new position, that communications were establish-ed, that though casualties enough had occurred there was no gun out of action, that the group of guns in H.24.b. had fired over 5,000 rounds in support of 21st Division Infantry,[1] and that a quantity of ammunition had been salved. It had been a trying day, perhaps the most trying during the period covered by Part II, and the batteries were very tired; between 25th and 27th three complete brigade posi-tions had been occupied, stocked with ammunition, and heavily used in battle—not to mention the share taken in the outpost operations.

The early morning of the 27th was blessedly quiet, for we were not yet allowed to register our real S.O.S. line, lest we should disclose the withdrawal of the outposts; however, at 10.30 the enemy were advancing about Verbranden-molen (I.28.d.). From 15.00 to 20.00 there was considerable fighting about Voormezeele and soon after 20.00 every gun was firing on enemy advancing about Manor Farm (I.22.c.). The 149th Brigade R.F.A. (30th Div. Artillery) had become our neighbours. From 03.30 till 03.40 on 28th, 2nd Bde. R.F.A. took part in a raid by the 11/Essex R. from the new 'outpost line.'

Before dawn on 28th an officer had been detailed to go forward to Zillebeke O.P. as 'brigade sniping officer'; special arrangements had been made as regards communications, including direct lines to certain batteries and a direct line to a Heavy Artillery F.O.O., and the party was plugged through to Brigade Headquarters. The venture was very successful; from 06.00 at intervals throughout the day this officer was engaging with effect the numerous targets which offered themselves as the enemy felt his way forward.

At 09.00 the enemy had unexpectedly attacked and captured Lankhof Farm (I.26.d.1/1) and our line ran Lock 8—Iron Bridge (I.26.c.)—Hazlebury Farm (I.26.d.)—Gunners Lodge. A prisoner prophesied a further big enemy attack on the morrow.[2] At 10.00 we were informed 2nd Brigade R.F.A. would be under 49 D.A. for tactical purposes from dawn 29th; at 11.00 a B.C's conference was held without undue enemy interference.[3] At 16.00 the enemy showed signs of advance from the east, but by 16.30 our artillery fire com-pletely broke up this first effort and he made no further ones. At 21.50 we were again assisting 49th D.A. to the south, from 21.00 till 04.00 on 29th we were harassing, and from 04.30 to 05.15 C.P.N. was on the books.

At 03.00 on 29th a terrific enemy bombardment started; at 05.58 there was an S.O.S. at Voormezeele; by 06.00 every air-line in the place was 'dis,' but the 'bury' served us well, officers from each battery

---

[1] Detached infantry brigades of 30th Div. were fighting under the 21st Div.
[2] The warning hardly ever failed to come.
[3] Only some more "W's" arrived.—"I presume."

being kept at the local test-boxes. We had an extra O.P. on the top of Belgian Château (H.23.b.)[1] and batteries were continually firing either on information from Segard O.P. or in answer to wireless aeroplane calls. Patrols sent out to our right again brought in useful information, but the officer who had taken this work in hand was unfortunately wounded; his place was taken by an intelligent corporal—but we do not train our N.C.O's to deal with other units and they seem shy of enquiring from strangers.

It became apparent about 10.30 that Voormezeele was lost and that there was some kind of a gap in our line about I.25. central; whereas the main battle to our right seemed to die down about 11.00, trouble kept flaring up all day from the smouldering embers to the south of us. The barraging of all roads from 17.00 onwards was very heavy. To the east things remained quiet all day. The first news of the main fighting, received about 12 noon, was far from satisfactory, but later it became known that except at Voormezeele the enemy had been completely repulsed; it was some time before it was realised that the great German effort to reach the Channel Ports had been defeated.

The wagon-lines had spent a hard day dodging German M.P.I.'s; ever since the possession of Mount Kemmel had given the enemy such good observation, they had been suffering considerably, which accounts for the large number of horse-casualties especially on 29th. Casualties between April 20th and 29th totalled approximately 5 officers,[2] 62 other ranks, and 73 horses.

## COMMENTS.

The chief interest of this Chapter lies in the practical illustration it affords of the difficulties of emplacing artillery in a salient; to perform its double task, the 2nd Bde. R.F.A. in the S.E. corner of the salient, was strictly confined as regards choice of positions. As salients will keep occurring in war, the solution appears to be to keep the guns as far back as possible, which necessitates the use of a very long range.

From a broader point of view, the holding of a salient necessitates the enemy also holding one and imposes upon him the task of widening; it was this further task which brought our Cambrai effort in November 1917 to an end. If the attacker wishes to continue the offensive, he has to launch it from a harassed salient—a most inconvenient proceeding, as the Germans found to their cost during the months of May and June 1918. The whole question affords one more example of the truth of the old saying 'Everything has the defects of its qualities and the qualities of its defects.'

It was freely suggested at the time that Mount Kemmel had been lost owing to the want of liaison between the French division

---

[1] We shared this O.P. with the Heavy Artillery, but the "bury" did not help him as it did us; the unusual situation had arisen that (buried) communications in the forward area were working well, while (air) lines in the rearward were gone.

[2] 23 battle-casualties since 21st March among the officers of a Brigade R.F.A.

REFERENCE.

SCALE.
Yds 500 0 500 1000 2000 3000 4000.

Roads or Tracks.
Contours or Form Lines.
British Lines.
German Lines.
Headquarters.
Position occupied by Right Group.
Outposts after April 20th.

REAR WAGON LINES.

SQUARES ARE
[i] LARGE LETTERED SQUARES SUCH AS H.
[ii] SMALL DITTO. SUCH AS H1.
[iii] QUARTER SQUARES H1C.
[iv] FIGURES READ FROM LEFT HAND BOTTOM CORNER.
(A) TO RIGHT FIRST.
(B) THEN UPWARDS.
SUCH AS X. H1.C.9¼.

THE VLAMPOP ROAD.
SCREENED ALL THE WAY AFTER APRIL AGAINST KEMMEL.

POPERINGHE.
VLAMERTINGHE.
BUSSEBOOM.
OUDERDOOM.
RENINGHELST.
DICKEBUSCH.
HALLEBAST.
CLYTTE.
KEMMEL.
WYTSCHAETE.
ST. ELOI.
THE BLUFF.
ZILLEBEKE.
YPRES.
YPRES COMINES CANAL.
ZONNEBEKE.
GHELUVELT.
MENIN ROAD.
HOOGE.
MANOR FARM.
HELL FIRE CORNER.
K2 OBSERVATORY RIDGE.
LINE OF HEIGHTS.
BRITISH LINE.
WOESTRAAT.
APPROXIMATE LINE OF HEIGHTS.
APPROXIMATE FRONT LINE APRIL 8.
ORIGINAL FRONT LINE APRIL 5.
FRONT LINE WHICH OUTPOSTS RETIRED NIGHT 15/16.
FIRST POSITION RIGHT GROUP 5-9 APRIL.
SECOND AND OUTPOST ARTILLERY POSITIONS.
2500 YDS TO RESCHENDAELE.

holding the mountain and the British troops holding Kemmel and Dranoutre Villages[1] in the low ground flanking the approaches to the mountain. A single mountain of no great width[2] can be regarded as a narrow salient; its defence is best conducted not by a mass of troops on the top of the mountain or within the salient, but rather by the action of troops flanking the approaches; and those troops should be *under the same command* as the detachment directly defending the mountain or salient.

The decision, on the strength of a promise from the French to recapture Mount Kemmel, still to include Hill 60 in our front system —therefore to advance both infantry and guns further beyond the bottle neck—caused surprise and was costly; but Hill 60 was an important pivot, not to be lightly given up.

## CHAPTER VI.—After 29th April.

### ARRANGEMENTS TO MEET A FURTHER ENEMY OFFENSIVE.

Though not coming within the period covered by Part II, a study of "The F.A. Group in Retreat" would scarcely be complete without such a chapter, as showing how far we had progressed in the practice of Defence since our first experience in March.

The arrangements fall under the headings (a) actual operations in the forward area, (b) preparations to defend the battle zone, (c) preparations for withdrawal, (d) counter-offensive.

(a) Actual operations. Mount Kemmel was never retaken; in September, as a result of failure elsewhere, it was evacuated by the enemy. Throughout the summer its baneful influence affected all artillery operations, but a liberal bombardment rendered its possession of the least possible value to him. Fortunately for us, summer foliage began to appear almost directly we had lost it, else it is difficult to see how we could have emplaced sufficient artillery; one position the writer has in mind whose value depended solely on whether certain trees would or would not 'bear.' The result of enemy possession of this remarkable hill was to force an undue amount of guns into the cramped area between Diskebusch and Vlamertinghe; this was well enough when the extra batteries were of a horizon-blue tint and courtesy forbade protest; it was quite another matter when British batteries came trespasseing over the mystic boundary drawn in an office tens of miles away! The fact is, defending artillery cannot be tied down by chalk lines, but one must recognise that over many guns crowded into one area cause much inconvenience to its rightful occupants.

With French reinforcements, their area kept extending to its left until they and the 6th Division became next-door neighbours. Our allies disappeared early in July for the Marne.

---

[1] Written 1919 and not strictly accurate; see Vol. II. of "Sir Douglas Haig's Command," Chapter VIII., pp. 192—197, from which it would appear that Dranoutre was in French hands on the morning of April 25.

[2] Mount Kemmel is about 2 miles from N.E. to S.W.

Ridge Wood[1] had been marked in April as a crucial spot; violent fighting went on for its possession throughout May and June, for it would have given the enemy most valuable observation. There were at least half a dozen local attacks, in every one of which the enemy gained temporary possession of the heights, only to be driven out again next day; these attacks usually coincided with some great effort on his part elsewhere. It was not until the 18th I.B. attacked in strength on 14th July, that the situation became less palpitating; no counter-attack followed this success, for the enemy was otherwise engaged.

2nd Bde. R.F.A. remained the nucleus of a reinforced Right Group (7 batteries); after a short period of rest in June, 6th Division re-entered the line further to the west and the 2nd Bde. R.F.A. then became the Left Group. Enemy counter-battery work was severe, as was to be expected in such circumstances; the actual days of battle are sometimes restful for the artillery; the two opponents were like wrestlers seeking for hold, the German ambition being to start their offensive with Ridge Wood in their hands; in between their efforts, each side devoted its energies to the weakening of its opponent artillery. Camouflage was therefore of the first importance; it was not difficult to effect here, if the principle of 'silent positions' was rigorously adhered to; never a shot was fired from them, day or night, unless every gun in the area was busy. Nasty place though it was, we kept observation going from Segard until on return to the line after 'rest-and-training' we moved our O.P.'s further west along the Segard Ridge.

There was a lot of enemy bombing by night, but at this period he confined his attentions to rearward areas, and it was the wagon-lines which were affected.

(b) Preparations for Defence of the Battle Zone : It was thought that over such terrain tanks would make poor progress, so the authorities dismissed the idea of an enemy tank attack. Trench mortars were always placed for counter-attack in case of penetration; they were not employed for daily trench warfare—of which indeed there was remarkably little. An important development took place in the S.O.S. policy; in April the rule had been "3 minutes intense and 12 minutes normal, to be repeated if the S.O.S. signal was repeated within the last five of these fifteen minutes"; by July it had been laid down that batteries were to continue on their S.O.S. lines until ordered off by *superior authority*, the idea being to cut off the

---

[1] Early in July a section of the Right group was emplaced well to the East whose task was to enfilade the enemy line immediately opposite Ridge Wood. One hopes it was effective; great trouble was taken in the selection of the position and meticulous calculatiᴄn was necessary to ensure not only correct line, but also whether the shells would clear Scottish Wood over which they had to pass. Such enfilade positions sound better than they are in practice; communication in battle would have been impossible; the Group Commander must lose control of such guns, and the officer on the spot has a very difficult task in acting according to information which it is always so hard to procure.

enemy's advanced troops from his supports[1]; fire on the front penetrated was to be increased by the employment of certain batteries detailed as 'swingers,' whose fire was left at the disposal of officers on the spot. This policy killed the 'pious hope' that F.O.O. could bring back the barrage to meet circumstances; but it was far more practicable from the point of view of the group-commander (the first fire-controller), enabled battery commanders to go on in the event of non-receipt of orders, and seemed to us an advance in thought. Several barrages were arranged behind our front line. Observation was planned out in depth right back to the gun positions, F.O.O's being instructed to withdraw when it became impossible any longer to communicate. The difficulty of sorting ammunition was now at its height; little progress appeared to have been made with the idea of sorting ammunition in rearward areas; one never had any idea what nature of ammunition would reach one, other than whether it was shrapnel, H.E. or gas; we favoured the principle of providing one gun with ammunition of the same group, if possible (which it seldom was), rather than dividing up each of the various groups amongst all the guns on any one position—decentralising thus the duty of making corrections.

(c) Preparations for Withdrawal: This was of course by far the hardest work. Higher authority attempted to supervise, but positions were few and batteries many; Divisions were supervising Field Artillery positions, while the Corps looked after the Heavy Artillery; the attack might come from north-east, east, or south; the art of "looking after No. 1," somewhat thoughtlessly cultivated by those in power, which reached alarming proportions before the end of the war, and which has perhaps accounted for some of the present indiscipline at home, resulted in such things as batteries substituting their own boards for those of their neighbours. It seemed sometimes as if the only desideratum was to be able to mark a green, blue or yellow circle on a wall map; that, this done, all would be well and responsibility ceased—which is not the case. It is to be feared that there would have been much confusion in the event—but, after all, this is one of the known disadvantages of a salient in the defence.

Right Group Commander, adhering closely to the limitations imposed as regards areas, tried to organise positions to meet every contingency; it was not expected that things would turn out exactly as arranged, but what was hoped was that reconnaissance had been done by so many people in this effort (which lasted over months), that the whole area would be intimately known to batteries when a crisis arrived—which is, after all, the one essential; it was a simple aim for such complex and voluminous instructions as littered our office tables.

Cross-country routes were reconnoitred, marked out, and *prepared*, avoiding roads and known danger spots. No attempt was

---

[1] See Part I., Chapter III., para. (xxxv).

made to stock the positions with ammunition. The Survey Companies were indeed asked to prepare fighting maps for every rearward position, but it was rather a hopeless task in such circumstances, and such as were seen did not inspire confidence. The entire area was searched, and successfully searched, for observation.

One can say that, wherever and whenever the attack came, there were a whole series of positions *in depth*, going back several miles, which had been reconnoitred. For all the actual lines of defence barrages had been arranged and allotted to batteries on a basis of *zones of responsibility*, keeping in each case a battery or two in hand. Of course there were no buried communications, but there were ditches along which to lay wire, O.P's were close to hand, and Infantry-cum-group headquarters were ready. As the result of our fears rather than our virtues, we had progressed.

Forward wagon-lines were maintained to the end, in spite of their obvious disadvantages as regards condition of horses; the rear wagon-lines were altogether too far back.

(d) Counter-Offensive. During May and June the counter-offensive consisted in violent harassing by night and counter-preparation at dawn; intelligence summaries led one to believe that it was this harassing which staved off Prince Rupprecht's offensive until events elsewhere rendered it impossible. From time to time there were raids, developing into daylight raids, and eventually (on 14 July) into a quite considerable local attack. The purely defensive artillery work strengthened up into bold sniping, and the use of gas shell on a fairly large scale became more frequent with increased supply. Up to 22nd July or so, Prince Rupprecht's attack was 'cried' almost daily, but most people realised his chance was gone when the extent of the German failure at Rheims on 15th and the French success on 18th had become known. No one will forget the revulsion of feeling which all ranks, almost it seemed the horses, felt when the crisis had passed and a new era was proclaimed by the 4th Army attack on the 8th August.

"Awake! for Morning in the Bowl of Night has cast the Stone which puts the Stars to Flight."

\* \* \* \* \* \* \* \*

With reference to remarks in Part I, Chapter III, para. (xvi), there is appended a copy of Right Group Standing Orders forming part of the early July Defence Scheme. Stress was laid in para. 24 (records of fire) in the hope of being able to locate the source of short shells.[1]

There were now 4 Lewis guns per battery, generally distributed 1 at each gun position (2 in the gun area), 1 at forward wagon-lines, 1 at rear wagon-lines; this arrangement suited the batteries and provided higher authority with anti-aircraft defence in depth.

---

[1] Compare Part I., Chapter IV., A Comment (ix).

From the commencement of June, it was once more possible to hope for good wagon-lines; but personnel was short in spite of leave not being open, and the maintenance of forward wagon-lines interfered with administration; comfortable wagon-lines form the basis of a good battery, but with increased bombing they were no longer the resting-place they had been in the early part of the war. Supply of ammunition was mostly by light railway, but the system does not work well in shelled areas at night, and the drivers had, as ever, long hard nights on the roads, with little opportunity for distinction and often very little supervision. In stationary warfare the subaltern is apt to become an 'O.P. boy'; the captain and battery sergeant-major have a hard task and earn their pay if it is well done.

\* \* \* \* \* \* \* \*

APPENDIX "B" TO JULY DEFENCE SCHEME.

· GROUP STANDING ORDERS.

### I. Alarm Arrangements.

1. One officer will sleep in the telephone pit, or alongside a telephone in the immediate vicinity of the position.

2. Two men will sleep in, or in the immediate vicinity of each gun-pit.

3. Every position will be equipped with rocket indicator showing (a) flanks of battery zone; (b) Group O.P. (c) magnetic north. A look-out man will be on duty at this board watching for enemy aircraft by day and S.O.S. signals at night.

4. 18-pounders will be kept loaded at night.

### II. Detached Section Orders.

5. An officer will sleep at a detached section position and will ring up the main position at dawn.

5a. Visual will be arranged to Battery or Group Headquarters and will be checked daily.

### III. Silent Positions.

6. Silent positions will not be used for calibration, harassing fire, or ordinary S.O.S. Tests. Registration will be covered by fire from the active position.

7. Ammunition will be 'turned over' from time to time.

### IV. Gun Pits.

8. Gun pits will be strengthened to the greatest extent that local circumstances allow.

9. Gun pits will be prepared so far as possible to allow of engagements of Tanks.

10. 3 rifles and 50 rounds per rifle will be kept in each pit.

11. Every pit will have a scheme-board in it signed by an officer showing S.O.S. angles and angles for such concentrations, etc., as are thought desirable. One of these will be the northern point of Scottish Wood (within our own lines).

A separate board should show gun and daily atmosphere corrections.

12. Every pit must have good facilities for egress and a platform marked for use in the open.

### V. Guns.

13. Every gun to have painted on the piece its most reliable calibration for each nature of charge, giving date of calibration. Subsidiary information will be painted on the shield.

14. Every gun will be painted for anti-tank engagement.

15. Sights will be checked daily.

### VI. Ammunition.

16. As far as possible only one group of ammunition will be provided for each gun.

17. Not more than 200 rounds will be kept in any pit, and not more than 100 rounds 4·5″ cartridges.

18. 18-pounder ammunition is not to be stored more than 3 deep and must be stacked on a wooden or tin flooring.

19. Ammunition from the echelon and from silent positions is to be turned over from time to time

20. The echelon will be kept full. The gun limbers will be filled with shrapnel. The shrapnel and H.E. will be kept in separate wagons divided between (a) the various subsections (b) the firing battery and first-line wagons. Clips and nose-caps will be kept on all rounds.

### VII. All Positions.

21. Alternative methods of egress will be generally known and thoroughly prepared. High roads to be avoided.

22. Limbers will be kept at or near the gun-position. Forward Wagon-Lines will be maintained.

23. Movement is to be restricted as far as possible during periods of high visibility. Men are not to leave the position in daylight, except on duty. Exposed work must be carried out at night.

24. A book is to be kept showing daily rounds fired, target, time of commencement and time of ceasing fire.

25. A 'Defence File' is to be kept, including the defence scheme, and all definite instructions reference the operation in force at the time.

Abstract instructions will be kept together in a 'Tactical Instructions File.'

### VIII. Observation Posts.

26. Each O.P. will maintain a fighting map, marked to show grid bearings, and dead ground, and provided with a pointer. Also a list of code calls, a log-book, and available information reference Heavy Artillery.

27. O.P's are arranged in depth. When one becomes unusable the F.O.O. withdraws to the next and reopens communication as soon as possible.

28. Each battery will establish a local O.P.—if possible within sound of voice of the battery.

29. O.P. party will always be armed and carry ammunition; officer with revolver, men with rifles.

### IX. Liaison.

30. A liaison officer must be fully acquainted with all Artillery information concerning the whole of the units he represents, their S.O.S. lines, geographical capabilities, etc.  ·

31. Normally the party consists of an officer anu two signallers and a lamp; they will be armed.

32. When a liaison officer can no longer help in co-operation, his duty is to go to the nearest telephone and ask for orders from the Group.

### X. Training, Inspection, and General.

33. Training of layers and in anti-tank drill at the gun-line, and drivers and signallers at the wagon-lines is to go on daily as can be effected.

34. Continual inspection of equipment, especially gas respirators is to be carried out. This is particularly necessary at wagon-lines and detached section positions.

35. Officers will impart information as advisable to responsible N.C.O.'s.

36. All officers will initial tactical instructions, routine orders, etc.

# PART III.

## CONCLUSIONS AND SOME PLATITUDES.

In drawing the following conclusions from Parts I and II it should be remarked that they refer to conditions where the front is continuous and opportunities for the display of brilliant initiative by a subordinate are few and far between, though the need of it may not be less than in the past. The modern great war is an affair of organisation from behind, even from those parts of the belligerent countries not externally affected by the conflict; it cannot be waged without the goodwill of the people; success, it has been said, comes to the finest national character. For all that, when one belligerent or the other initiates an offensive, there occur on the battle front situations calling for resolute decision which is all the harder to come by when one has become accustomed to the receipt of orders and advice from superior authority.

There is little originality in the conclusions, and no attempt to set the military world right in a few choice phrases. But the attitude that "we have done well, let us change nothing" cannot be right; the writer, having been lucky enough to get certain experiences, before he in his turn "whither hurries hence," can only record certain impressions made on him, for what they may be worth. His remarks are confined as far as possible to points which have been discussed in the previous chapters; they seem best grouped under the headings :—

(a). Preparations to meet a first-class offensive.
(b). The Field Artillery in Battle.
(c). Training in Peace.
(d). General.

### A. Preparations to meet a First Class Offensive.

(i). *Distribution as affected by communications.* Control of artillery in the defence is an affair of communications; visual is not to be trusted; pigeons may be useful from O.P's and at times one could employ a message-rocket apparatus; the alternatives are buried lines and wireless. The enemy attacked our communications on March 21st, 1918, in his preliminary bombardment, abandoning perhaps the idea of many shells per gun in favour of a larger number of guns[1] to fire the available ammunition on many targets. On the defensive the simplest plan would appear to be a few masses of guns with trustworthy communications to central spots in those masses;

---

[1] Compare Major-Genl. Sir F. R. Bingham's remark that at first the cry was "Oh! those hungry guns," whereas later it changed to "Oh! that hungry ammunition." Yet a German staff officer of high rank once said to the writer "No matter how you try to decentralise, the question of supply of ammunition always re-induces centralisation."

as, however, such a plan would offer opportunity to the enemy counter-battery organisation, it would be wise to concentrate labour and material to ensure communication to such positions as it is believed the enemy has not located; this condition is fulfilled by really well-concealed 'silent' positions, or by positions selected but not occupied until the shortest possible time before the attack; the latter alternative is especially suitable to field artillery and may solve the problem of rest and training. Developments in wireless may modify this problem.

*Reliability of communications is the decisive factor in effect produced.*

(ii). *Camouflage and the Development of Aircraft.* A premium is thus put upon camouflage—not only against the camera, but also the bombing and short-range attack from the air to be expected with the development of aircraft. 'Silent' positions are useless unless they can be concealed—the personnel is better occupied in rest and training and labour; the idea of positions to be occupied when the assault is impending, offers much; it trends towards the covering of such positions, not with strips, but (so to speak) acres of veiling,[1] so that enemy aircraft would not notice a difference in the landscape when the positions were occupied. Of course flashes would be seen through the veil, but by the time such positions have been located and reported to enemy headquarters, a decision will probably have been reached in the infantry combat.

It is just possible that the development of large aircraft may in time allow of quick concentration of troops on the defence, but not much progress in this direction has as yet been made. Generally speaking, the development favours the offensive, and appears to threaten the rearward services of the defenders, even the civilian population, rather than the forward area. Of course, improvement in the artillery attack of enemy aircraft offers the most immediate field for assistance to the defence; failure to get one's shells anywhere near the hostile aeroplane is so terribly obvious to the upturned eyes of the troops.

(iii). *S.O.S. Policy.* The S.O.S. policy announced in July 1918 [see Part II Chapter VI (b)] was a confession of failure to ensure communications, but there is no doubt, when one considers the difficulty of hitting small bodies of advanced (attacking) troops, that even under conditions favourable to the defending artillery, fire is better directed to the denial of passage to enemy supports; at the least, one will complicate matters for the enemy by making him deploy his supports and reserves. The policy of keeping the bulk of the guns on the S.O.S. line and leaving a proportion at the disposal of the officers on the spot, seems the most satisfactory one; it is a corollary of that policy that barrages behind our front line should be pre-arranged, so that at a given signal competent authority can turn on to rearward barrage-lines such lengths of artillery frontage as seem necessary.

---

[1] The writer has heard of a large field in the French area completely so covered.

(iv). *Observation.* Observation on the defence must be considered, not as it often was—a chance of 'sniping' movement and watching enemy flashes and machine-guns, but (a) to view a large area of ground, (b) having regard to facilities for communication, and (c) with special consideration for the counter-attack. Reconnaissance for observation should commence from the gun-position forwards, not from the front line back, as trench warfare falsely taught us. It should be possible even at the present stage of development to organise wireless from initial O.P's; pigeons are suitable to O.P's as the reports of a trained F.O.O. are valuable to Headquarters located near the pigeon-loft as well as to the group or battery finding the party. The best conditions for defending artillery are where there is a high ridge close in front of the gun-line from which the enemy forward area and our own front line can be seen. The modern F.O.O. must be able to range his battery, be an expert signaller, an intelligence officer, and a liaison officer.

(v). *Distribution on the defence as affected by enemy action.* The probability is that the assault will succeed in its earliest stages, that it may reach the defending gun-line (the Germans included it in their first day's objective), and that it will be accompanied by tanks. For offensive work and trench warfare, dispersion is advantageous for enfilade fire; for a defensive battle, one needs to control, which in practice means concentration in one's own area; nevertheless, defending artillery must not be too much tied by those mystic boundary-lines. A good proportion of the guns should use extreme range to allow for covering the withdrawal of forward troops and to give time for the development of the action; such guns need not be able to fire beyond the enemy front system.

The question of enemy tanks must now be considered. To attack them, we have as yet seen nothing better than a few suitable guns placed as far away from the actual trenches as possible, in sites providing a fine field of fire; the gun should have a high muzzle velocity and a special shell and be a quick-firer; the Germans organised anti-tank forts, employing anti-tank rifles and land mines: they successfully defeated our tanks when the element of surprise was absent—to quote an example, at the 'quadrilateral' N.W. of St. Quentin in September 1918.[1] The writer does not believe in the idea of detailing one gun per defending battery to go out against a tank attack—there is not time to do this; but it is wise to bear penetration in mind and it is an advantage for defending batteries to have a few hundred yards field of fire in front of their muzzles,[2] which generally means emplacement on the forward (or inner) slope of a valley; and it seems sound to detail special mobile units from resting or reserve artillery to deal with tanks that have penetrated.

For protective purposes, instead of surrounding each battery with a few strands of wire, the bulk of the defending artillery should

---

[1] Vide Article II., Part I.
[2] The holding-up of our tanks on the Flesquières Ridge on November 20th 1918, by a few German guns thus placed, offers an historic example. Vide Article III.

# DIAGRAM TO ILLUSTRATE SECTION (A) OF PART III.

Buried Communications,
(to be extended as
labour admits).

O.P. with air-line..........
Pigeons (p) and
Wireless (w).

=A   Anti-Tank Gun.

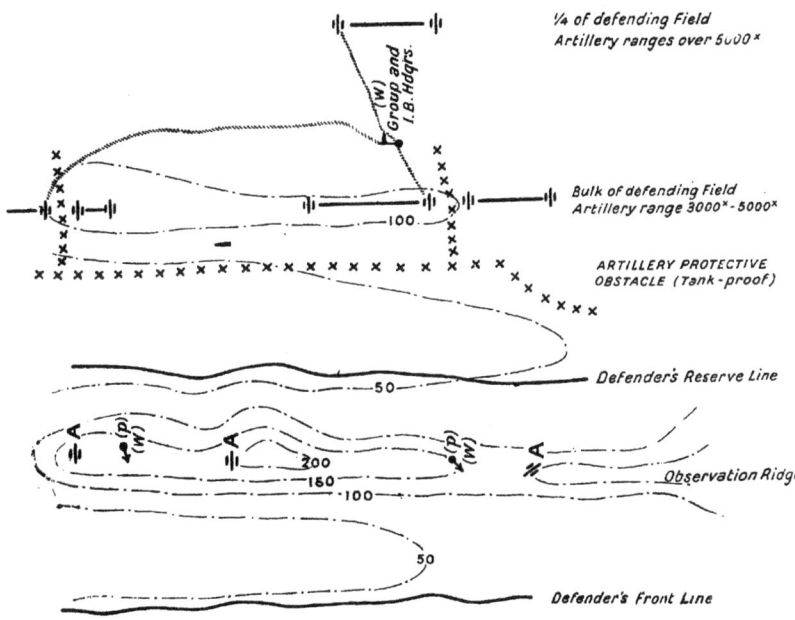

Main Gun-Line has a field of fire in front of
its muzzle.

Observation Ridge not in front system and not
in any special trenches, approachable from behind.

Artillery protective obstacle hidden in hollow.

Trench Mortars could either be in a Support
Line West of Observation Ridge, placed to bombard the Front System; or in Reserve Line placed
to bombard Observation Ridge.

Of the defending Artillery, perhaps ¼ would be
in normal 'active' positions; ¼ may be in strictly
concealed silent positions; at least ¼ at rest and
training until expectancy of attack causes occupation of selected positions.

¼ of defending Field
Artillery ranges over 5000ˣ

Group and
I.B. Hdqrs.
(W)

Bulk of defending Field
Artillery range 3000ˣ-5000ˣ

100

ARTILLERY PROTECTIVE
OBSTACLE (Tank-proof)

50

Defender's Reserve Line

(p)
(W)
A
200
150
100
A
(p)
(W)
A

Observation Ridge

50

Defender's Front Line

be behind an obstacle such as the Germans called their "artillery protective wire," from which transverse legs leading rearwards could be constructed at intervals on the principle of watertight compartments; this obstacle might nowadays include something in the nature of a tank trap; the tendency of the Germans at the end of the war was to get behind a water-way.

(vi). *Gun-pits versus Camouflage.* The question of gun-pits versus camouflage is controversial; it is too much to say that the object of entrenchments is to save troops for the decisive moment; everyone knows that cover gives a man an ostrich-like sense of security, which induces better performance of duties, even when he knows the cover to be insecure; shelter from weather for both men *and material* must be considered; a gun-pit can give cover against splinters even if not proof against a direct hit. The troubles of a gun-pit are that it is immobile, often difficult to get out of, obvious and dangerous to the occupants when hit, apart from the danger of the shell itself; flooring and drainage are hard to manage and there is a tendency to limit the arc of fire. Where guns are emplaced under cover which existed before, such as a stable or a house, there is no excuse for not strengthening the position by every possible means, including concrete; but such conditions cannot always be found and, to meet an expected attack, mobility and camouflage seem better suited to the characteristics of field artillery. Whether a gun stands under a net or an 8″-proof roof, each gun emplacement requires a set of standing orders suitable to its position and the tactical situation.

(vii). *Gas.* Assuming that the offensive will obtain some initial success, and that one of its conditions is the bringing up into the assailant's forward area of large reserves, it would appear that the defenders are well placed to use gas; not out of cylinders—for the cylinders would get captured or destroyed by enemy bombardment to the defender's disadvantage, but by long-range projectiles.

As regards defence against gas, every conceivable regulation was made during the war to limit casualties. The writer saw at Salisbury Plain in 1918 a gas-proof gun-pit; but at present the best protection appears to be the respirator; if one side or the other invents some new method of inflicting casualties, it will be for the scientist to invent a remedy; so many chemical devices have been prophesied—blinding, germs, etc.

(viii). *Trench Mortars.* T.M's appear best placed well back, in the idea of the counter-offensive—it depends on the terrain where. It is a controversial question whether they should be 'run' by the General Staff or the Artillery; there are certain obvious advantages and certain great inconveniences in the latter scheme. If they are to be run by the Field Artillery Group Commander, they form a sub-group in another echelon of defence and need a sub-group commander with the usual staff and paraphernalia for control. The arrangements which obtained in 1917 and 1918 for the provision of personnel were unsatisfactory and reacted against successful handling of a weapon so exceedingly important in trench warfare as the T.M. Development may be expected as regards the use of mobile T.M's in the offensive.

(ix). *Heavy Artillery.* Especially before an expected hostile offensive, the relation of the Heavy Artillery units to the Field Artillery should be clearly determined. Even if the present organisation is to continue, there is no reason whatever why the group should not be called a 'Mobile Artillery Group' (instead of Field ditto) and the Group Commander be a Heavy Artilleryman. It is unsound that an infantry brigadier should have to hold separate conclaves with two artillery commanders, and the "comedy of co-operative hate" should not appear upon the boards.

(x). *Field Artillery in a Salient.* Artillery is difficult to place well where a salient is concerned; its work is much harder, it is difficult to supply and still more difficult to extricate. The ideal is to keep the bulk of the batteries not farther forward than the bottle-neck line, which will probably require guns with a long range. Any units within the salient must be specially mobile.

(xi). *Preparations for withdrawal.* Preparations to meet a decisive attack must include preparations for retreat. The first necessity is for all ranks to be acquainted with the area through which a withdrawal might take place; the next is to prevent units clashing during the withdrawal by allotment of areas, positions and routes. Between necessity and convenience come certain preparations such as provision of (a) wire for future communications, (b) ammunition in the First Reserve positions, (c) fighting-maps, (d) shelter for headquarters. The digging of positions may do harm by disclosing them to enemy aircraft and will very likely prove to be labour wasted. Every rearward position should be supplied with a *carnet de tir,* of which one copy should be kept by the battery most likely to occupy it, and another copy at some accessible place like Group Headquarters; it would be best if each battery made out its own fighting map or maps instead of leaving the work to someone not personally interested in the work; the locking up of records and reconnaissance reports, etc., when those reports might be required at any moment, in headquarter and departmental offices, is a cardinal sin. *Quand le vice se masque, il est le plus dangereux.* Rearward positions should be sited in contemplation of a *gradual* withdrawal, i.e., in depth, each set connecting with the set in front of it, and *not* on a linear basis which provides only for the defence of certain prepared systems. The one absolute essential is reconnaissance.

B. *The Field Artillery during a Defensive Battle*

(xii). *Conditions necessary properly to support the Infantry.* There are nine conditions to fulfil in order to support the Infantry:

(a) Good equipment, kept in order, and enough ammunition.

(b) Good gunnery, which means sights properly tested, ammunition well sorted, and good gun-pit standing orders.

(c) The safety and comfort of detachments with cover from shell, gas, weather, implying concealment; good wagon-lines.

(d)  Good communications.

(e)  Good observation, which means capable F.O.O's.

(f)  Good liaison, above and below; one can include under this heading good alarm arrangements; *no short shooting*.

(g)  A good system of command—not more units than one man can command with the staff at his disposal.

(h)  Good distribution, suitable to the tactical situation and considering flanks.

(i)  Mobility.

(xiii).  *Zones of responsibility.*  Artillery units function best in a defensive battle on a system of zones of responsibility; if suitably allotted they can offer efficient support within those zones, but attack coming from a flank will upset the arrangements; it is better to keep the guns doing satisfactory work on their own frontages than to attempt too much fire-concentration to a flank. Artillery must *watch* its own flanks, however.

(xiv).  *A Rapid Retreat.*  In case of withdrawal when at grips with the hostile infantry, it would seem best to leave a homogeneous detachment under a suitable officer to act as local C.R.A. to the Infantry rearguard commander; the bulk of the guns should be withdrawn to prepare a proper defence of some new line; an artillery force must be seen by its commander in position before he can efficiently use it; a local C.R.A. should have his permanent headquarters alongside the commander of whatever infantry he is supporting, but the latter officer must consider the demands of artillery communications in the choice of those headquarters. There is an awkward period of inefficiency after a battery has changed its position; everything possible should be done by means of standing orders to reduce this period to a minimum. The half-covered position probably remains the best and it is practically impossible to work otherwise than by zones, or lanes, of responsibility.

(xv).  *The personal touch.*  As personal leadership is admittedly the secret of command, and since 'time spent in reconnaissance is seldom wasted,' an artillery brigade commander needs at least a sidecar (so long as roads exist) to carry out his duties *in time*.

(xvi).  *Ammunition Supply.*  At a practice-camp in 1910, the writer saw a horse artillery battery lose its 'special' for being without ammunition when an important target appeared; the decision caused an outcry; a strike was feared but of course the other batteries would not come out. Remembering our pre-war training, in seems absurd to remark that, on the move, the firing battery is inseparable; yet an 23rd March, the writer was asked to send *all* wagons away and rely upon dumps! In a moving battle dumps cease to exist and the firing battery wagon is part and parcel of the gun-detachment; going further, the wagon lines are an integral portion of the battery. Granting that separation between the firing-battery and the first line wagons is inevitable, responsibility for liaison rests primarily with the first-line wagons; a similar principle applies to headquarter units.

It is not till one starts moving that one really feels the need of the Brigade Ammunition Column; the D.A.C. is doubtless more suitable for trench warfare.

### C. Training in Peace.

(xvii). *Practice Camps for Gunnery and Manœuvres for Tactics.* Practical Gunnery has shown itself so much more technical than most people imagined, that we shall probably have to devote the whole or almost the whole of our 'practice' ammunition to that branch of training. The ammunition expended is nothing but an insurance premium. Prince Kraft's cry 'to hit and again to hit' has received additional justification in a war where daylight movement was at a discount in all but exceptional periods. Short shells should be highly penalised at our 'practice camps' and the writer humbly expresses an opinion in favour of the competitive system.

Infinitely more might be done at manœuvres as regards training for open warfare; if the umpiring were carried out with one quarter of the care devoted to umpiring at practice camps, we should progress and we could afford to dispense with tactical days at 'practice.' It is not a difficult sort of umpiring; no 'casualising'; just a judgment on the following points :—

(a)   Is the battery concealed? Was it exposed before coming into action?

(b)   Were the initial orders efficiently given out?

(c)   Is the position tactically suitable?

(d)   Was the fire timely?

(e)   Is the observation satisfactory?

(f)   Are communications working?

(g)   Is the liaison satisfactory?

A simple system of marks would help the senior artillery umpire to form a judgment, and that judgment must be weighed in the decision as to who wins. The writer knows of no other means than manœuvres to acquire 'the tactical sense'; he has in his mind a battery commander whose battery, in attack or defence, seemed always able at the critical moment to perform the task demanded by an unexpected set of circumstances.

(xviii). *Heavy and Field Artillery Co-operation.* Heavy and Field Artillery must be trained to work as one Regiment. There is no intention to discuss amalgamation or to suggest alteration of armament here. Officially asked for an opinion, the writer suggested an increased Mobile Artillery Group composed of the usual field artillery, one battery of 6″ Hows. or 60-pdrs., a Brigade Ammunition Column, and, where necessary, a Trench Mortar Battery. His reason was co-operation in battle; who commands is merely a personal question; the heavier armament was to be Corps Artillery[1] and can claim the services of the 6″ and 60-pdrs. The system which obtained in France—extreme centralisation—grew up directly from trench warfare

---

[1] Some think the task of the very heavy artillery will be taken over by bombing planes.

and the constant trench *offensives* of 1916 and 1917; were defence and movement sufficiently considered?

(xix). *Co-operation with aircraft.* A great deal of practical training is required in the co-operation of field artillery and aircraft; field batteries never got enough practice with *trained* observers and inexperienced observers found it hard to see the small shells; intercommunication was often unsatisfactory.

(xx). *Training of the young Officer.* A young officer should receive training :—

(a) To make him more of a professional artilleryman (much increased knowledge of ballistics) and a reasonably expert armament officer, which is largely mechanics. The writer confesses to scandalous ignorance of gunnery as a subaltern and his armament capabilities were almost limited to taking the breechblock to pieces. Borrowing from "Henry Clay"[1] an artillery officer should be capable of advertising the British Artillery to foreign missions, to get orders from abroad.

(b). In staff-work; the writing of operation messages is a drill; the tendency of an untrained man on getting an order is to lock it up in his mind instead of distributing a certain amount to his subordinates; the upkeep of records was neglected—it is difficult now to discover where pre-war battery property is located and almost impossible to find out what officers have passed through batteries; the daily fire record is an important document if accurately kept; training is dependent on study of military history, which is ultimately based on war-diaries. It does not demean a man to be able to run a good office, or to write a useful intelligence-summary.

(c) Besides being a horse master, he should have a working knowledge of mechanical transport; nowadays the latter has priority.

(xxi). *Training of N.C.O's.* Could we not make more use of our N.C.O's? Generally speaking they could not compete with most of the so-called "officer's jobs" because they were never allowed to perform them! A good N.C.O. can run a wagon-line, take an exercise, supervise a stable-hour, manage his equipment, test his sights, write a letter or operation message, handle the director, give a lecture, shoot a section, or do F.O.O. If they are thus trained, we can do without so many officers, like the French Artillery (where the officers do not exist in such numbers). The officer should be supervisor and advisor; for instance, the 'standing' F.O.O. could be a N.C.O., while an officer supervises the observation, talks to the infantry, and carries out the usual liaison.

Something in the nature of 'The Shop' is required to correct the haphazards of promotion within the unit; at any rate a man should not be able to reach the Sergeant's Mess without the 'vision' engendered by such training; this should not be unfeasible; compare the Guards' Depôt at Caterham.

(xxii). *Principles of training.* We must start our hunting-seasons with fat horses and our wars with trained batteries. What should be the principles of training? They must vary somewhat to meet circumstances, but surely the basis should be decentralisation.

---

[1] "Journal of the Royal Artillery," May and June, 1919.

Nothing teaches one the need of it more than a defensive battle. It is true that a capable man gets quicker effect by running everything himself and that it is a bitter experience to receive criticism because a subordinate has failed; it is also quite useless to argue that the critic is an ignoramus. Have we not seen again and again the disadvantage of a one-man show, kept alive perhaps beyond its span by a clever idler? On the other hand a first-class supervisor is often adjudged idle even by those who should know better. Supervising demands great patience from an able man, but it is a far better use of his abilities, for in the process not only are a number of men trained to run their special jobs, but that number of minds and more are trained to think for themselves, and, further, a system has been started which will outlast many a hard trial. How to train for decentralisation? The obvious method is to deal only with one's immediate subordinates, giving credit or blame by results. Much could be done with the 'running account,' which can be applied to equipment, harness, horses, forage, clothing, barrack furniture, barrack construction; something has been done in this way, but it is positive humiliating to see the troops inconvenienced for want of some useful building and then in the last weeks of a financial year see some less useful indulgence permitted so that there may be no balance to hand back to a Treasury which (naturally) regards the Army as a 'spending department.' [1] A battery commander should be primarily responsible for the good shooting of his guns, and there should be more direct liaison between the ordnance authorities and the gun-line; in peace as well as war, a commander should be able so to distribute his personnel as to allow him to obtain the efficiency for which he is responsible—i.e., direct liaison between 'Records' or the Depôt and the Brigade Commander. The principle under which a soldier is taught to find his food, his furniture, his equipment, etc., with no trouble at all, and by which he is in no way penalised for waste, causes atrophy of mind and character; whereas a reasonable amount of worry in getting a good show out of the local conditions is a tonic and trains the mind to responsibility. *But*, one must guard against the encouragement thoughtlessly, but only too often, given to the 'greatest pincher.' The writer suggests the orchard-robbing by the garrison nearest to his present residence, accompanied as it is by stoning of the unfortunate proprietor, as a direct result of official teaching in France to obtain what one wants by any means to hand.

### D.   Some General Platitudes.

(xxiii). *Surprise.* In strategy or tactics, in peace and in war, almost if not quite the most important element of success is surprise. In 1914 there was the direction of the German advance; at Neuve Chapelle the enemy apparently did not expect attack; in April 1915 he used poison-gas; in May 1915 there was no surprise on our front and little success—September was scarcely better. The Germans expected a British attack in 1916; success only occurred on or near

---

[1] See articles by Lieut.-Colonel Sir John Keane, Bart., in "Nineteenth Century" Magazine and elsewhere on Public Accounts.

the French front. In April 1917 a succession of daylight raids near Arras put the enemy off his guard; in June 1917 our miners provided the surprise; modified success in Flanders was dearly purchased without surprise by masses of men and huge expenditure of life and ammunition. At Cambrai we obtained success by a surprise tank attack in force, while the enemy got his later by a surprise 'counter.'

What surprise did the Germans achieve in March? First of all there was concealment of the date which led to the cry of 'Wolf,' affecting a distinctly tired army; secondly they made astute use of the weather-forecast; thirdly they adopted new tactics—penetration at all costs, penetrators to wheel outwards widening the salient under support from machine guns and mobile trench mortars. As regards artillery? Ludendorff speaks of the creeping barrage; but we had it fully developed by the autumn of 1916 and the writer's opinion from what he saw is to the effect that the German 'creeper' was not as efficient as ours. Ludendorff speaks of calibration behind the line so as to open fire without registration, but we had done that at Cambrai *in imitation* of the Central Powers' effort on the Caporetto! It seems to the writer that there was nothing new in the German artillery methods except the extraordinary distribution of their bombardment and the use of long range guns against all communications. Very effective it was, too! [1]

Our success in the 100 Days' Battle was largely due to the constant change of front of attack without any preliminary bombardment to give away our intentions—which had been the talk of the army two years before, only that we presumably had not the means to put it into effect.[2]

Some surprise, some change of method, is essential to success in the offensive. It is possible also on the defence[3] and one can get no better example than General Gouraud's battle about Rheims on July 15th, 1918; such surprise makes opportunity for that counter-attack which is "the soul of the defence." In plain words what is the counter-attack but the exploitation of surprise?

(xxiv). *Artillery and the General Staff.* There have always been two divergent tendencies, one to let the artillery run itself, the other to embody it in mixed Formations; a lecturer at Camberley headed his lecture "Artillery must be controlled, but the principle of control is subordinate to that of co-operation." After the Boer War we formed Divisions of all arms; just before 1914 an article in the Army review favoured Mixed Brigades, or something very like it. Trench warfare tended towards separation from one's Infantry because such great powers of control became vested in Corps Artillery offices: this tendency was increased when experience on the Somme in 1916

---

[1] But read article entitled "German Artillery in the Break through," "R.A. Journal," June, 1923, a summarised translation from the German.

[2] This would have necessitated offensive preparations all along this front; a considered offensive policy is necessary—a sort of Offence Scheme.

[3] Other examples of surprise in the defence were the German booby-traps during their withdrawal in the spring of 1917, and (of far greater importance) their delay-action mines in 1918.

showed that divisional artilleries hardly ever supported their own infantry after the early phases of an offensive; consequently divisional artilleries were reduced and Army Brigades R.F.A. created. There are doubtless advantages in allowing the Artillery to run itself, but the deciding factor appears to be that unless you have training together and close neighbourhood in peace, you will not get genuine co-operation in war.

The lowest mixed formation is, we all know, the Division. Within the division, the field artillery is commanded by a C.R.A. and the same divergent ideas appear; in some divisions the Divl. Commander left the management of the field artillery to the C.R.A., while in others it was treated like an infantry brigade, to which however it is not similar, because it naturally gets split up in the battle. The question arises, how far should the Divisional Command retain control so as to keep a finger on the artillery pulse? in other words, having *initiated* co-operation by divisional orders, how far should the G.S. fulfil its duty to criticise the carrying out of its policy by the artillery? The subject has been discussed at some length in the R.U.S.I. Journal of August 1919.

Of the nine conditions of artillery support mentioned in para. (xii), *the Divisional Commander* is responsible for all but the first three. The influence of the general staff has been suggested (or referred to) several times in the course of these pages; (i) as regards priority of labour; (ii) as regards fixing of combined infantry and artillery headquarters so as to ensure liaison; (iii) as regards S.O.S. policy. In the offensive, changes at the last moment in the line of departure or first barrage line often made their task dangerously difficult for the batteries; zero was sometimes fixed at too short notice. It used to be thought, probably most unjustly, that "the Division" was not always as careful about the artillery getting rest as about the infantry[1]; the arrival of the artillery to rejoin its infantry after a period of separation was not always greeted with music and bunting. Infantry and Artillery interests must clash from time to time; the clashing can usually be foreseen and discussed if the commanders meet frequently in the normal procedure of the day—which is quite a different thing to the one making a special journey to see the other, for the favourable moment can be chosen; in other words it is in most cases highly conducive to efficient liaison if parochial difficulties can be overcome so far as to permit of the two chiefs 'living' together. The divisional artillery does no worse in battle for an occasional touch of the Divisional Commander's spur, and the writer believes that the batteries appreciate his personal attention.

The General Staff has a good "jumping-off ground" in the genuine keenness of the artillery to support its infantry well—nor will sacrifices be grudged by the gunners to effect this; on the other hand the artillery possibly thinks that its real efforts towards co-operation have not always met with perfervid response—the word 'co-operation'

---

[1] Reserve Infantry units rest and train and provide labour; Reserve Artillery units often occupied so called "silent positions" which they dared not use. More rest than the R.F.A. got 1916—1918, must be catered for in the future.

implies mutual help. The G.S. have two great fields in which to display their influence in the future—(i) the inculcation of both Arms in peace, by every possible method (such as attachments, lectures, classes, tactical exercises, attendance at musketry and practice camps, criticism of schemes), of the pecularities of those Arms and of the principles of co-operation; (ii) a correct appreciation at manœuvres of the influence on the mimic battle of the artillery of either side. Only too often one sees a G.S. memorandum, a training scheme, or an operation order, so worded that it was transparently written without a thought of artillery in the author's mind; no Operation Order at any rate should be issued to the troops without some reference, however slight, to the existence of the artillery.

(xxv). *Signal Service.* It can scarcely be denied that communications are the secret of control and that control is more than ever necessary when we are trying to defeat *the will of the enemy*, as in a defensive battle; it seems to follow that we must organise accordingly. It was inconceivably long before the authorities would admit that the divisional artillery needed a special signal detachment at all, and that in the face of unanimous demand from 1908 (when divisional artilleries first blossomed into existence) until 1912 or 1913. What is desired now is not so much increase in numbers as improvement in the average standard of efficiency—with these exceptions (a) that a battery having a detached section and finding an O.P. party (the normal defensive procedure) requires 12 trained telephonists, which is more than the establishment allows; and (b) that the F.A. Brigade signal subsection needs a wireless detachment. As regards quality, it is an education to visit a big signal office and see the men at their work during a busy hour; it is equally an education to see a lineman in the forward area mending the lines to an encouraging accompaniment of "five nines," brave to a degree but sometimes a most inefficient signaller. A proportion of the "stuff" which goes through that big signal office is not of very urgent importance, 'Priority' though it be marked—while in the forward area battle is perhaps being decided by the holding or giving of some one of those obstacles to movement, the above-ground cables. What is the solution? does the big signal office need all the best signallers? should we train more artillery-men or demand the services of more R.E.? The disadvantage of having R.E. personnel are that one introduces an outside element into the battery with a consequent chance of disturbing the peace, and that the sapper or pioneer cannot at a moment of pressure work the gun; are these really serious disadvantages, or could not they be overcome? In any case what the Field Artillery wants in battle is a certain increase in battery personnel, better-trained men, more signal discipline, and a development of wireless. To every organisation such as a Group *at least one D.R.* is an absolute necessity during a retreat.

(xxvi). *Horses, harness, and mechanical Transport.*[1] "Them

---

[1] Written early in 1919.

wimmin spiles the ball'' was a male dancer's historic remark; on a
quiet front, a similar remark could have been made of the mass of
horses and mules which lived *and ate* from 6 to 20 miles behind
the line.

Could we usefully introduce a proportion of mechanical transport
into the Field Artillery?   No doubt there exist countries in which it
would be possible to dispense, to a large extent, with horses by the
use of an ammunition-carrying tractor which draws a gun.   Is there
sufficient petrol to keep up such a standard?   How far towards the
front could mechanical transport be economically employed? to include
the D.A.C., the B.A.C. (if such exists), or to the first line wagons?
M.T. can be more quickly pooled in case of need on an active front
and takes up less room; on the whole it is less reliable than horses;
it is usually quicker but more easily put out of action.   We ought not,
one would think, if trench warfare ever supervenes again, to spend
such a mighty lot of money and grain on maintaining more horses
than are wanted—but the writer has not the means at his disposal to
justify a statement that in the end there was want of economy.   The
first consideration is, of course, the nature of the theatre of operations;
France and Belgium are well roaded and M.T. could have done the
work down to and including the ammunition columns.   What about
Gallipoli?

Allied to this subject is the question of harness for the horses,
and the metal equipment of the R.F.A. generally.   Doubtless in a
long war it is good for discipline to have harness and other steel-
work to clean, but the amount of labour devoted to what was
affectionately called 'eyewash' was enormous.   Could not the additional units which spring into existence with a great war be equipped
with some sort of oxydised or otherwise prepared metal-work which
could be treated with water?   *Pas magnifique, mais la guerre?*   The
barrack-square brightness which we had in defence of our reputations
to maintain is a positive disadvantage in battle—vide Marshal Foch's
order—and occasioned a demand for much expensive cleaning-
material.

(xxvii).   *Organisation.*   A few simple modifications in organisation would go far to easing the situation for artillery.

An improvement in the signal service within a F.A. Brigade was
suggested in para. (xxv.)   In Part I, Chapter VIII, it was endeavoured to present a case for the provision of a side-car to enable the
brigade commander to carry out absolutely necessary reconnaissance
in a short space of time.   A battery should be mobilised at the beginning of the war with a proportion of tradesmen; a clerk, a draughtsman, a tailor, a shoe-maker; this should not be difficult to arrange,
though when we were trying to smarten up for the Rhine, tailors
were not to be had at any price, and we were in a really bad way for
clothes, those of us who were far forward.

It is to be doubted whether anyone foresaw the enormous amount of work which would be involved in an attempt to account for ammunition. The staff-captain on the D.A. Staff is, or could be, wholly occupied in attending to the comfort and other administration of the batteries, especially during a withdrawal; the brigade-major and the reconnaissance officer have their hands full of 'G' work; an officer for ammunition duties, whose work was partly 'G' and partly 'Q' and always of a 'priority' nature, was found necessary by many D.A's on the Western front.

(xxviii). *Equipment*[1]. For the defending artillery engaged against a first-class offensive, especially where a salient is concerned, a long-range weapon is necessary; it would probably take the attacking infantry $3\frac{1}{2}$ hours at the least to reach a defending gun-position emplaced at 7,000ˣ from the assailant's front line. Both the French and Germans realised this, and put the British Field Artillery to a great disadvantage, never more felt than when we were supporting the French infantry; the lack of long range was acutely felt too at a time when the object was by intensive harassing to stave off an enemy attack (see Part II, Chapter VI). This disadvantage still existed when the armistice was signed, as it had existed all through the South African war—due perhaps to dismissal of the idea of shooting by the map, on the plea that it was of no use to be able to shoot further than one could observe.

Variety in ammunition involved work at the gun-position which can scarcely be grasped by those unacquainted with the battlefield, and to some extent affected the morale of the artillery in the close support of their infantry—by 'close support' is meant creeping barrages in the attack and S.O.S. barrage in defence. Whether we should not be wise to save labour by providing Field Artillery with only one kind of ammunition in the future, H.E. and instantaneous fuze? It is not that shrapnel was a failure—far from it, *under favourable conditions;* but difficulty and cost of manufacture *must* be considered in a modern big war, and it is to be doubted if the most enthusiastic supporter of shrapnel would ask for more than a proportion to be shrapnel, for use in creeping barrages,[2] defensive S.O.S. when conditions allow of good storage, and occasionally during a 'moving' battle. In other things besides ammunition, the armies of the future will cry for simple and fool-proof equipment.

The introduction of labour-saving as regards metal work has been suggested in para. 25; there are other labour-saving devices, too, such as the excellent aluminium 'graphs' and sliding-scales (not, however, always 'simple and fool-proof'), with which the German batteries, especially their howitzers, were equipped.

(xxix). *Efficiency and Tradition.* A well-trained battery starts a war efficient, but loses efficiency in proportion as it suffers casualties; on the other hand it gains experience. Between the middle of

[1] Written in 1919.
[2] More than one authority favoured H.E. even for the Creeping Barrage.

November, 1917 and the end of April 1918, the 2nd Brigade R.F.A. lost no less than 39 officers and over 200 other ranks in battle— casualties alone; yet the writer would be hard put to it to say that the brigade was less efficient at the end of that period.   This is due to the fact that personnel does not change all at once; a proportion is always left to hand over that elusive element of efficiency, a mixture of pride, vanity, and custom called 'tradition.'   The 'Tradition of the Regiment, sounds, *and is,* magnificent, but it requires someone to hand it over; it is an error to suppose it begins at the top, where much else is considered; it begins at the bottom with the gunner and driver as regards his gun or his horses; it builds up and combines in a section and, later, in the battery, where it probably reaches its maximum so far as the R.F.A. is concerned.   No sane soldier could cast a doubt on its value as tending to efficiency.   It is to be regretted that old regular units which there was never any intention to disband could not have been re-organised so as to retain a certain proportion of their officers and men to hand over to a new generation the tradition they had inherited and so splendidly and gallantly maintained![1]

---

[1] The writer, in his humble capacity as brigade commander, endeavoured to put this into practice, but the gigantic and complicated task of simultaneous demobilisation and re-organisation no doubt rendered such a thing impossible.   In fact, there is no connection between 2nd Bde. R.F.A. of 1923 and that of 1918 other than the name. In 1919 the Nth Bde. R.F.A., was presented with the title 2nd Bde. R.F.A., and in 1922 the (N+1)th Bde. R.F.A.   It's composition by batteries is not even nominally the same to-day as in 1918.   Change is unavoidable, alas! but one may be sure that, as far as gallantry and efficiency are concerned, it is a case of 'Plus ça change, plus c'est la même chose.'

# ARTICLE II.

# A FIELD ARTILLERY

# GROUP IN ADVANCE.

In three parts;

Part I—The Approach to a Fortress.

Part II—Movement.

Part III—Summary.   The Transformations of War.

*Reprinted from the Journal of the Royal Artillery.*
*Vol. XLIX.   Nos. 7 and 8.*
*(By kind permission of the Royal Artillery Institution.)*

# PRELIMINARY.

The Brigade Commander arrived back in the Ypres Area from Shoeburyness in the first week of September, to find 6th Divisional Artillery withdrawn from the Line preparatory to moving into the Somme district, and himself acting C.R.A. The elaborate arrangements to meet the expected attack by Prince Rupprecht of Bavaria had, fortunately, never been tested. On the contrary the enemy was retiring and Mount Kemmel fell into our hands once more. (The author has since heard from sundry German sources, how very unpleasant we had made his Hazebrouck salient for the enemy during the months of May, June, July and August.)

The Fourth Army had attacked on August 8tn and achieved a brilliant success. The French were fighting steadily on its right. The Third Army had joined in the attack (on the Ancre) on August 21st, and the First Army had broken the Queant—Drocourt Line E. of Arras on August 26th. On the Somme we had almost regained the ground lost during the German offensive; the First Army was an important step in front of its 1917 line.

The author would summarise as follows the psychological attitude of troops reaching the Somme battlefield at this time. The Somme held bitter memories for 6th Division, but the Fourth Army seemed "on the win." Recent successes on the Western Front seemed to offer more than previous 'victories.' The Americans were seriously engaged and were present in France in great force, in spite of submarines. It was probably possible after all to drive the enemy out of France and the war might really be ended before so very long. Things were looking better in other theatres of operations. British troops had had a breathing space in which to recover from the severe blow dealt them in the Spring. The third battle of Ypres (or Passchendaele) followed by the German offensive, had entirely altered the constitution of units, but some experience had been gained with the new personnel. We had not forgotten our offensive lessons of 1916-1917 and we had learned something during the year of defence; but always of the trench warfare and limited objective type of fighting. There might be open warfare before us, but of that we had no experience; such personnel left as had been trained in open warfare had forgotten it.[1] Put into other words, we expected ample time to prepare for action, expected our food and ammunition to reach us according to plan, looked for reasonable comfort, and should fight by the map with the help of a barrage scheme which freed regimental officers of need for decisive independent action. One cannot have things both ways; we had grown used to "control cake."

---

[1] But experiences at Cambrai in Nov. and Dec. 1917 had been useful.

On September 6th, the Bde. Commander summarised lessons gathered from the troops already in battle as follows :—

(i) Not many casualties, but hard work, and short sleep.

(ii) Forward reconnaissance, as well as observation and liaison, to arrange for.

(iii) Necessity of 2/3rds artillery being always ready to lay down a protective or creeping barrage; not more than 1/3rd to be on the move.

(iv) Possibility of advanced sections with battalion headquarters.

(v) Shooting oneself in from observation, rather than by use of map.

(vi) Infantry jumping-off places to conform to artillery barrage possibilities; direct attack on obstacles in preference to turning movements.

It was just possible to hold[1] 4 battery exercises and one brigade exercise, with full staffs, and one sub-section present per battery, other subsections represented by their "Numbers One," to inculcate the forgotten principles of open warfare, before 2nd Bde. R.F.A. moved to battle on Sept. 13th.

\* \* \* \* \* \* \* \*

We heard, from those we relieved, of pursuit and infantry guns; very little of the kind was to come our way, at any rate at first. Theirs had been the long drive; were were to make the approach shot; our neighbours were to hole out across the Canal de St. Quentin at Bellenglise.

---

[1] We also held our long-promised, but time after time deferred, sports; the luck was against us, for the weather was wet, but not the refreshments.

# PART I.

## THE APPROACH TO A FORTRESS.

### CHAPTER I. Sept. 13/17.

One must consider the Hindenburg line as the wall of a fortress, plans for the defence of which had long been prepared. From the point of view of the artillery supporting the attack, then, we were in for none too easy a task.

The outline of events during this period is given in pages 122—125 of Major General Sir A. A. Montgomery's "Story of the Fourth Army" and in slightly more detail on p. 59 of Major-General T. O. Marden's "Short History of 6th Division." The general trend of these events will only be briefly mentioned in this paper.

On the 13th September, 2nd Bde. R.F.A. marched out of Corbie, spending the night 13/14 West of the Somme; we had opportunity there to witness determined, though to themselves disastrous, efforts of enemy airmen to destroy the rough bridge at St. Christ—Briost. It was on this night that 6th Division relieved 32nd Division (IX Corps) on the Holnon Wood front.

On the night of 14th September 2nd Brigade was in action in a supporting position S. of Villeveque (Position No. 1), ready to fire a long-range defensive barrage. 24th Brigade, R.F.A., the other 6th Divisional Artillery unit, was in front and already engaged in some rather confused infantry operations along the Eastern edge of St. Quentin and Holnon Woods; the village of Holnon long remained a disputed point.

The 15th September was spent in reconnoitring the area X 4, R 34 and 35 (Position No. 2), for emplacement in the coming battle of the Left Group (to consist of 3 brigades), and in reconnaissance for passages through the woods; the enemy artillery made this duty unpleasant, especially within the confines of the wood. The defensive barrage prepared for the night was along the line X 22 b 5/0—X 17 a—X 11 c—X 4 d 3/5.

Instructions No.1, issued by the Brigade Commander on 16th gave :—

(i) Approximate time and date of attack (dawn September 18th).

(ii) First and second objectives and a further objective for patrols.

(iii) Composition of Left Group—2nd Bde. R.F.A. (1),[1] 14th Army Horse Artillery Bde. (consisting of four 18-pdr. batteries), 161st Bde., R.F.A.

(iv) Allotment of tasks to Sub-groups, complicated by the necessity of advancing part of the Group whilst the barrage was in progress.

---

[1] Figures in brackets refer to comments at end of each chapter.

- (v) Map co-ordinates of tracks being prepared by R.E. through the woods.
- (vi) Orders to prepare O.P's at X 6 a 4/0 and R 35 d 5/8.
- (vii) Allotment of liaison duties, as far as was possible at the moment.
- (viii) Orders for dumping ammunition (18-prs. 300 r.p.g. 60% H.E. and 40% shrapnel with 50 r.p.g. smoke; 4·5″ Howitzers 250 r.p.g. fuze 106).
- (ix) Intentions reference wagon-lines (2) and location of battle hdqrs. (3), with orders as to synchronisation (4).
- (x) And asked for "reconnaissance reports" from all 3 subgroups on the areas into which they would have to advance during the battle, exact location of their intended battle headquarters, and information reference clearing the crests.

Special circumstances of the moment included the following :—

(a) An operation[1] had to be carried out on 17th to capture our intended Line of Departure, which involved action by the French about Savy on our right (5).

(b) 2nd Bde., R.F.A., could not occupy its battle position till night 17/18 because of its defensive responsibilities. 14th A.H.A. Bde. (still some distance away) was not to be allowed to use the roads forward on night 17/18 because of other traffic,—must therefore choose between spending 17th at some half-way halt, or occupying its battle position at once, with risk of giving it away. 161st Bde., R.F.A. was already engaged on or near its battle position.

(c) Ammunition supply was presenting difficulties and there was no "smoke" available.

Instruction No. 2, issued late on 16th, explained briefly 16th Infantry Brigade plan of attack, viz :——Capture of First Objective by 2/York & Lancaster Regiment (161st Bde., R.F.A. to find liaison); Capture of Second Objective by 1/Buffs on right (2nd Bde., R.F.A.) and 1/K.S.L.I. on left (14th A.H.A. Bde.).

Relying on known intentions, as would later be laid down in the barrage map, the Group plan was :—

*2nd Bde. R.F.A.*

- (i) Centre portion of barrage up to protective line second objective.
- (ii) Take over 161st Barrage (on protective line first objective) while latter were on the move.
- (iii) Advance immediately after reaching the protective line second objective.

---

[1] Progress in this preliminary operation was not wholly satisfactory, which caused much trouble on the 18th.

*14th A.H.A. Bde.*

  (i)  Left portion of barrage all through.
  (ii) Be prepared to advance sections to support further objective of patrols.

*161st Bde., R.F.A.*

  (i)   Right portion of barrage up to protective line first objective.
  (ii)  Advance.
  (iii) Take over 2nd Bde. barrage (on protective line second objective) while latter were on the move.

A formal Group Operation Order was issued with an Objective Map during the morning of 17th. The Barrage Map did not come till much later in the day. The O.O. :—

  (a) Ordered the manning of the permanent O.P's, and that each sub-group should find a travelling F.O.O. in addition and a Forward Intelligence Officer. (6)
  (b) Announced definite arrangements with R.E. and No. 1 Section D.A.C.
  (c) Announced contemplated participation of Y/6 Trench Mortar Battery.
  (d) Allotted valley in X 8 (a) and (c) for "forward wagon lines"; said that "rear wagon lines" would not move East of valley lying S.S.E. of Villeveque pending developments; subject to these principles, sub-group commanders could use their discretion as regards moves of wagon-lines. (2)
  (e) Headquarters Left Group X 4 d 1/7, then with 16th I.B.; 2nd Bde. R.F.A. R 34 c 3/5; 14th A.H.A. Bde. near level crossing in X 3 a; 161st Bde. R.F.A. X 3 a 2/3.
  (f) All parties to be in position by midnight 17/18.
      Fourteen copies of this O.O. had to be issued.

At a conference 2 p.m. 17th, the communication arrangements were explained.[1]

At the last moment it was necessary to issue special instructions to Y/6 T.M.B. (armed with mobile 6-inch Stokes Mortars). These instructions contemplated advance behind 2/York & Lancaster Regiment to the first objective and engagement of obstacles such as Fresnoy le Petit Cemetery between first and second objectives. (7)

Arrangements were now complete for the battle except :—

  (i)   Barrage map with rates of fire not yet arrived.[2]
  (ii)  Synchronisation hour not definitely settled.
  (iii) Zero hour not yet announced.

---

[1] Lateral communication with the group on our left was to be obtained through 14th A.H.A. Bde. (proved successful). Lateral communication with our Right Group was not possible except by orderly.

[2] Tasks for the howitzers and Rates of Fire for whole group only arrived at **19.45** hrs. The Meteor was received over the telephone at 00.05 hrs. on **18th** from D.A.

It had been difficult throughout the time, on account of distance, to obtain personal touch with Headquarters 16th Infantry Brigade, whom the Left Group was to support.

## COMMENTS ON CHAPTER I.

(1.) As usual when a large group is found, it was necessary to extemporise a staff for 2nd Bde. R.F.A. Sub-group. Such an arrangement cannot well be avoided, but tends to lessen efficiency. Group Commander took the Brigade Signal-Officer and a spare Subaltern as orderly-officer. 2nd Brigade was commanded by its senior major with the Brigade Orderly Officer as adjutant-and-signal officer (the adjutant was unfortunately sick at the time). In this case it was expected that the B.G.C. 16th Infantry Brigade would be much on the move, but everything had to give way to the principle that the group commander must be with the infantry commander.

(2.) It is always a question as to who should be responsible for moves of wagon-lines during a battle, the Divl. Artillery, the Group, the Brigade, or the Battery? The question has been already discussed in Article I, Part III.

(3). Both on this occasion and on many others, especially in October, delay in settling the location of infantry brigade headquatrers seriously hampered efficient preparation for artillery support, the basis of which is good communications.

(4.) By this time it had become the drill in the 6th Division to synchronise twice daily, whatever extra arrangements might be made for special occasons. The original idea was to prevent overhearing by the enemy, but from a general point of view the custom proved very satisfactory.

(5.) The French area included two localities known as Round Hill and Manchester Hill (further South), which dominated the glacis E. of Holnon Wood and whose possession by the enemy rendered our attack on the Quadrilateral (W. of Fayet and N. of Selency) most difficult. These two localities had already become famous during the German March offensive (a posthumous VC had been earned in connection with Manchester Hill). The French now found them a serious obstacle and only completed their capture on Sept. 26th; it was this which caused the trouble about the Quadrilateral, which in its turn impeded the efforts of the 16th Infantry Brigade against Fresnoy-le-Petit.

(6.) Information reaches Infantry Brigade Headquarters slowly in battle, and comes from infantry sources only. The permanent O.P's must remain manned, but cannot see all localities. From this date on, as a result of his experiences in March and April 1918, the Brigade Commander invariably detailed (a) travelling F.O.O's, whose duty was to procure artillery support to meet special circumstances, by any means available, also (b) Forward Intelligence officers, who reported events direct to Group Hdqtrs. Their task was difficult and uncertain, and success depended almost entirely on the individuality of the officers thus employed. Some reports were quite invaluable. It was lucky we had almost always enough spare subalterns to allow of such extra work not contemplated in the Training Manuals.

(7.) Y/6 T.M.B. section did not arrive in time to take part in the battle. There was no doubt a failure of organisation here; Brigade Commander pressed very hard for (and would have been given) permanent affiliation to 2nd Bde. R.F.A. of at least a section of mobile trench mortars. During the period Sept. 19/23 he put up the section commander at Bde. Headquarters, endeavoured to train the section, carrying out practice shoots, and providing drivers from 2nd Bde. to take charge of the animals lent (by order) to Y/6 T.M.B. It was rather surprising that, in spite of the lessons taught us by the Germans in their Spring offensive in the use of mobile T.M's, we made a poor show with them when our turn came. One supposes it was the transport question; but all requests for suggestions began "No extra transport can be provided," which presented an impasse. On this occasion they would without doubt have proved helpful.

## CHAPTER II.  Sept. 18/19.

At 04.00 hrs. on 18th, B.G.C. 16th Infantry Bde. decided to move into St. Quentin Wood (1). Group Commander accompanied him with one officer and two orderlies and ran out a line to Group Hdqtrs. X 4 d 1/3. It was raining in torrents and the wood was under a fairly heavy fire.

The barrage opened well at 05.20 hrs., and, when the pause on the first objective arrived, all seemed well. 161st Bde. R.F.A. moved up, battery by battery at 5 minutes' interval, without interference, into the area R 36a (Position No. 3), whence it took part in a portion of the next barrage.

The dark and the mist had however caused loss of direction and confusion amongst infantry units. It was soon known that things had not gone too well for 71st Infantry Bde. on our right. When the second barrage had been completed, information was almost entirely lacking, and it became a question what to do about the advance of 2nd Bde. R.F.A. This sub-group was of course the nucleus of Left Group; the other brigades might be called away at any moment; one had to think of a possible counter-attack. Group Commander decided to keep 53rd Battery at R 35 a 2/2 (7) and advance the remainder of 2nd Bde. to area R 35 d and X 5 b (Position No. 3); the advance was carried out by batteries (by sections of 87th How. Battery) between 11.00 and 11.30 hrs.

B.G.C. 16th Infantry Bde. now moved his headquarters to the Quarry X 5 b 9/9, where his three battalion commanders were. (1) Casualties in and round about the quarry had obviously been heavy and continued to occur all day[1]; there was also some gas.

The information obtained from 12 specially detailed officers (3 F.O.O's., 3 F.I.O's., 3 "travelling" F.O.O's., and 3 Liaison Officers)

---

[1] 30 men were killed at the Quarries before noon.

was poor (2), but in time things got clearer. Between 11.55 and 12.25 hrs. it was possible to issue a provisional protective barrage line, with a considerable amount of information, to all three sub-groups; this barrage line ran S 3 central—M 34 a 5/0—M 28 central—M 22 central; it was thought we held Fresnoy—and probably we did at that time; the situation at Holnon village was not known. The above line was amended at 13.37 hrs. to read Western point of Fayet—M 28 d 9/5—M 28 b 5/8—M 22 d 1/0—M 22 central (i.e. along Argonne Trench). A provisional Group Operation Order issued later confirmed this and ordered 14th A.H.A. Bde. to remain where it was, 161st Bde. R.F.A. to withdraw two batteries to their old position in X 4, 2nd Bde. R.F.A. to withdraw 1 battery 18-prs. and 1 section 4·5″ Hows. to original positions; Group Commander would continue as Group Liaison Officer (3) with 16th Infantry Bde., but Group Headquarters would remain at 4 d 1/3.

Later, the whole 2nd and 161st Bdes. R.F.A. were withdrawn to their original positions, except 2 forward sections each. (Position No. 4.) The defensive barrage for the night was fixed at 21. 45 hrs. on the protective line to the morning's First Objective. It was difficult to communicate with the Right Group in order to fix a junction point. Ammunition had to be obtained and some guns sent to I.O.M.; casualties had been fairly heavy, especially in 14th A.H.A. Bde., one of whose battery commanders had been killed. Harassing fire was arranged for the night.

Group Commander had been able during the afternoon to visit most of the batteries in their forward positions, but was not altogether satisfied with the steps taken to attain tactical efficiency, such as "shooting themselves in," local observation, etc. (4)

The R.E. had not been required. No. 1 Section 6 D.A.C. had done excellently. Y/6 T.M.B. had failed because the animals provided could not bring the mortars into action.

Things were settling down and one was thinking of some rest, when at 23.55 hrs. arrived an order to renew the attack under a barrage at 05.30 hrs. on 19th (5).

The infantry knew but vaguely where their men were, so mixed were units; the forward area was under heavy and continuous machine-gun fire and air-bombing—no doubt in accordance with the plans for defence of the Hindenburg Line; it was not feasible for a company commander to light a match to read an order. Group Commander's line to Group Headquarters was smashed at 23.50 hrs.; there were no new maps to issue, and most of the old barrage maps had been destroyed by the rain. The original barrage must be modified to meet the Right Group barrage and had become more than complicated. (6) But what does one go fighting for except to meet such difficulties?

Warning was given at once and an Operation Order prepared by 01.40 hrs., but—what was better—it proved possible to get Sub-group Commanders 2nd and 161st Bdes., R.F.A., to visit Group Commander at Infantry Bde. Headquarters; the former left the Quarry at

03.00 hrs. and the latter at 04.25 hrs. The new divisional order had transferred 14th A.H.A. Bde. to Right Group. As already said, a complication lay in applying the new barrage lines to the old barrage-map, for Right Group had had their orders many hours earlier (and the Right Infantry Bde. had not made as much progress). In the event, all batteries of 2nd Bde., R.F.A., and two of 161 carried out the whole barrage, sheets for the later stages being prepared while the earlier ones were being fired; the remainder of 161 batteries joined in after a time. The attack failed[1]—but what could one expect under such circumstances? (6)

On 19th, Group Commander, having now only two sub-groups, resumed personal command of 2nd Bde., R.F.A., replacing himself for the time at Infantry Bde. Headquaters by a senior major. During the afternoon instructions were issued for re-organisation of the newly constituted group, based on a temporarily defensive policy.

The batteries were now disposed (Position No. 4.) :—

| | | |
|---|---|---|
| Two sections 161st Brigade, R.F.A. ... ... ... | In R 36 a | Range to Defensive Barrage Line 2800 yds. |
| Remainder 161st Brigade, R.F.A. ... ... ... | In X 4 | ,, ,, ,, ,, 5000 ,, |
| 21st Battery, 2nd Brigade, R.F.A. ... ... ... | R 34 d 9/6 | ,, ,, ,, ,, 4400 ,, |
| One Section, 42nd Battery, 2nd Brigade, R.F.A. ... | R 35 central | ,, ,, ,, ,, 3500 ,, |
| Remainder, 42nd Battery, 2nd Brigade, R.F.A. ... | R 34 a 7/2 | ,, ,, ,, ,, 4800 ,, |
| (7.) 53rd Battery, 2nd Brigade, R.F.A. ... ... | R 35 a 2/2 | ,, ,, ,, ,, 3800 ,, |
| 1 Section, 87th How. Battery ... | N.W. Corner of Copse R 35 Central | ,, ,, ,, ,, 3500 ,, |
| Remainder ,, ,, ,, ... | R 34 d 5/8 | ,, ,, ,, ,, 4500 ,, |

Forward sections to maintain active sniping policy in closest possible liaison with the infantry; remainder (at request of the infantry) to keep as quiet as possible. Observation, reconnaissance, and communications required early re-organisation. A dividing line for bombardment was given, 161st on right, 2nd on left. The line being consolidated by the infantry ran junction of Douai Trench and American Alley (M 33d 8/6)——old C.T. about M 27 d 1/3—spur in M 27 a and c—M 21 c 3/2. Infantry Bde. Hdqrs. in Quarry, Group Hdqrs. at present R.34 c 3/5.

It had been a hectic time.

---

[1] We lost also the ground which had to be evacuated to allow the barrage to be fired at all. At least one company never received its orders to attack.

The French to the South had been unsuccessful. Our right (71st) Infantry Bde. had failed against the Quadrilateral, tanks having proved unable to provide the necessary support. The left (16th) Infantry Bde. had gained its first objective as had the right brigade of the 1st Division on our left, while the latter's left brigade was well forward connecting up with the Australians beyond their second objective. The mischief had been the continued possession by the enemy of Round and Manchester Hills, which permitted a very fine defence by 280th I.R. of 82nd (German) Reserve Division of an 'advanced post' viz., the Quadrilateral. The 6th Div. Infantry were not to be denied, however, as time would show.

### Comments on Chapter II.

(1.) These moves of Infantry Bde. Headquarters might have been settled beforehand, but, to the very end, the artillery was expected to bring instant fire to bear wherever wanted without being given a fair chance to lay the necessary communications.

(2.) It should be one of our chief training-duties to insist on good information in battle from batteries, and on messages correctly timed, dated, etc.

(3.) No matter how inconvenient, it was here as everywhere the first necessity for Infantry and Artillery Commanders to be together. Only in a limited operation, when everything goes according to plan, can the gunner remain at home; it follows his home should be alongside the infantry home; if the infantry are to chose the home, they must chose it in time. As a matter of fact this *should*, if in any way possible, *be arranged by Divisonal Headquarters* when organsing the battle?

(4.) In Article I, the writer laid great stress on the danger of allowing a certain inertia to overcome the personnel of a battery after changing position. It is the time of all others "to get a move on" and it is essentially the duty of the Brigade Commander to ensure this.

(5.) It was a matter for regret that the *one* (Divisional) orderly who brought this highly important operation message, came last of all to the only Infantry Brigade (16th) which had not had previous warning that the attack had to be renewed.

(6.) Throughout his experience the author has never met a case in which an attack, renewed at such short notice and after initial failure, has succeeded—unless the circumstances have been exceptional. Such an attack has frequently been ordered, but the outcry of those who have to carry it out has generally availed to cancel the order. A special circumstance is, when an objective has been already gained and is solidly held in certain places, which become pivots for the renewed attack, and provide flanking fire; a case of this kind comes to the author's mind in which a party of Highlanders had established itself on the final objective—and was thought to have gone West (or rather

East!); as a result of their determination, on a whole divisional frontage, troops were enabled to occupy the original objective several hours late but (in their second effort) almost unopposed.

(7.) We had become so used to attack with a limited objective, in which all could be arranged beforehand, during the early years of the war. The guns, more often than not, remained in their original position until the captured ground had been thoroughly consolidated. In a battle of movement, one may have to turn at any moment from attack to defence, or vice-versâ. It is sound to dispose a brigade or group of field artillery, to a certain extent, in depth. 53rd Battery position in this instance presents a good example of the advantages to be gained thereby—it was suitable for close support or defence. The officer at this time commanding 53rd Battery had a singular gift for finding positions of tactical value for both offence and defence. Such positions have generally to be kept fairly quiet and are not much used for harassing fie, etc., consequently they require less haulage of ammunition and should be popular.

## CHAPTER III.   September 20/24.

There was much to do during the interval before the next attack (to complete IX Corps objectives of 18th). 3rd Infantry Brigade (1st Div.) extended its zone towards us, and was for a time covered by our Left Group—which meant a lot of visiting. There was some fear of counter-attack; advanced sections would have to repeat S.O.S. rocket signals for information of the main positions (because of the woods); a deal of counter-preparation (CPN) and harassing fire. Observation was organised by each sub-group in depth, very careful arrangements being necessary to ensure that certain specified areas could be seen; direct communication between certain O.P's and Infantry Bde. Headquarters was established. It required constant attention to achieve the maximum effiiciency from the Signal Section. (1) Positions had to be selected for the next attack, which would allow of emplacement of other (1st Div.) batteries in the Left Group area. 16th Infantry Bde. plan of attack was not decided for some time, because counter-attack from the Hindenburg Line against any initial success needed consideration. It is pleasant to relate that the infantry seemed particularly well satisfied with our support on 18/19 and had written specially to the Divisional Commander; we knew what a difficult task was theirs, and there was great keenness in all ranks of the artillery to help them, based on long-established Divisional *esprit de corps* and a lucky lack of unfortunate incidents.

Orders were issued on September 23rd for the attack on 24th.

The barrage instructions were in greater detail and of more complicated nature than usual; in view of likelihood of counter-attack, one 18-pr. battery of each brigade was super-imposed over the sub-group front, ready for eventualities; there were quite a number of special "tasks" to be allotted; gas was to be used on certain areas under

H

particular sets of circumstances[1] (wind, early success, etc.).  Y/6
T.M.B. followed 14th A.H.A. Bde. to the Right Group. 16th
Infantry Brigade had a first and second objective; 2 battalions in line
with certain special flanking parties; Infantry Brigade Headquarters
in the old Quarry and all battalion headquarters in Trout Copse. The
new "Loop (wireless) Set" was placed in a selected Group O.P. as an
alternative method of communication with either 16th Infantry or
Group Headquarters; the various observation, intelligence, and liaison,
officers were chosen with particular attention to their individualities;
the Travelling F.O.O's and F.I.O's were instructed to report personally
in case of a serious hold-up with the most detailed information obtain-
able.    All sorts of arrangements were made for early news of counter-
attack, involving rockets, aeroplane signals, etc. The new positions
(Position No. 5)[2] were to be occupied early in the night of 23/24, leaving
sections in the old positions to carry out certain fire-concentrations,
which sections must join their batteries after completion of tasks.
Batteries were to be ready to move directly the barrage had been fired
into already-reconnoitred forward areas; the eventual distribution of
Left Group to be in depth, this object being attained by withdrawal
(if necessary) of a portion of 161st Bde., R.F.A., to a range of 5500ˣ
from the final protective barrage line.    And so we come to the attack.

The general trend of events on 24th was, briefly as follows.  The
French captured Round Hill and a part of Manchester Hill; the 18th
Infantry Bde. on our right was, in spite of considerable tank rein-
forcement, again held up by the Quadrilateral. but 11th Essex on its
extreme left got a precarious footing in the S.W. corner of it; 16th
Infantry Bde. did well getting its objectives, and securing the whole
Northern face of the Quadrilateral; 1st Division captured Fresnoy-le-
Petit[3] and Gricourt.    All was not yet over, however, for 1/Leicester-
shire Regt. of 21st Infantry Bde., attached to 18th I.B., made a gallant
and successful moonlight attack on Douai Trench at 23.00 hours, from
which, during the 25th, the 18th Infantry Brigade completed the
capture of the Quadrilateral by as fine a bit of genuine infantry trench-
fighting as could be found in the history of the war.    It is strange that
on both occasions on which the old 6th Div. came down to the Somme,
it should have had to run its head against a "Quadrilateral"!

As for the Group—the barrage, one may hope, was fired according
to plan and assisted the infantry.  161st Bde., R.F.A., put down a
heavy fire against alleged enemy reinforcements in the course of
the morning, and 1st Divisional Artillery smashed an attempted

---

[1] One has heard of a horse called "Circumstances," because no one ever had any
control over it.

[2] Position No. 5 as marked on map shows not only the positions occupied for the
battle of 24th., but includes a number of positions occupied by forward sections on
the night 24/25 and used for sniping purposes during the period 25/28.

[3] A "pocket" of Germans held out in the N.E. corner till night, giving much
trouble.  During night 24/25 they surrendered to the number of five officers and over
one hundred men.

# MAP TO ILLUSTRATE ARTICLE II., PART I.

SCALE:- 1/40000

YARDS 1000 800 0 100 200 300 400

NOTE:- GROUP HEAD QUARTERS INDICATED THUS:- ▲

GRICOURT

To PONTRUET

FAYET

Dee Copse

Dee Dunn Copse

Cemetery

FRESNOY TRENCH

FRESNOY LE PETIT

SELENCY

HOLNON

Olive Copse

Badger Copse

Trout of ♦ Copse

QUADRILATERAL

HILL CANAL

RAILWAY

POSITION Nº 5

GROUP

MIDDAY 18

MARTEVILLE

RIVET

ATTILLY

VILLEVEQUE

RFA

POSITION

SEPT 11

FROM MONCHY LAGACHE

TO ST QUENTIN

10 KILLENAISE 1000 YARDS

counter-attack in M 17c; later 1st D.A. Right Group requested our assistance in a minor operation about Dum Copse. At 16.10 hrs. during a personal liaison visit, the Group Commander was asked to support a local offensive by 3rd Infantry Brigade, to be flanked by 16th I.B.; B.G.C. 16th concurred; it proved possible to give orders verbally to most batteries and the barrage was fired at 17.30 hrs. Our howitzers answered a few "zone calls." It was 02.00 hrs. before a personal visit to Right Group made it possible to fix the barrage for the night.

The search for information had this time been far more successful—but then the infantry had succeeded, which makes all the difference; two or three first-class reports were received; but unfortunately we lost an officer wounded at an O.P.—perhaps the most experienced of those detailed for intelligence duties. 2nd Bde., R.F.A., was lucky not to lose also the services of one of its battery commanders, who was hit about this time, but only very slightly; anyway we lost same for a time when he went on leave. (2)

### COMMENTS ON CHAPTER III.

(1.) The composition of a Field Artillery Brigade Headquarters[1] including as it did personnel from two separate corps, tended perhaps towards a certain strife. The brigade commander was not, strictly speaking, the brigade staff signaller's C.O. (as he was of the battery signallers). One did at times find a little difficulty in insistence on the best signal discipline plus perfect harmony. No doubt all this has been considered in the new organisation, though the millenium may not be yet.

(2.) Not the least of a regimental commander's tasks was to fill *suitably* temporary vacancies in responsible posts. The moment under consideration provides a good example; the Brigade Staff was in a crisis consequent on sickness and leave; two battery commanders' leave overlapped; one captain was suddenly promoted and another wounded. Leave was so much looked forward to, and so invaluable in its effects, that few C.O's would have thought of keeping an officer back whose turn for the shore had come; besides one could reasonably rely on his being alive for the next affray.

"He who three-monthly got his leave,
Did live to share more battle's grief."

### CHAPTER IV.     September 25/30.

By dawn 25th, Left Group had been reduced to 2nd. Bde., R.F.A. alone; from 10.33 to 11.15 hrs. it was engaged in answering an S.O.S. call. News arrived that during the previous night the horses, especially those of 87th Battery ("forward" wagon-lines, up against the railway embankment near Marteville) had suffered severe (46) casualties from air-bombing; it became advisable on "flying nights" to move horses after dusk and to disperse them in the open—extra work and incon-

---

[1] Not peculiar to field artillery.

venience; what made things worse was the great distance back of the rear wagon-lines, due to "circumstances over which Group Commander had no control." (1)

On 26th dispositions were modified; 21st and 42nd batteries were to cover right and left battalions respectively—night lines to be arranged in consultation with battalion commanders; 53rd and 87th batteries were retained in the Group Commanders hands; forward sections to do as much as possible of the necessary shooting; defensively, batteries in case of S.O.S. were to fire on their night lines till otherwise ordered. Lewis Guns were now distributed, two at gun-line, one at forward and one at rear wagon-line. (2)

Very heavy harassing fire was ordered by IX Corps for night 26/27. (3.)

On 27th it was notified that 6th Division might have to advance in sympathy with troops on its left, and arrangements for cutting passages through the wire had to be considered; also to push sections forward in close touch with the advancing infantry; these preparations were decentralised on to the shoulders of O's.C. 21st and 42nd batteries. Two German 77 $^{m/m}$ guns had been salved by us the previous night and were put into action.

On 28th the enemy disappeared from our front, probably, we thought (and correctly thought), to a line[1] just E. of Fayet; the infantry brigade on our right established patrols on three sides of Fayet. The rear wagon-lines were at last moved up to about some 4 miles behind the gun-line. (1) An Operation Order was issued for co-operation by 6th Div. with the attack further north; it might be necessary for our infantry to advance, but the O.O. contemplated principally a prolonged barrage against enemy reinforcements moving N. towards the centre of disturbance—i.e. the intended crossing of the canal at Bellenglise by 46th Div. There were three points of special notice in the O.O., (i) Action to be undertaken by the French, and possibility of action by the enemy against our right; (ii) extension of front by Left Group (2nd Bde., R.F.A.) to cover also 71st Infantry Brigade coming in on the left of 16th Infantry Brigade in relief of 3rd Infantry Brigade; (iii) possibility of advance by 6th Div., which was interpreted at Divisional Headquarters into an order to 2nd Bde., R.F.A., to move during night 28/29 to more forward positions whence the morrow's barrage would be fired—though it was perfectly possible to fire it effectively from present positions. To (iii) Left Group Commander put in an objection, not only for the reason given, and that batteries would have to advance at the moment when, and into the area where, enemy harassing was at its height, but also because there was still a certain instability on our immediate right, Southern, flank. The objection was overruled; the batteries advanced by sections (Position No. 6). so as to leave at any moment 4 guns per battery capable of firing on their night lines. A good few casualties occurred, as expected, during this move, which called for able battery-leading. (4) Group Headquarters also moved, to Quarry X 5 b 9/9 alongside 16th Infantry Bde.

---

[1] Such a line was marked on a just-captured map.

The Bde. Signal Officer was wounded in an unsuccessful attempt in company with a wireless officer (also wounded) to get the C.W. (wireless) set into position. (5)

The night 28/29 had been an unpleasant one—very dark and wet, everyone on the move, heavy shelling and much gas, and quite a number of casualties; but the morning found us merrily firing our barrage, which lasted several hours (3000 rounds by zero + 512') and left us in the immediate necessity to bring up more ammunition.[1] News arrived that the French would relieve 6th Div. (infantry) during night 29/30 and that the French artillery would come in when the French commander was satisfied. The whole afternoon was spent in getting things ship-shape for them to take over our new area as a "going concern,"and in preparing as best we could for our own relief; there was much to do in clearing ammunition, for by this time the countryside, in which we had been fighting since 18th, was littered with small dumps.

During night 29/30 the French Infantry (47th Chasseur Division) duly relieved ours. Our hearts were gladdened with knowledge of 46th Div. success at Bellenglise, by a rumour of American success further north, and by news of the advance of II Army in Flanders and of the retirement of the Germans before General Mangin from the Chemin des Dames; I Army had also achieved success in crossing the Canal du Nord on 27th and we knew the Canadians were moving.

At 13.35 hrs. on 30th arrived the French field artillery group commander (three 75 m/m batteries) who was to take over the whole 6th D.A. front (six 18-pr. and two 4·5″ How. batteries). He declined to look at the Right Group area, but walked with Left Group Commander round our positions, returning to Group Headquarters at 15.30 hrs.

At 15.48 hrs. he came into the office and said "We are going to attack under a creeping barrage at 17.00 hrs. I cannot help" and vanished. There was a perfect uproar in the (now French) quarry, but it was "la mauvaise humeur du maréchal"—and that was all to be said about it! Very little talk of objections, evidently. It was an interesting exposition of Gallic psychology and of the discipline insisted upon in their higher ranks.

By the grace of goodness the telephone lines held. At 16.00 hrs. the (French) infantry commander gave the (British) group commander his objectives and general instructions for the barrage. Between 16.20 and 16.30 hrs. it was possible to give all batteries of Left Group (now fourteen 18-prs., five howitzers, and two 77 mm's) the right and left flanks, the first line, the pause, the final protective line, lifts, and zero; and at last[2] at 16.50 hrs. connection was obtained

---

[1] 250 rounds per gun.

[2] This was the third time during the period covered by Part I. in which difficulty had been encountered over communication with our neighbours. It was due chiefly to the wood, but it was a warning against a similar contingency in the future. There is no idea of imparting blame to Right Group for this failure; Right Group had had its hands very full with the Quadrilateral in front of them, and the French to the right.

with Right Group, who promised to join in, while the British liaison officer with 47th Chasseur division notified the southern flank of a barrage about to be fired by 1st Division on our left.

At 17.00 hrs. the barrage commenced. At 17.10 hrs. the French commander said his infantry had not started; would we begin again at 17.10 hrs? Followed another hectic period and at 17.30 hrs. we re-opened. The frontage of Left Group barrage was 2000$^x$ contracting to about 1200$^x$; there were ten 3-minute 100-yd. lifts, then a pause of 15 minutes, then another twenty 100-yd. lifts to the final protective line. It began 'intense' and went through 'rapid' to 'normal,' using nominally about 360 rounds per gun.

At 19.30 hrs. the Group had finished its ammunition, reached the final protective line, and the utmost limit of gun-range (6). It was lucky "the Division" had insisted on advance, and Group Commander on the dumping of 250 rounds per gun after completion of the barrage of 29th! Whether this 'lightning' barrage was satisfactory, or what measure of immediate success the French achieved, has never come to the writer's knowledge; one was doubtful at the time, but the French entered St. Quentin next day without a fight. During the barrage the French batteries had pulled in alongside ours—with their long range, the positions were good enough; and at 19.45, the 2nd Bde., R.F.A., was allowed to go, spending the night in the wagon-lines and moving to Monchy Lagache next day.

Everyone knows Bairnsfather's picture of the battalion officers after completion of relief for the Nth time; but on this occasion there was some extra joy about. Good news had come from Palestine, Salonika and the Argonnes, as well as from our immediate neighbourhood; DOUBT had vanished. We had been engaged in 4 actions without any known loss of credit, and with, on the whole light casualties (except in horses).

The period had been chiefly remarkable for intense activity at night. Every fold in the ground had received enemy attention; it was what one would expect when approaching a fortress—and indeed part of the Hindenburg line defence scheme was published, which showed the areas needing the special attention of the German artillery and airmen, should the Allies ever attack the fortress. It is perfectly true that it does not matter where you meet the enemy, so long as you do meet him and beat him, but the Hindenburg line possessed a very material strength besides great moral value as an outer wall of the Fatherland. Many British divisions had learnt that!

### COMMENTS ON CHAPTER IV.

(1.) The distance of the rear wagon-lines from the front exceeded that of Ypres days, when the guns were on the Ypres—Dickebusch line and the wagon-lines some miles W. of Popperinghe.

(2.) The Lewis-guns provided for the artillery were considered a part of the divisional anti-aircraft defence and were echeloned accordingly.

(3.)  It was a 2nd Bde. custom to get foolscap-sized sketch maps hektographed, and to illustrate all orders for harassing fire, etc.  It gave a good deal of work in the brigade office and necessitated a draughtsman-clerk, but the result was undoubtedly worth it, for it checked mistakes as to map co-ordinates.

(4.)  The insistance of Divisional Headquarters on the advance of Left Group batteries was justified by the unexpected turn of events on 30th, as well as by the possibilities of 29th; but there were serious arguments against it, one of which (losses to the batteries) was also justified in the event.  The incident illustrates fairly well the principle that, in the offensive, supporting artillery must provide for the future by getting at least some of its guns as far forward as possible—in other words, distribution in depth.

(5.)  Complete decentralisation is not feasible where the battle is on a very wide front and each part dependent on its neighbour. Therefore one must control artillery.  To control, one must have good communications.  Communications were throughout the period covered by Part I a source of great difficulty.  This was no doubt due in part to the system of command organisation (i.e. the splitting up of 2nd Bde., R.F.A. staff into Sub-group Headquarters, Group Head-quarters, and Infantry Bde. liaison, on 18th September).  Another, technical, difficulty was the interference of the high trees of St. Quentin Wood with wireless arrangements.  But one certainly did at times think longingly after the old "bury" of trench-warfare days; one realised the need for that improvement in communications mentioned in the Preface (Lieut.-Col. Broad's article), especially in the efficient practice of wireless telegraphy.

(6.)  The simultaneous arrival at the end of ammunition, limit of range, and final protective line, was due to circumstances, and probably unique.

# PART II.—Movement.

## CHAPTER I—October 5/7.

October 5th found 2nd Bde R.F.A.[1] on the move again after a pleasant little holiday; we were to go further North this time, via Bellenglise. The nature of the fighting was expected to, and did, more nearly approach open warfare. Before marching, the Bde. Commander summoned up September lessons, such as were likely to be applicable to October, as follows :—

Support of Infantry and Economy of Force.

    (i)   4 guns in action and 2 in reserve (probably with forward wagon-line).

    (ii)  Not more than 1/3 of guns on move at the same time.

    (iii) Might be necessary to keep firing battery wagons with guns in action.

    (iv)  IX Corps Instructions contemplated possible exclusion of organised barrages in future.

Choice of positions and observation.

    (v)   Avoid banks or hedges marked on map or specially visible to the eye.

    (vi)  Avoid "Column of Route" during advance in battle.

    (vii) Report *immediately* occupation of a new position.

  (viii) Achieve efficiency without delay after occupation.

    (ix)  Probably have to shoot without help of the squared maps, with which we had been "spoilt" for years.

Reports and Reconnaissance.

    (x)   Every unit in Army responsible for touch with neighbours.

    (xi)  Patrols required for (a) Protection, (b) Information, (c) Reconnaissance of ground.

    (xii) Pass back information gained, personally if possible.

  (xiii) Drill of Operation Messages.

  (xiv) Great demand for mounted men (out-riders) with a battery.

Communications.

    (xv)  Economise wire for special occasions.

  (xvi) Lamp better than flags for visual.

 (xvii) Wireless.

General.

 (xviii) Constant testing of sights.

  (xix) Treatment of ammunition in changeable Autumn weather.

  (xx)  Be prepared to man captured guns.

  (xxi) 6-inch T.M's. will probably be affiliated to 2nd Bde.

---

[1] Adjutants had changed owing to an officer's promotion.

(xxii)  Splitting up of 2nd Bde. Staff to be avoided *if possible*.
(xxiii) Bde. Commander usually with Infantry Bde.; if not, with one (named) battery.
(xxiv)  Great Principle—*Take care of sights and ammunition*, and *Fight by Eye*.

On the evening of 5th, we found 46th Division in high fettle over their recent success. They say "everything comes to him who waits"; this Division had waited since February 1915, for a sensational success.

In view of the prevailing ideas as to employment of 2nd Bde., R.F.A., in the forthcoming attack, a large number of officers were engaged on 6th in reconnoitring the country from the high ground S.W. of Ramicourt as centre. Some excellent reports were rendered and the German line well established in our minds. Information was still uncertain as to who held Sequehart and Montbrehain. The enemy held Mannequin Hill, N.E. of Sequehart. Doon Copse was the highest feature in our area and there appeared to be a fine position for artillery along the Western slopes of the ridge Doon Copse— Mericourt, which could be modified to the ridge Doon Copse— Mannequin Hill. Once more, much would depend on the success of the French on our right about Sequehart. Two areas needed a watchful eye on the part of battery commanders, (i) high ground S.E. of Sequehart, (ii) that N.E. of Brancourt.

On the afternoon of 6th, it was notified that 2nd Bde., R.F.A., would be "in readiness" at the commencement of the attack, a detachment to move into action between Ramicourt and Doon Copse when the First Objective had been captured—remainder of Bde. to act according to circumstances.

Preliminary Instructions issued at 11.25 hrs. on 7th notified the place of assembly (Position No. 7) of 2nd Bde., R.F.A., as follows :— "Bde. Commander and O.C. 42nd Battery with O.C. section 87th Hows. (at a named locality) E. of Magny-la-Fosse; Batteries near Fosse Wood." Time of assembly depended upon a question of water supply, but midnight 7/8 at latest. Probable first position of Bde. would be in I 13, approx. 2000$^x$ S.W. of Doon Copse with headquarters alongside 16th Inf. Bde. at Preselles. Advance to be in 3 echelons, viz : (i) 4 guns and 4 wagons, (ii) 2 guns and 2 wagons, (iii) first-line wagons. Route of advance as reconnoitred yesterday, if possible by the valley S. of Preselles; special care in crossing the Lehaucourt Ridge. Liaison duties were forecasted. Firing battery wagons to dump at once after occupation of advanced positions, then to return and refill from D.A.C. Section about Fosse Wood; First-line wagons on arrival to remain on gun positions. Water would be a difficulty; petrol tins required. 24th Bde., R.F.A. would be with 71st Inf. Bde., assembling S. of Joncourt, moving between Ramicourt and Preselles, and taking up a position on our left (North).

The Operation Order issued later explained that 16th Infantry Bde. was to attack on the right, with its outer (right) flank covered by a special detachment of 18th Infantry Bde. provided with tanks.    16th Infantry Bde. attack to be exploited according to circumstances.    42nd Battery (with one section 87th Hows.[1]) was to advance directly the First Objective was captured to a position about I 13 b 8/1, to act in immediate touch with the infantry on the spot, communicating with 2nd Bde., R.F.A., by visual and orderly.    The protective barrage, over whatever line was eventually occupied by the exploiting infantry, would be fired by 42nd on right, 21st on left, 53rd and 87th superimposed.    1/K.S.L.I. would capture First Objective; 1 Buffs would advance through 1/K.S.L.I. (liaison 21st Battery); 2 York & Lancaster would attack Mericourt from N.W. (liaison 53rd Battery).

*Note on Chapter 1.*—The position down South was uncertain, the French having met with strong resistance E. of St. Quentin.    The French were faced with a difficult task; their objectives were such that, even in case of their success, our (6th Div.) frontage would be thrown back from left to right and 7,500$^\underline{x}$ in extent; it might be 10,000$^\underline{x}$; and the French were to start an hour later than we did.    The valley between us and them was to be the scene of operations of the special detachment 18th Inf. Bde. with its tanks.    A detachment of 46th Div. (left unrelieved at Sequehart) had to undertake a subsidiary attack[2] before our zero.    On our left, 30th American Division (who had relieved the Australians) was ahead of 6th Div. (who had relieved 46th Div.), thereby complicating the barrage.    The force of Field Artillery supporting 6th Div. totalled *eleven* Bdes., of which only 7 were to take part in the creeping barrage.    5th Cavalry Bde. was in attendance, and, as before, Life Guards' Machine Gun Battalion was attached to 6th Div.

The above Note seems necessary, properly to understand the course of events.    It is obvious therefrom that we were in for something different to the normal frontal attack of 1916/7 with its parallel lines, wired and entrenched, and its limited objectives.

## CHAPTER II.—OCTOBER 8/10.

NOTE.—The writer finds it difficult to describe the exact course of events (from the point of view of Right Group) during the next period, as almost all information came in personally and many orders were given verbally.    He has, however, *not* drawn on his imagination.

At 08.15 hrs. on 8th, batteries sent forward their R.O's to I 13 area.    At 08.30 hrs. 42nd Battery and attached section 87th Hows. were ordered forward according to plan, and passed through at 08.42. At 09.40 we received news of the capture of Cerise Wood by the French, which turned out to be inaccurate, for a subaltern of 21st Battery, sent on reconnaissance at 13.00 hrs., brought the first news that things were going better on that flank.    Three other officers went out at

---

[1] At special request of O.C. 2nd Bde., R.F.A.
[2] Unfortunately this subsidiary attack failed, twice over, but the great effort made enabled 6th Div. troops to cut the defenders off and compel them to surrender.

various times between 11.00 and 15.00 hrs., all bringing back useful reports to the Bde. Commander, which were of course passed to 16th Inf. Bde.   At length the special detachment 18th Inf. Bde. (1/West Yorks) secured Mannequin Wood, in spite of all three supporting whippet-tanks having been knocked out; the rest of 2nd Bde., R.F.A., was launched at 16.15 hrs., and at 17.00 hrs. headquarters 16th Inf. Bde. and 2nd Bde., R.F.A., shifted to Preselles Farm (Position No. 8).

42nd Battery had had some sensational shooting during the day, but unfortunately the battery commander was severly wounded by a rifle bullet and the battlefield knew him no more.

6th Div. had gained its final objectives by dark, including Mericourt; there had fallen into its hands over 30 officers and 1,100 men; casualties had been moderate, coming chiefly from the right flank previous to the capture of Mannequin Wood (the decisive incident) and the French success; 71st Inf. Bde. and 5th Cavalry Bde., on our left, had come under fire of German field-guns firing over open sights from about Jonnecourt Farm.

Followed an indescribably hard night! Communication to be established; night-lines to be decided and notified (eventually Orme Copse—L'Esperance—then directly towards Brancourt); 2nd Bde., R.F.A. to be reinforced to form a large Group; "remaining efficiency" (1.) of the various units to be studied; and orders to be issued for an attack under a barrage at dawn. It was pitch dark and the accommodation at Preselles bad (after our shelling), but there was a dug-out.

Right Group was at first increased only by 5th Army Bde., R.F.A., but later by 23rd Army Bde. also. Somehow or other, orders were prepared and issued (verbally, for the most part); somehow or other, 16th Inf. Bde. handed over ground on its right to 46th Div. and side-slipped to the left (N.); and somehow or other, we attacked at 05.30 hrs. on 9th under a respectable barrage. The attack, whose object was to complete capture of the "area of exploitation," met with considerable success.

At 06.10 hrs on 9th, it was notified to all concerned that 16th Inf. Bde. was to reach and hold a road leading approximately from Jonnecourt Farm to Beaufegard and to form a defensive flank facing Fresnoy-te-Grand; then, while maintaining the defensive flank, 6th Div was to gain the Fresnoy—Bohain railway line.

At 08.00 B.G.C. 16th Inf. Bde. unexpectedly moved (without informing the artillery). Group Commander, having lost his Infantry Brigadier, experienced delay in meeting unit representatives at the appointed place (Doon Copse), but eventually Right Group disposed itself to meet existing circumstances, as shown on the map (Position No. 9); it might have to fire E. or S.[1] Touch was regained with headquarters 16th Inf. Bde. in the afternoon and we settled down

---

[1] When 46th Div. had occupied Fresnoy-le-Grand, the southern line of fire was, of course, eliminated

together in Doon Mill. Some registration had been done by the artillery, but in view of the fact that our patrols and those of 46th Div. on our right were now out, it was not possible to do the harassing fire ordered and arranged. It had been a hard but interesting day without any sensational events after the affair of the morning. The ground traversed was freely covered with dead, dispersed in open-warfare fashion, mostly German. Night lines had been ordained running from N. outskirts of Fresnoy and along E. side of the railway, but the success of 46th Div., who occupied Fresnoy before night, altered things—and during the night 9/10 6th Div. entered Bohain.

Very late on the evening 9th, an order arrived grouping the division into 3 mobile mixed brigades, 2nd Bde., R.F.A., being affiiliated with 16th Inf. Bde. 5th and 23rd Army Bdes., R.F.A., had left the Right Group during the later hours of the afternoon. As 16th Inf. Bde. was relieved by 71st Inf. Bde. during the night and went out to rest, O.C. 2nd Bde., R.F.A., determined to accompany them (in accordance, as he thought, with the spirit of the new grouping order) and took his batteries to Ramicourt early on 10th. This was apparently not intended and considered 'ultra vires'; we had to suffer for it by a very early start on 11th. In future, a Brigade, R.F.A., though affiliated to an infantry brigade in the second, or even third, line, was to remain in its forward position and watch developments. (2.) Any how, Ramicourt was a fairly well preserved village—much better than anything we had seen for a long, long time—and the pleasure of spending an afternoon and part of a night under such conditions compensated for a certain coolness towards us on the part of superior authority.

Here we can pause, after our first bout of something like open warfare.

## COMMENTS ON CHAPTER II.

(1.) The "table of remaining efficiency" at about 21.00 hrs. on 8th read as follows :—

| No. | Question. | 5th Army Bde. | 23rd Army Bde. | 21st Battery | 42nd Battery | 53rd Battery | 87th (How.) Battery |
|---|---|---|---|---|---|---|---|
| 1 | Number of guns in action? | 13 | | 6 | 6 | 6 | 6 |
| 2 | Ammunition—(a) echelons | Full | | Full | Full | Full | Full (except 1 Section |
| | (b) dumped on position | Over 200 | | None yet | 309 | 200 | 208 |
| 3 | Observation? ... ... | Not yet Selected | Not yet reported to Right Group. | Local | Local | Local | Local |
| 4 | Has battery shot itself in? | Not yet | | Yes | Yes | Yes | Yes |
| 5 | Casualties ? ... ... ... | None | | None | B.C. and 2 Gunners | None | |
| 6 | Any shelling going on? ... | A little | | Yes, on O.P. | Slight | A little | Quiet |
| 7 | Horses? ... ... ... | — | | — | — | — | — |

(2.) Possibly an opportunity was missed to give a third of the artillery some rest; but it must be remembered that each minor operation was supported by the *whole* artillery, and that minor operations

# MAP TO ILLUSTRATE ARTICLE II, PART II. CHAPTERS I TO III.

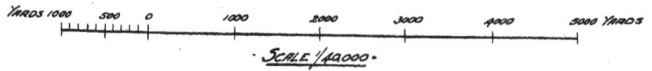

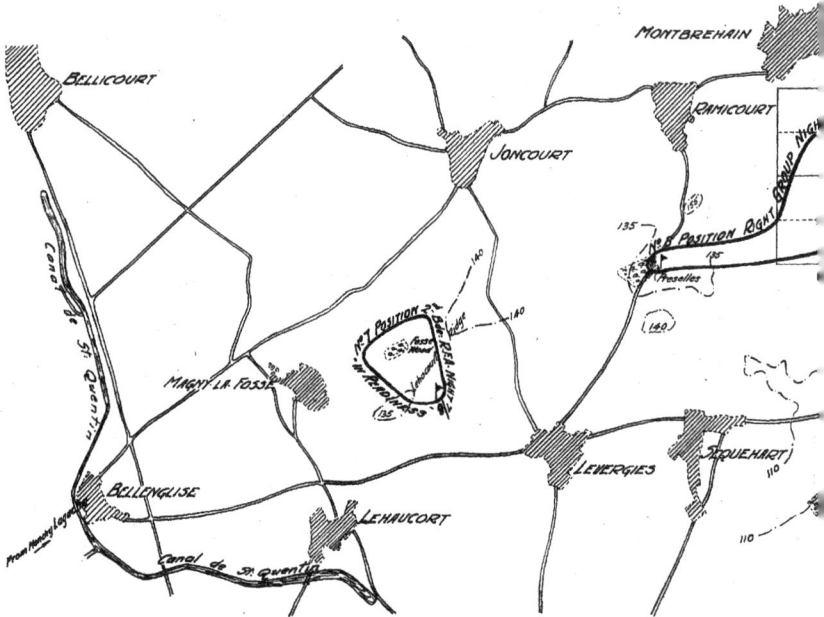

No. II Position 2ND BDE: R.K.R. Oct: III

To Vaux Andigny

Béguyot Farm

BOHAIN

No. 10 Position
2ND BDE: R.F.A
MORNING
Oct: II
IN OBSERVATION

REG

Le Bois de Riquerval

...ANCOURT

Oct 9...

Jonnecourt Farm

RAILWAY

...SNOY-LE-GRAND

L'Esperance

...PICOURT

To St. Quentin

were occurring freely and at short notice. The point is, that the artillery needs its breathing spaces as much as the infantry.

## CHAPTER III. Oct. 11/16.

2nd Bde. left Ramicourt at 03.45 hrs. on 11th and came into action "in observation" soon after 06.00 hrs., just S.W. of Bohain (Position No. 10). Bde. Headquarters established itself in the outskirts of the town,[1] which contained almost its normal inhabitants, so far as we could judge. Liaison was established with 71st Infantry Bde., at the moment the "brigade in the Line," and the day was spent in re-connaissance for positions to suit action contemplated for 12th. At dusk batteries moved their guns on to the selected positions N.E. of Bohain (Position No. 11), but only a few men passed the night there. 18th Infantry Bde. relieved 71st Inf. Bde. in "the Line," 24th Bde., R.F.A., taking up duty accordingly.

On the morning of 12th, 2nd Bde., R.F.A., Headquarters moved (early) to a small farm-house about 1 mile N.E. of Bohain; routes of approach to the new positions were chosen, which would avoid passage through the town; the ammunition dump was completed to meet the latest instructions; batteries registered (on *targets other than their barrage objectives*); operation orders and barrage tables were issued.

The position was as follows. The Americans held Vaux Andigny on our left and were considerably ahead of 6th Div. 71st Inf. Bde. in spite of tank support, had failed to reach the alignment on 11th. 46th Div. was held up by Riqueval Wood on our right and were still further behind. The object of to-day's minor operation (by 6th & 46th Divs.) was to come into line with the Americans; the special objective 6th Div (18th Inf. Bde.) was a footing on Bellevue Ridge.

The attack took place at 16.30 hrs. in heavy rain. Except for some success on the extreme left, by 2/D.L.I., it failed all along the line. It was useful, for it disclosed a new enemy position, provided with a considerable amount of wire; it showed also that our maps were, for once, rather inaccurate. The opening of our barrage produced an unexpectedly heavy retaliation on the battery positions and caused a number of casualties, in which Bde. Headquarters shared.[2] It was evident that the enemy intended to stand along the Selle River.

The next days were spent in constant conferences and recon-naissance; in addition to the normal harassing, and so on, batteries had to cut wire on 13th, in view of a probable renewal of the attack on

---

[1] Whence it was brusquely ejected after a couple of hours by "four two's."

[2] The brigade commander had an old Irish hunter, of marked personality—like most Crackenthorpe stock. He had apparently been very lame for weeks past; vets had advised his destruction, but he was a favourite; the brigade orderly officer had maintained that the horse was "swinging it." On this occasion a shell burst in the brigade staff lines; the animal in question, *very* slightly wounded, broke loose and led the lot off on a trotting tour. Pausing to graze, he was easily caught with the aid of a feed-tin, but it took the whole afternoon to re-capture the others. Our friend never went lame again from that day to this, when he still carries his mistress to hounds.

a large scale on 15th; but late in the evening (13th), a temporarily defensive attitude was ordained. Tactically, a special condition was present, comparable to that of 29th September; we were very close up to the front line, and the position on our right (S.) flank was uncertain and that flank refused.

A new commander[1] had arrived on 11th for 42nd Battery. Life was rendered more pleasant during this lull by the existence of a fine crop of vegetables considerately grown for us during the summer by the enemy.

On 14th, a new plan was explained to eight field artillery brigade commanders. The Bellevue Ridge was to be attacked in enfilade from N.W.—entailing a preliminary flank move, surely a sign that the war of position was over. 6th Div. was to effect penetration from Vaux Andigny, 1st Div. to exploit. The attack was to be made under a barrage of eight brigades R.F.A. and eighty machine guns, and to be supported by 172 60-prs. and heavy howitzers. 2nd Bde., R.F.A., was to be the nucleus of the Right Group of 4 Bdes., R.F.A. (2, 5, 161, 298). 6th Div. infantry had to commence their attack on a frontage of $1500^x$, which (in the course of an advance of less than $3000^x$) extended to $5000^x$; there were several enemy strong points in this fan-shaped area.

The problem was not too simple, either, for the Field Artillery. The area allotted Right Group (Position No. 12) was an exceptionally difficult one in which to emplace so many batteries; it was chiefly occupied by scrubby woodland, of most uneven terrain, called Bois de Busigny and for the most part on a forward slope. The opening lines of No. 1 Barrage were, in some instances, at a range of under $2000^x$ (without registration) (1.), the final lines at an almost prohibitively long distance. Two of the four brigades had to move, after capture of the First Objective, in order to cover the forming-up of 1st Div. infantry by No. 2 Barrage. The other two had to move later (on capture of the Second Objective) to take part in No. 3 Barrage to cover the advance of 1st Div. This arrangement was modified; the moves were now to be by time-table, subject to orders from the Group Commander, and *trusting to their own patrols for security*. It was, of course, necessary yet once again to split up 2nd Bde., R.F.A. staff;[2] for Group Commander would have at least 4 Brigades under him—in a battle of movement, too.

Within the Group, the barrage of 2nd and 5th (Army) Bdes. were to be superimposed on one another; similarly 161st and 298th Bdes on the left (Northern) half; each Bde. to keep a battery ready to answer zone calls. The moves were to be by one battery per brigade first; remainders of brigades to follow on successful occupation of advanced position by the first battery; units behind to keep touch

---

[1] Formerly staff-captain 6th D.A., so no stranger. This officer acted as O.C. 2nd Bde., R.F.A., during most of the remaining period covered by this narrative.

[2] 2nd Brigade sub-group was remarkably well handled during period Oct. 17/20.

with those gone forward. Group Headquarters to be at Becquigny from 15.00 hrs. on 16th; communication after the start of the battle entirely by mounted orderlies. Wagons to dump on new positions, return to refill, and be replaced by First Line Wagons which would refill in their turn. There were amendments to the arrangements (arriving up to the last moments) so frequent and so complicated, that in order to simplify this narrative further details as to the Group Task have been omitted, but the writer does not remember an occasion which necessitated more meticulous attention to the requirements of superior authority or more care on the part of battery commanders.

Another serious, and avoidable, complication was the decision at a late hour (on 16th) of our Infantry Brigadier to change his battle head-quarters (2); the artillery communications had all been laid; nor did the brigadier in question inform his artillery of the change. The result thereof was felt throughout the whole two days' fighting, and must have been serious had the attack failed, as it at one time threaten-ed to do, or the enemy been active.

At the last, Right Group was ordered to emplace a single section[1] to enfilade the enemy opposite 46th Div. on our right. (3) Its target was a length of enemy trench just W. of Regnicourt.

Careful arrangements were necessary to ensure that the old front was covered during the emplacement of Right Group for the new battle.

The night 16/17 at Becquigny was saddened by the serious wound-ing near Group Headquarters of the B.G.C. 16th Inf. Bde., who lost his arm. 2nd Bde., R.F.A., was not working with him on this occasion, but had been in almost constant liaison with him since the Autumn of 1917; he was alway sympathetic in his dealings with the Gunners and we missed him very much.

### Comments on Chapter III.

(1.)   At this period of the war, preliminary registration never took place as such; the practice of firing unregistered barrages had been initiated at Cambrai in November 1917.

(2.)   Without wishing to insist too much, the change of plans here recorded was the most inconvenient instance in the writer's experience of the "headquarters" difficulty. The new Infantry Brigade Head-quarters were $1\frac{1}{2}$ miles from those originally fixed and rather inaccess-ible. The change was made so that the 6th Div. Brigadier could be alongside the 1st Div. Brigadiers, the importance of which is not for a moment underrated.

(3.)   This was the third occasion in the writer's experience on which he was asked to perform an enfilade task. Enfilade artillery fire reads better on paper than it works out in practice. On the whole it would seem to be best carried out by a detachment of the formation which requires it; the task is not easy (from a gunnery point of view

---

[1] The task was duly performed but the position chosen turned out to be in a very hot spot. The section commander was most unfortunately killed, for he was a par-ticularly able officer, and there were a number of other casualties.

often quite difficult), accidents can easily happen, and any consequent unpleasantness is best kept within one Formation. Secondly, it is more suitable to offensive than to defensive conditions, because an outlying detachment is difficult to control, and control is usually easier to maintain in the attack than on defence, unless the enemy is very active.

CHAPTER IV.   Oct. 17/20.

At 05.20 hrs. on 17th the attack was launched, in thick fog. At a time not recorded[1] in any papers at disposal, information was considered good enough to advance 21st Battery of 2nd Bde. R.F.A., together with one battery 298th Bde. to the valley running due South from Vaux Andigny and lying at the foot of the Bellevue Ridge (Position No. 13). At 08.20 the rest of these two Bdes. was ordered forward to join their advanced batteries. Group Headquarters, which after the start of the barrage had been located on the railway embankment between Becquigny and Vaux Andigny, moved later to the above-mentioned valley. It was a rare and exhilarating sight to watch the long lines of guns trotting down the slope into action in the open. On arrival in the valley, Group Commander was soon able, on a pre-arranged plan, to connect up by telephone with 6th D.A.—not a bad performance on the part of 2nd Bde. Signal Officer. (1.)

Things had not gone perfectly with the infantry. The assembly of 18th Inf. Bde. just outside Vaux Audigny, and the passage of supports through the village, had been seriously interfered with by enemy gas shells. In spite of tapes laid out to show the initial lines of advance—which, it will be remembered, was fan-shaped—direction was lost. 16th Inf. Bde. (on the left) got its objective without delay, except on its extreme right; but 18th Inf. Bde. in the low ground (one of whose battalions actually advanced arm-in-arm, the better to ensure direction) became involved in the fog with 46th Div. troops on their right. It was the advance of 1st Div. which definitely secured the First Objective all along the line, while troops of 1st, 6th, and 46 Divs. met in Andigny-les-Fermes (in 46th Div. area).

It may be asked whether it was safe to advance the battteries under such conditions, but at this period of the war no one took counsel of his fears, and enough information was brought in personally by selected F.I.O.'s., or forwarded by liaison officers with the infantry, to satisfy the Group Commander that *advance was justifiable, if the batteries used patrols properly.* The F.I.O's accurately located advanced positions of 16th Inf. Bde, 46th Div., and the French; but immediately in front of us the position was uncertain.

At 09.50 hrs. Group Commander ordered forward 5th Army and 161st Bdes., R.F.A., to the Bois St. Pierre-Pres Des Vaux valley on the other side of the Bellevue Ridge (Position No. 14), to fire No. 3

---

[1] The exact position and moves on Oct. 17 of the various units in this large group are found most difficult to follow in the available records. Map shows only those of which the writer can be certain.

# MAP TO ILLUSTRATE ARTICLE II PART II. CHAPTERS III & IV.

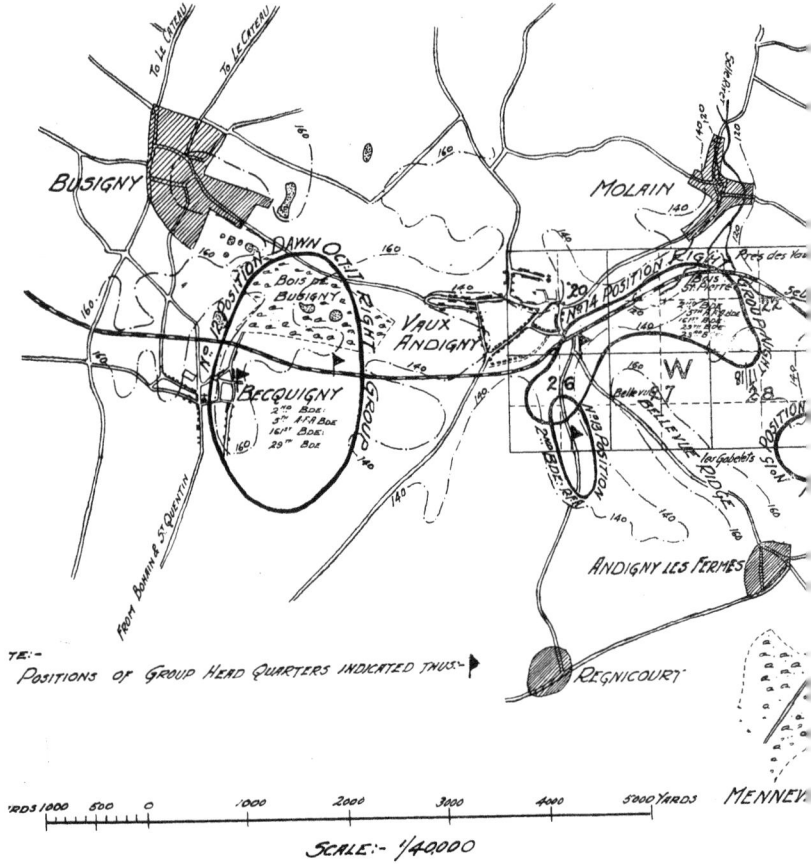

TE:-
POSITIONS OF GROUP HEAD QUARTERS INDICATED THUS:-▶

'RDS 1000    500    0    1000    2000    3000    4000    5000 YARDS    MENNEV

SCALE:- 1/40,000

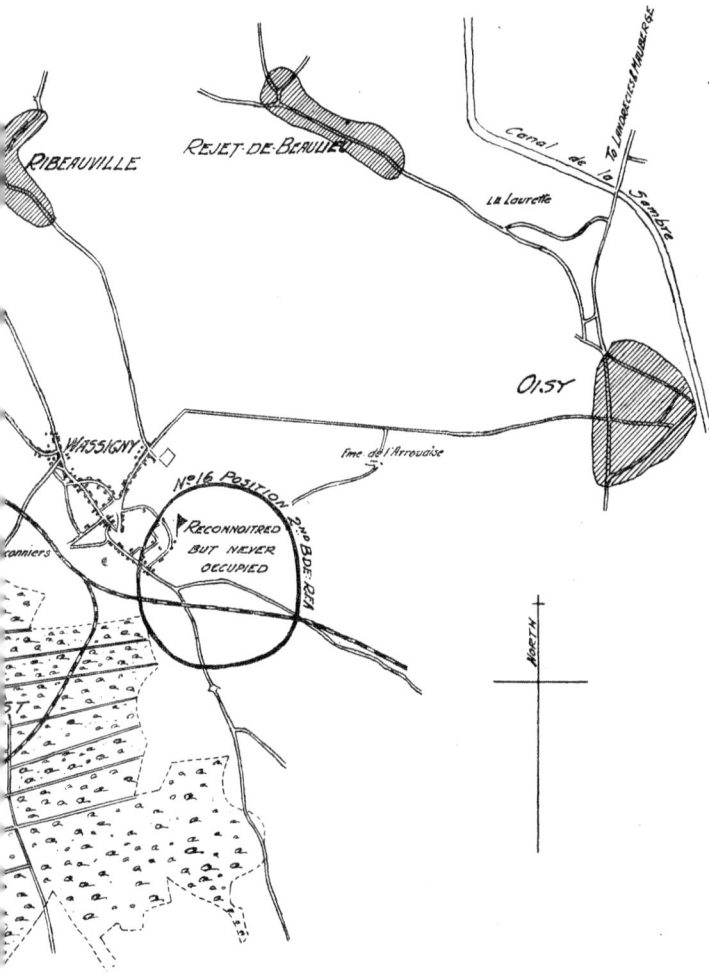

RIBEAUVILLE

REJET·DE·BEAULIEU

Canal de la Sambre

To LANDRECIES & MAUBEUGE

La Lourette

OISY

WASSIGNY

Fme de l'Arrouaise

Nº16 POSITION 2ND BDE R.F.A.

RECONNOITRED
BUT NEVER
OCCUPIED

onniers

NORTH

Barrage (due to last till 12.52 hrs.).  At 10.37 hrs. 2nd and 298th commenced their No. 2 Barrage, after the completion of which (up to the limit of their range)[1] 23rd Army Bde., R.F.A., which was by now in the valley W 26, came under the Right Group Commander.  As two Heavy Artillery representatives were, about this time, offering their services and asking for information, which Group Commander was able to give in considerable detail, there were at this moment under his leadership between 120 and 130 guns—and it was a "moment of movement."  Group Headquarters established itself in the Southern outskirts of Vaux Andigny, at a spot where no projectiles were falling.

There was now a pause in the battle; 6th Div. infantry were being gradually eliminated; 1st Div. had taken over command, but C.R.A. 6th Div. remained on duty.  The time was occupied by Group Headquarters in gathering and sifting information from various sources, and by the batteries in improving their positions and in management of ammunition.  This information, in unusual detail, showed 1st Div. infantry as held up on a line along the Eastern edge of La Vallée Mulâtre and the W. edge of Andigny Forest.  The last report, particularly clear,was brought in personally by a captain, formerly adjutant 2nd Bde., R.F.A., at about 16.00 hrs.

There now occurred an incident, of interest as showing what may occcur on such occasions; it was entirely *due to the separation of infantry and artillery headquarters*.  At 16.25 hrs. a message, considerably mutilated, was received over the 'phone from the C.R.A. 6th Div., ordering Right Group to fire a barrage to cover a renewed attack by 1st Div. Infantry; the barrage was to start at 17.15 hrs. from a line about one thousand yards distant from that on which the Group Commander believed that infantry to be held up.  The Group Commander, on receiving the (mutilated) message, sent for the (five) Sub-group Commanders, and went at once to the telephone; but at this critical moment it had gone 'dis.'  He sent two officers in succession to first Div. Infantry Brigadier's headquarters; the first to ask whether the line of resistance as known to Group Headquarters, vide 16.00 hrs. report, suited 1st Div. for the first line of the barrage; the second to ask simply when and where the barrage was to begin.  Both officers were long delayed at the infantry headquarters, but returned with the following answers, (i) that 1st Div. infantry line had changed somewhat since that given in the 16.00 hrs. report and quoted by the Group Commander, (ii) that 1st Div. Artillery was firing the barrage and that nothing was known of our Right Group co-operating. Information to be gathered by Group Commander from his immediate neighbourhood was conflicting beyond hope of usefulness.  It was now past 17.00 hrs. and impossible to fire the barrage as ordered in the (mutilated) message; but a long 'concentration' was put down on absolutely 'safe' localities at 17.15 hrs., at which hour some kind of special fire could be distinguished from the general din.  At 17.24 hrs.

---

[1] Eighteen-pounder batteries of 2nd Bde. moved forward after reaching their range-limit to Position No. 14.

arrived written orders confirming the (mutilated) message; and about the same time two F.I.O's rendered reports showing the modification to the 1st Div. infantry line since the 16.00 hrs. report, thus confirming the answer sent from 1st Div. infantry headquarters. This incident, itself of little practical importance, has been narrated at some length because it illustrates very well the situations which come to an artillery commander in moving warfare; above all he should be at Infantry Headquarters. One sees here the problem, such as it was, and the action taken; in the cool reflection of to-day, the proper solution was (i) to issue instructions for barrage in accordance with the (mutilated) telephone message, (ii) to order the barrage not to be actually fired without further confirmation from Group Headquarters, (iii) *then*, to leave someone else in temporary charge, ride at once to 1st Div. Infantry Headquarters, and obtain their wishes personally? But "it is easy to be wise, etc." (2.)

As a matter of fact, the line was little different at dark from that given in the 16.00 hrs. report. We knew that 46th Div. were safely established about Andigny-les-Fermes and that the French were close up to Menevret. Right Group was reduced by departure of 23rd Army Bde. before midnight to 2nd, 5th (Army), and 161st Bdes., R.F.A., and was to act as a stand-by to 1st D.A. 6th Div. Infantry were gone. It had been a vastly interesting day!

At 09.30 hrs. on 18th orders were received, still from 6th D.A., for a barrage to commence at 11.30 hrs. This barrage was duly fired; the attack was everywhere successful; the French got Mennevret, the (British) 1st Div. Wassigny, and the Americans Ribeauville. Immediately afterwards, 2nd Bde., R.F.A., and part of 5th (Army) Bde. advanced to the neighbourhood of La Vallée Mulâtre (Position No. 15).

On 19th, 6th D.A. Headquarters were eliminated and our Group came under 1st D.A., who gave orders for the advance of 2nd and 5th (Army) Bdes., R.F.A., to positions whence to cover the crossing of the Oise Canal; 161st Bde., R.F.A. was kept "in readiness." Group Headquarters was moving to Wassigny when a message was received from 6th D.A. that 2nd Bde., R.F.A., was to pull out and rejoin 6th Div.; this was not agreed to by 1st D.A. who were on the spot. The arrival of the message had caused Group Headquarters to remain in Vaux Andigny (where by now Headquarters 1st D.A. had established themselves); by a mischance, the (verbal) orders to 2nd and 5th (Army) Bdes., R.F.A., had miscarried (3.); so no one moved though Position No 16 had been reconnoitred. It was luckily of no importance that the orders had miscarried, for an immediate crossing of the Oise Canal was not contemplated; and early next morning 5th Army Bde. joined 1st D.A., while, by 14.00 hrs. on 20th, 2nd Bde. R.F.A., was in IX Corps Reserve on its way to Becquigny. The battle line was at this moment, Oisy (French)—La Laurette—Reget (American).

COMMENTS ON CHAPTER IV.

(1.) It would seem that if a unit advances in a battle of this nature, responsibility for touch between it and superior authority behind should be maintained from back to front. There was really insufficient personnel to lay and maintain communications within such a large Group after Group Headquarters had once advanced, though the utmost economy was observed. The mounted orderlies, too, were still unused to their new work.

(2.)    The conditions under which a soldier may disobey an order are (a) that he must believe himself to have such information as to enable him to appreciate the situation better than the issuer of the order can do; (b) that he cannot refer to the issuer at the moment, but that he must inform the latter at the earliest possible moment, that the order has not been carried out; (c) that he must bear the responsibility for non-compliance. All these conditions were of course fulfilled in this instance; and it must be remembered that the original message was considerably mutilated. It has three times happened in the writer's experience that a battle-order has arrived which it seemed to the recipient should not be carried out; on the first occasion it was clearly impossible to do so owing to fresh conditions; on the second occasion the recipient was admitted by the issuer to have acted correctly; on this, third, occasion, the recipient was probably wrong—a solution to the problem has already been suggested.

(3.)    There is surely no more fruitful source of trouble than verbal orders! It was perhaps the personality of two officers, hitherto unknown to one another, which brought about this miscarriage of orders; one must be thankful that the occasion was not more important. If the man who is carrying the verbal order has time to transmit it to paper (in his own interest), so has the issuer time to write the order. Indeed, with many personalities, it takes less time to write than to dictate an order, and their written orders are the best.

## CHAPTER V.—Oct. 21/Armistice.

NOTE.—The following pages are based on a written record; the author of this article was called away on urgent private affairs and was therefore, unfortunately, not present during these, the last, actions of the war in which 2nd Bde., R.F.A. participated.

The evening of Oct. 20th, found 2nd Bde. R.F.A. at rest in Becquigny, where we had a new and rather unexpected experience;[1] for war had not passed through the country since Autumn 1914, and some inhabitants resented its inconveniences—not so much the shells, of which they said philosophically "C'est la guerre," but rather that four years of warfare had taught all armies to get the greatest possible value out of any luxuries available—arm-chairs and pianos, for example.

On Oct. 22nd the Bde. Commander went on leave; on Oct. 23rd, 2nd Bde., R.F.A., was called upon (unexpectedly) to relieve artillery of 4th Australian Div. The positions were S. and W. of Bazuel, headquarters in Le Cateau[2] (Position No. 17): batteries were at the call of

---

[1] i.e. An old dame expressed her preference for German occupants!
[2] The terrain E. of Le Cateau, becomes suddenly of an enclosed nature, divided into small fields bounded by fly-fences.

24th Bde., R.F.A. A barrage was fired at 00.30 hrs. on Oct. 24th and the following night 2nd Bde., R.F.A., moved to positions N.E. of Bazuel (Position No. 18). On Oct. 30th it participated in a successful minor operation W. of Landrecies. There was a lot of 'harassing' on both sides during this period and batteries had rather a bad time.

On Oct. 31st, 2nd Bde., R.F.A., became part of a Sub-group under O.C. 16th Bde., R.H.A., the Group Commander being C.R.A. 4th Austr. D.A. On Nov. 2nd a minor operation was undertaken to secure a forming-up place (on the Happegarbe spur) for the general attack on Nov. 4th; a barrage was fired early in the morning and the attack succeeded, but at 09.00 hrs. a counter-attack developed; there was protective S.O.S. fire at frequent intervals during the morning, but by 15.30 hrs. the spur was definitely lost.

Nov 3rd produced an almost exact replica of the events of the previous day. (1.) The offcer temporarily commanding 42nd Battery (its major was acting as Bde. Commander) was wounded. The shooting in connection with these two days' fighting had used up a deal of ammunition and it was a heavy task to collect the necessary dump (400 r.p.g.) by zero Nov. 4th.

During the last minutes before zero on 4th, 2nd Bde., R.F.A., was taken out of the pre-arranged barrage to repeat its barrages[1] of Nov. 2nd and 3rd in support of 96th Infantry Bde., who took the Happegarbe spur without trouble *in their stride* (1.). Things were not very easy on the left, where 14th Inf. Bde. found difficulty in crossing the Canal about Ors owing to enemy machine-guns, whose activity formed the principal feature of this battle. At 09.05 hrs. the main barrage had to be brought back to meet this condition. The opposition was eventually overcome by moving troops (already across the Canal) Northwards along the Eastern bank. At 13.45 hrs. "Stop Firing" was ordered and the Bde. Commander went forward to reconnoitre; there was still, however, trouble coming from enemy machine-guns passed by our troops in the advance, and it was 16.30 hrs. before the batteries of 2nd Bde. were advancing (to Position No. 19). At 19.00 hrs. 2nd Bde was placed under 161st Bde., R.F.A., which was already across the Canal at Ors, and there was a prospect of having to support exploitation on Nov. 5th. But the enemy retired, and some harassing of his line of retreat during the night were the last rounds of the war fired by 2nd Bde., R.F.A.

On Nov. 5th, the Brigade crossed the Canal and came into "observation" about Favril (Position) No. 20); it crossed the River Petite Helpe on Nov. 7th and was again "in observation" (Position No. 21). There was to have been a barrage on Nov. 8th, but the enemy had again retired.

On Nov. 9th, 2nd Bde., R.F.A., was disposed E. of Avesnes (Position No. 22) with the enemy some 8—10 kilometres distant; the

---

[1] The fifteenth organised barrage since 17 Sept.

# MAP TO ILLUSTRATE ARTICLE II, PART II.

MILE 1  0  1  2  3  4  5  6  7  8  9  10 MILES

• SCALE ¹/₁₀₀,₀₀₀ OR 1 INCH TO 1·58 MILES·

NOTE:-
   SINGLE LINE RAILWAYS SHEWN THUS :- +++++++
   DOUBLE  "    "      "    " :- ━━━━━

BOIS L'EVEQUE
HARDEG
ORS
LE CATEAU
POSITION N°17
POS. N°10
POS. N°12
BAZUEL
CATILLON
BUSIGNY
REJET
VAUX INDIGNY
LA VALLEE MULATRE
OISY
WASSIGNY
CANAL

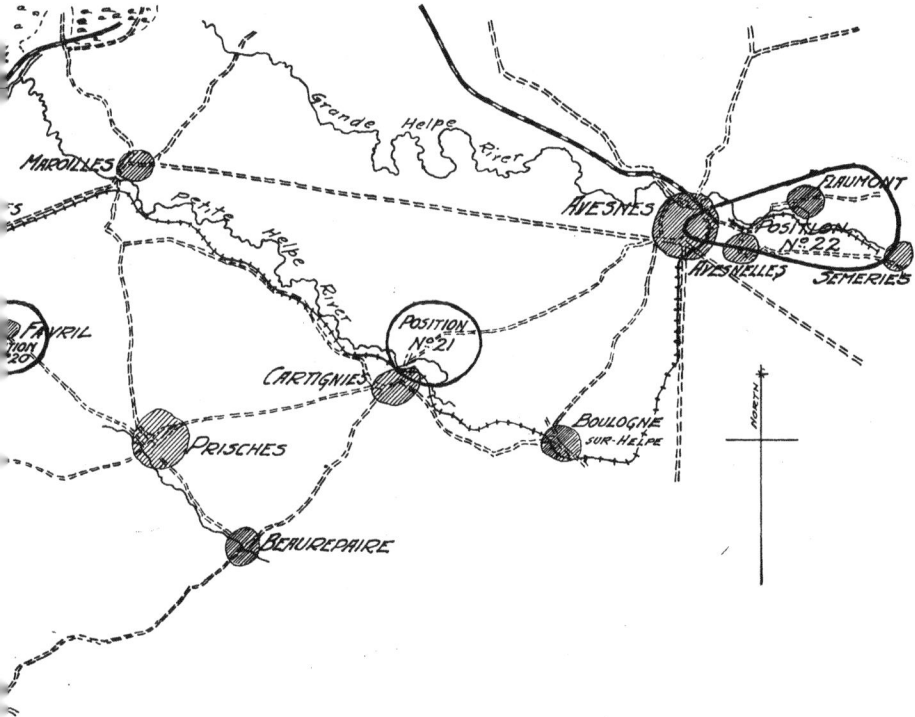

Bde. Commander returned from leave[1] in time to order the last advance on Nov. 10th. There were no squared maps of the country in which we were now fighting, but we never came nearer to battle after Nov. 10th than "positions of readiness." The remarkable features of the period covered by Chapter V. were (a) enemy use of delay-action mines (2.), (b) the able handling of his machine-guns, and (c) the bad weather, one result of which was that, in the last battle-position occupied, 2nd Bde. R.F.A. was split in two by an unfordable river; one had to go back into Avesnes. All things considered, casualties in this fortnight's advance had been fairly heavy—1 officer, 20 O.R., and 34 horses.

On Nov. 11th came the Armistice; at 10.59 hrs. the not-yet-completely-conquered, -in-Defence-of-his- Fatherland-so-brave, -but-now with-republican-Ideas-imbued, german Machine-Gun-Man, fired his last belt, took off his helmet, bowed, and walked away; the psychological effect on the soldiery of this sudden cessation of active warfare is tempting to discuss, but too ambitious for the author. Also it has nothing to do with field artillery tactics.

### COMMENTS ON CHAPTER V.

(1.) There are some positions in battle, as in Life, which one cannot occupy without going straight on; one must "either go on or go back." Such a one was the Happegarbe spur; another was Trones Wood on the Somme, which lay in an enemy re-entrant, and which was attacked and occupied half a dozen times between 7th and 13th July, 1916, by 30th and 18th Divs. in succession, before finally passing into British hands when the whole IV Army line advanced on 14th.

(2.) The effect of delay-action mines was more strategical than tactical, for it interfered principally with the supply system; one cannot feed huge armies by hand or by aeroplane during the advance. The railway lines about Avesnes were freely adorned with these instruments of war; every road-culvert, if not already destroyed, was probably mined; even if it was already blown up, there might be another explosion impending. These mines kept going off for long after the fighting was over, which caused great delay during the advance to the Rhine; they would perhaps have prevented pursuit, if the fighting had continued; may they have even influenced the decision to grant an Armistice? It would be interesting to know the date on which the last mine exploded, and the date, too, on which the last was timed to go off had not enemy representatives arrived to disclose them.

---

[1] Methods of transit were many and various at such times; on this occasion they included, besides the usual lorry-jumping, a journey on the footboard of a pilot-engine testing a stretch of railway-line for mines, and a motor-car drive with the Army Commander at the wheel!

## PART III.   Summary.   The Transformations of War.

NOTE :—In the following pages, the writer has endeavoured to confine himself to a few deductions from the events recorded in Parts I and II of this Article, and to interweave these lessons with the military tendencies of to-day; and this briefly.  He has not forgotten the financial side of the question—the cost of changing armaments; but when a national crisis arrives, money gets freely spent to secure victory; nor has finality been reached in the development of the tank, the heavy gun, or aircraft.

A.   THE INFLUENCE OF ARTILLERY UPON THE BATTLE AND THE FUNCTION

OF FIELD ARTILLERY IN PARTICULAR.

Throughout the 58 days' fighting recorded, the function of the Field Artillery was almost entirely protective; i.e. the creeping barrage to cover the infantry during advance and the defensive S.O.S. barrage. There may at times have been some pushing forward of sections with the infantry for offensive tasks; there was harassing (and a little sniping) fire; generally speaking, the offensive duties were still performed by the heavier armament, though of course the duty of exploitation did to a certain extent increase the importance of field artillery support.  In war-time, the cry must always be for a further-shooting, harder-hitting, and more reliable weapon that the enemy has got; hence the fifteen-inch howitzer and the tank, hence the battleship, hence the Zeppelin and the Handley-Page.  The answer to the demand is governed largely by what the nation can produce or purchase and by the nature of the theatre of operations.  It has happened that armament has become so heavy as to render its possessor defenceless through immobility; viz., the armoured knights of the middle ages and the heavy fighting ships of the Armada; it is not quite the same thing in the case of the battleship, because of the invention of the torpedo; otherwise, too, with the surrender of the Zeppelin to the aeroplane.

On the Western Front was a maximum of productivity plus purchasing power and a minimum of natural obstacles, so that the influence of auxiliaries (artillery and tanks) dominated at times that of infantry power.  Frontages of offensive were chosen by the Allies (from fairly early in the war), according to where the attacker could produce the greatest artillery-power with the maximum surprise; the objectives were sometimes limited or arranged according to where the attacking artillery could support, or the defending artillery could not produce its full effect upon, the attacking infantry;  the Germans endeavoured, when attacking, to extend their objectives to the capture of the defending gun-line.  At the end of the war, the appearance of the tank affected, decisively no doubt, the course of the war.  On only one occasion in the latter part of the war on the Western Front did a combatant rely primarily on his infantry to achieve his object— i.e. when the Germans practised on us in the Spring of 1918 the tactics already tried and approved at Riga; but then the Germans had no tanks.

The last thing the writer wants to suggest is that, even under the most favourable conditions, heavy armament (guns or armour), or new inventions, do anything but modify war—though of course, as in the case of gas and tanks, their influence is temporarily enormous; success must depend on national character, training, and resources. He does not hold that the basis of an army will ever be other than well-trained infantry, even if "mopping-up" (nettoyage), and the act of occupation, become at times its chief functions.

Away from the Western Front, the story was rather a different one. There were no tanks and few heavy guns. In rough countries, whose roughness is due to terrain or the uncivilised nature of the inhabitants, offensive duties no doubt did, and probably again will, fall to the lot of field artillerry, which can generally be landed and used with *some* form of traction.

Warfare reached its highest (or lowest?) development on the Western Front *after an extended period of training and improvement.* There it would seem that the centre of the battlefield was a wall of fire, against or behind which the infantry moved, and which was created by the lighter guns, which we can group under the name "field artillery," but much of which was manned in our Army by the misnamed Royal Garrison Artillery. People say the "Creeper" was the outcome of stationary warfare; that it will not be feasible in a war of real movement; that it will be replaced by "Concentrations," though this form of artillery fire needs as much control as does the organisation of a creeping barrage. No doubt there will be a period of movement early in any future war—*though not necessarily at once,* for, is it not conceivable that the initial conditions following mobilisation may necessitate a preliminary period of position warfare *on the land front?* one must remember also that a single night's work digging goes far to produce a battle of position. In the humble opinion of the writer, we shall do well to expect that infantry will demand some form of "wall of fire," both in attack and defence; but he admits that in a war of movement the supply of the necessary ammunition to provide this wall will be the difficulty, as it is also the principal argument for the maintenance of what we now call field artillery, because of the cheapness, ease of manufacture, and portability of the field artillery shell. Obviously, the heavier the armament, the less density will the wall of fire have, not only because of the increased difficulty in provision of ammunition on the battlefield, but also because of the increased physical exertion on the part of the gun detachments.

If one could easily move thirty-inch howitzers, their platforms, and their ammunition, and afford and carry an unlimited amount of both, would there be anything to prevent the entire armament of an army being thus composed? each weapon, for security hence for reliability, in its own steel fortress. But here we enter dreamland; nevertheless "If you can dream yet not make dreams your master . . . ."

A tank containing a field artillery gun is with us, the real object of the tank being reliability by securing the personnel and equipment from destruction. Surely this combination of gun, shield, and power of movement, may one day provide a possible solution of the problem of the "infantry gun"? the object of which is to provide attacking infantry with an artillery weapon for immediate assistance wherever they go. Note the old cry for a heavier weapon than the enemy's rifle or machine-gun! It is worth consideration whether some pack artillery[2] of howitzer type should not be provided to form a reserve to the close-supporting weapons, to remain "in readiness" at direct disposal of infantry commanders on the spot. Defensively thinking, infantry will need support against the attacker's tanks; that support is not likely to be supplied by field artillery as we know it, or knew it yesterday, but rather by armoured anti-armour guns—viz. another form of tank, possibly firing fore and aft. (One should not, however, forget that a moving tank provides a poor platform for a gun, which puts it at the same disadvantage against a stationary weapon, which the ship-gun suffers as compared with the coast defence weapon.)

The deduction would appear to be that 18-pr. (or 75 $^{m/m}$) armed field artillery (organised in batteries) will give place to tanks[1] in front (attached to infantry formations) and to heavier,[2] probably mechanically drawn, and perhaps armoured, weapons behind—their size being limited by (i) the feasibility of providing (in the field) enough ammunition to create the wall of fire, (ii) the question of moveable platforms or possibility of their use on the natural surface of the ground.[3]

### B. MECHANICAL TRACTION AND HORSE DRAUGHT.

There is no deed recorded in these pages which could not have been equally well performed by a reliable tractor—the terrain was, in fact, particularly easy to negotiate. Nor is there anything to show that substitution of mechanical traction for horse draught would have been an advantage. The writer cannot see that the arrival of the tractor will alter field artillery tactics. But of course this is not the last word to be spoken on the subject.

Can a tractor go where a team of six horses can? Bad weather, causing boggy ground or a greasy surface, obviously gives preference to horse draught; steep mountain tracks, such as we had on the High Veldt in the Transvaal, call for the tractor; experiment will decide this point.

Will the tractor be able to get away after unlimbering as quickly as a six-horse team? Was there any necessity for such quickness on (say) the Western Front? One thinks of a tournament display by a

---

[1] Subject, of course, to the far-reaching proviso that a suitable type of tank is evolved.

[2] See Colonel Schirmer's remarks contained in an article entitled "The German Artillery in the Break-through," "R.A. Journal," June, 1923. Note.—This article was written early in 1922, before provision of pack artillery to certain formations at home.

[3] A quite different set of ideas is suggested by General Percin in his "Le Massacre de Notre Infanterie."

well-trained horse artillery battery—of "Saving the guns at Maiwand";
but under close-range fire of the modern machine-gun or the Q.F.,
both team and tractor would probably come to grief. It is possible
that some of the dash in limbering-up and unlimbering came under
the head of showing-off; the practical utility thereof, some people
might say, was based on an attractive hypothesis. Demonstrations
of quick and perfect drill are useful if superimposed on efficiency:
there exists a danger of their becoming a substitute for it, and it is
interesting to note that a common complaint to-day amongst German
ex-officers (*of other arms*) is that their field artillery posed as cavalry
rather than as gunners.

But there is one result of the change possible, which is more
interesting. The cry in peace-time is always for mobility, as it is in
war-time for weight—at least it always has been throughout the
writer's military life and studies. It is the old struggle of weight *v.*
mobility, comparable to that between the gun and armour in the
Navies of the World. Now that we have the tractor, *we shall not be
limited by the weight* which can be drawn by six horses (as much are
convenient to manage at a trot); the supporters of mobility will be
deprived of their chief argument. So far as the possibility to draw it is
concerned, the field gun of the future may be a considerably heavier
weapon, from which the conclusion seems again to present itself that
the 18-pr. and its opposite numbers will disappear before the heaviest
gun that can be emplaced and moved about at a slow pace on the
battlefield.

Some of us must naturally regret this, but progress demands a
certain sacrifice from tradition. In such a question sentiment carries
no weight. For a time finance will say its powerful word, but another
day of stress will surely come. Small wars must be considered, but
will there be any conditions in which it is possible to use the horse-
drawn field-gun and feed the horses, when it is impossible to use and
supply an improved tractor?

### C. Control and Communications.

Again to quote the precept once given in a lecture on Artillery at
Camberley—"guns must be controlled, but the principle of control is
subordinate to that of co-operation." The practice is harder than the
precept, unless you evade the problem by saying that control is a means
to co-operation.

Against a brave, highly,trained, well-armed, enemy, advance is
no easy matter; either you must conceal yourself or provide yourself
with armour as impenetrable as will still permit of movement. The
18-pr. of 1918 was not suitable for such an advance; the tank of to-day
possesses the elements of suitability. The object of decentralisation
(or decontrol) is more immediate co-operation, and there is, one would
think, no reason why the latter should not be attainable by means of
the tank.

It is otherwise with the "wall of fire" which forms one main
obstacle to preservation of life in a modern pitched battle; this wall

needs organisation before, and some control during, its period of existence; so do "concentrations" on selected localities. On the Western Front the battle-line was continuous, no portion independent of events to either flank,—another reason for control. Leaving aside consideration of war against an untrained enemy, it was a favourite theme of the present writer (before the war) that a battle of encounter would begin, as regards artillery, with decentralisation; but as the battle stabilised, decentralisation would give place to control, which would not disappear until one side retreated; decentralisation, of course, in the pursuit. But we had no battles of encounter or pursuits after the first few few weeks; it was only at the very end that, on the Western Front, regimental commanders began to have responsibility other than as regards organisation and administration; the artillery was always controlled.

How can a commander control on a modern battlefield without artificial communications? They are the very essence of management of artillery other than armoured guns accompanying the infantry. No doubt the heavier artillery suffered at times from failure of communications, but it was generally outside the zone of *constant* breaks, and it was less often on the move. There is no more desperate case that that of a field artillery commander, whose group is close up to the line and dispersed over a wide area, when he is asked to bring fire to bear here and there in a moving battle; the infantry, long accustomed to trench warfare conditions (the principal of which was for, field artillery, buried lines), hardly seemed to appreciate this; it is for that reason that the writer has laid so much stress on the early location of combined infantry and artillery battle headquarters. It will probably be admitted that heavy guns are usually disposed in an area where mounted orderlies can be maintained; even visual is often possible; neither of these means are generally available for the advanced artillery elements. The training manuals grant that infantry once launched is out of control; but really it is the same with field artillery, especially on the defence or during a not perfectly successful attack.

The solution would appear to lie in the direction of wireless, *especially for field artillery*, which is generally long enough in each position to make it worth while to put up a wireless installation. It is not suggested that this is an easy solution; a great deal of experence, technical improvement, and training, is required; but it seems to the writer that in this direction there is hope for solution of the problem. The problem should be more easily solved the further the guns are back from the zone of smoke and close-range; fire i.e. if the function of close support devolves on tanks, and that of the wall of fire on field artillery armed with a heavier and a longer-ranged weapon.

### D.    Disposition of Field Artillery on the Offensive.

In Part III of Article I, the writer recounted nine conditions governing good support by artillery; he begs leave to repeat them here :—

1.  A good system of command. *N.B.* The splitting up of a Brigade staff to command a large Group militates against this first condition, unavoidable though it may be.

2.  Good distribution. Suitability to the most probable course of the battle. Think also of the possibility of counter-attack. What is afoot to either flank of your area? Reconnoitre advanced and alternative positions.

3.  Mobility. Concealed approach and easy exit.

4.  Good observation. This includes arrangements against alarm by day or night. It is an essential, especially on the defensive (even if only temporary).

5.  Good liaison—with superior authority as well as with units of the Group—with the infantry, ça va sans dire— with any heavy artillery units in the neighbourhood.
    It includes the collection and sifting of information from all available sources. It is the duty of every unit in an army to keep touch with its neighbours.

6.  Good communications.

7.  Safety and comfort of personnel, including that of wagon-lines. Camouflage. Enemy gas. Rations.

8.  Good Gunnery. Sights tested daily. Care of ammunition.

9.  Good Equipment, well maintained. Good relations with representatives of Mobile Workshops.

It is a platitude to observe that the general offensive may easily turn for a time into the local defensive. In the latter days of March 1918, it did not seem to us that we were in position to do much counter-attacking, but counter-attacks do take place even when troops are hard pressed—the battle of Guise for example in 1914; it is just a question of reserves. One is not in a position to know whether the enemy is hard pressed, when he is fighting about a long-prepared defensive line of great strength; in Part I of this article (Article II), it was a question of the approach to an as yet unpunctured fortress. A group-commander must bear in mind the possibility of such a contingency, to meet which his batteries must be dispersed in depth,— and this holds good whatever the nature of the guns composing the group armament. Positions suitable to the close support of an attack in the open do not perhaps suit when it is a case of attacking an enemy holding advanced posts in front of a main position. The old-fashioned *very close* support is indeed rarely possible under modern conditions; the flat trajectory of the field-gun of to-day renders it difficult; but the mobile trench mortar was used with good effect in the great German offensive, a thing which we might have done well to imitate.

The writer suggests that about 25% of the Group should start the action close up, so that it can continue to have efficient range for a proportionately long time: and that (say) 25%, starting at a longish range, should be kept ready to move at once. Diagramatically put :—

```
Enemy line of resistance. |  <····································>  25% to 4% including some whole units.  <····································>  Over | 4,000 yards. <····································>  25% of strength at most, including if possible, one complete unit.
                          |       1,500 to 2,500 yards.                                                           About half the Group.
                          |  <····················>
                          |  <····································>       2,500 to | 4,000 yards.  <····················>
```

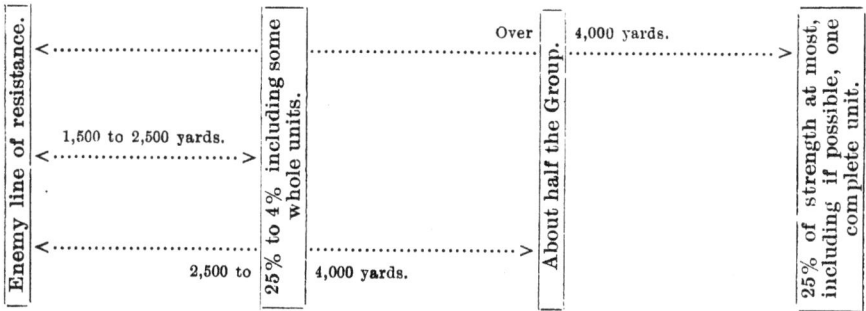

If there is a serious hold-up which shows signs of lasting through the night or longer, it would seem best to re-dispose the Group forthwith, so that it can fire an efficient S.O.S. defensive barrage, even if a few guns have to be withdrawn; the idea that the sight of artillery withdrawing at leisure will alarm the infantry is an insult to the latter; it comes down to us from a past century. (There are of course exceptional cases.)

Change of position in the advance is not altogether the same as change of position during the retirement. In the latter case, it is certain one will have to fight on the new position—probably at once, in the writer's opinion, as expressed in the earlier article, it is better to send back one section per battery to "warm" the new position—i.e. to make such arrangements as will ensure that effective fire can be opened from it at the earliest possible moment. One can pursue the same method in the slow advance on a limited objective. But where there is a possibility that the enemy may break, it is easier to achieve efficiency quickly; moral is at its height; there may be no need for concealment at all—flash cover at any rate need not be so carefully studied; one wants the most efficient fire-unit on the new position as early as possible, and the most efficient fire-unit is the whole battery. The advance, therefore, seems better carried out by the whole batteries within each brigade.

Even in the only-half-open warfare of the last days of the war, the need of reconnoitring the country in front of them while still in action, of choosing new positions against time, and of "shooting themselves in" quickly on arrival thereat, discovered weak points in the military ability of many a battery commander who had reached his post in slower times. Many officers got quickly used to the new conditions; but a B.C. with a real talent for the work was a jewel of great price. It can be taught; the map at home, then visiting the ground itself. The brigade commander alone (in most cases) can decide, by means of his intelligence service, the moment to advance, but he cannot do more than indicate the valley (or other area) where the new position is to be; the niceties of choice must be left to the battery commander, as well as local security. Indeed, the writer himself made a principle of never laying down the *exact* position for a battery, except very rarely when an officer was temporarily in command, of whose judgment he was uncertain; suggestion is quite a different matter.

It might not be out of place here to remark that in the advance the wagon-lines are often far behind; the supply of ammunition under such circumstances gives hard work, and the unit commanders get no opportunity to visit the unit "homes from home"; administration must not be forgotten.

### E.  Observation.

It is true that the principal duty of field artillery in the latter part of the war was the Creeping Barrage, fired off the map. Nevertheless, good observation is an essential for support to the infantry. Terrain has a great deal to say; it was easier in Picardy or Artois than in Flanders; ground observation is however, *always difficult to obtain in satisfactory measure*. On the whole it is easier when the battle moves; there is less hostile fire, except at certain periods, when indeed all observation fails owing to the smoke of the battlefield; what hostile fire there is, is directed chiefly against infantry masses and main roads; when directed at likely O.P's, it is neither so well considered, nor so well registered. Again, our F.O.O. finds more obvious targets.

With all this, there remains the bugbear of communications; and that the battle has a way of becoming important at just that point which one cannot see.

One's thoughts fly to the air. The Heavy Artillery of course had the advantage over the R.F.A., with their Observation planes working for the Counter-battery officer, and their "Sausage" ballons. It is not likely that field batteries will obtain the services of many planes; perhaps not a very great deal is to be expected of air observers as regards small-calibre shells. One of the best-known of Ole Lukoi's stories in "The Green Curve" is based on the doings of a kite attached to a Field Artillery Group Headquarters; it really seems as if more might have been attempted in this direction during a war of new inventions; for the use of the kite rids us at once of two great difficulties— one can see all the ground and one gets immediate and direct information of what the observer has seen. But, indeed, the writer has no personal experience of kite-work; or perhaps he would not have lived thus to trouble the reader.

### F.  Separation of Heavy and Field Artillery.[1]

About 1896 the Regiment was split into "Horse and Field" and "Garrison," which event was (the writer believes) the occasion for the publication of Captain Cleeve's never-to-be-forgotten "Creed." Presumably, what was in the minds of the then Authorities, was Training. It was, and has been ever since, a subject of controversy. The writer can only quote his experience as a General Staff Officer not higher than in a Division and as a Field Artillery Commander; this limited

---

[1] See Colonel Bruchmüller's remarks, published in "R.A. Journal" for June, 1923.

experience has produced in his mind two arguments *for* almagamation
and none against it.   These two arguments are, (i) inexperience by
each branch of the other's limitations and capabilities, of its "conditions of efficiency" so to speak; and (ii) a certain rivalry, due—shall
we say?—to competition for the good opinion of the Infantry (equally
revered by both branches), but often misunderstood by the latter,
especially when they find themselves obliged to deal with two separate
artillery authorities.   The two branches are really one, wherever it
concerns weapons which can move with reasonable ease over the battlefield; in the writer's opinion, they are now more than ever likely to
have the same sort of work.   Whatever be the final decision of the
Authorities of to-day (or the Future?), one would think it should not
be influenced by such a thing as temporary inconvenience in the
adjustment of personnel.   It is, however, much easier to generalise on
such a point than to make a responsible decision, and the writer craves
pardon for his generalisation.

G.   NEW DEVICES OF WAR AND THE STAGE OF DEVELOPMENT REACHED
BY THEM IN AUTUMN, 1918.

Briefly to summarise these developments as illustrated by the
narrative in the foregoing pages.

In doing so we must remember that 6th Division was not engaged
at a decisive point; that is to say, it was not a spear-head; its importance lay rather in its proximity to our Allies.

We will take first the Creeping Barrage (the story of whose
development would fill many pages), as being the one thing which
maintained the importance of the British Field Artillery to the very end
of the war.   The Germans had rather neglected their field guns; they
had been used for some time past for plastering our area with mustard
gas, but played a fairly important rôle (in sections) during the retirement; in the German army, during the last half of the war, field artillery seemed scarcely a first-class arm.   The French field artillery
maintained its influence, at any rate in part, by the national sentiment
towards the soixante-quinz.   We see in these pages (Sept. 19, 24, 30,
Oct 9 and 18, Nov. 4) that the "drill" of the Creeper was understood
in our army; that a barrage could be fired with only the briefest
instructions at short notice, provided the ammunition was availabie—
provided also that the Infantry would give way as regards their line of
departure.   Registration was hardly ever thought of in these days;
lack of range was what most hampered us—compare the ease of the
task of the French "75" group on Sept. 30.   There was a development
at the end, however; the period of limited objectives was dying; there
was now exploitation and, in the absence of heavier guns, exploitation
demanded from the field artillery offensive action as well as the protective duty of the Creeper; in fact, movement increased the importance
of field artillery in *all* armies.   The writer believes that the Creeping
Barrage has come to stay (in some form); what is really against it as
a device of war is the amount of ammunition it uses.

The writer had little to do with the Heavy Artillery during the period of the general advance—not nearly so much as during the German Spring offensive or the Summer's defensive about Ypres. A Heavy Artillery Brigade was now more or less an integral part of (nominally "attached to") each Divisional Artillery; we knew it could move almost as easily as the field artillery; in other words a portion of the Heavy Artillery had become heavy field artillery. It kept improving in what was perhaps its primary duty, counter-battery work, in which the field artillery (4·5 inch howitzers) lent an occasional hand—but the latter needed practice in this department, as well as longer range, and perhaps also more attention to platforms. The development of heavy artillery was surely one of the important things of the war?[1] Heavy artillery seems to be a weapon of the future, whereas field artillery may be one of the past; why else did the peace treaty (Treaty of Versailles) abolish the German Heavy Artillery?[2]

What was *our* experience of Tanks? We had participated in a tank attack on a grand scale at Cambrai in November 1917,[3] on which occasion it had seemed that the creeping barrage might almost have been dispensed with as regards man-killing projectiles; such an attack demands (a) surprise as regards concentration of the tanks, (b) smoke to screen the advance—a field artillery duty, (c) good counter-battery work to knock out what the enemy may use as anti-tank weapons. In the period covered by this narrative, tanks, in small numbers only, had on two occasions (Sept. 18 and 24) supported attacks on the Quadrilateral, which became a tank cemetery, and was eventually captured by infantry unaided. Some whippets were told off to assist W. Yorks Regiment on Oct. 8, but were knocked out; the task was performed by infantry with the assistance of field artillery using some smoke. Tanks failed again to assist 71st Inf. Bde. on Oct. 11. When we came up against waterways (Sept. 29, Oct. 20, and Nov. 4) we had of course to do without their help, whatever the tank of the future may be capable of. The prospective use of tanks as close-supporting artillery will call for much technical development; and the problem of co-operation between these tanks and the infantry they are supporting, is not so simple as it looks. But improvements will come with time and training; it certainly seems to the writer that in this direction we may expect novelties; and if tanks are to provide the close-supporting artillery of the future, let us hope the Royal Regiment will get its just share in the development of this new arm.

Little has been said here about Gas and Smoke. We used mustard gas for the first time on Sept. 29, but one knows nothing of its success or otherwise, for it was against an area which we were not to occupy. Altogether, in our experience, the use of gas was generally limited to "harassing" in between our own, or in assistance to our neighbours, attacks. The writer remarked in his previous (The Group in Retreat)

---

[1] So strongly did the writer hold an opinion that the Heavy Artillery was the more tactically important of the two branches that on two occasions he was engaging for transfer thereto.

[2] But compare Percin's "Le Massacre de Notre Infanterie."

[3] See Article III.

paper that a suitable opportunity for the use of gas was against the enemy's area of assembly, and we had a good example of this when the Germans used gas shells with effect against the assembly of 18th Infantry Bde. about Vaux Andigny on the night Oct. 16/17. Captain Lefebure in his "Riddle of the Rhine" suggests its use as an anti-aircraft weapon. There is obvious scope for use of gas in bombing attacks on manufacturing centres. There was much talk of Smoke, but the ammunition was not always available. Everyone must have seen for himself how smoke blears the battlefield; at the moment when one is attacking, everything which makes for ease in obtaining and communicating information is demanded, even though such conditions may also help the enemy; it is notorious that the use of smoke interfered with the counter-battery service. One would deduce that the use of smoke should be confined to certain definite occasions. With both gas and smoke climatic conditions have (in battle) the last say, and the use of either must often be left to the initiative of the responsible commander on the spot at the last moment.

Now for the Air—and here indeed is an occasion for the Dreamer! Who can tell what the future may bring? Let us confine ourselves to the period covered by this narrative. Enemy aircraft was, so far as we could judge, chiefly employed in bombing (a) depressions in our forward area—against personnel, (b) roads, bridges, wagon-lines, and probable rest camps—principally against our supply system; and that chiefly at night, and very well carried out. Our aircraft was presumably engaged in photography, the counter-battery service, and bombing raids. The development of aeronautics has reintroduced the artillery duel, in which "God is on the side of the strongest Artillery"; the attacking artillery is presumably the strongest at the moment of attack; good air-work therefore assists the attacker most and should continue to do so until someone invents a satisfactory anti-aircraft weapon, device or method. If a good anti-aircraft gun is forthcoming, one may expect to see one in the equipment of, at least, every brigade of field artillery; pending that day we must pay all possible attention to camouflage and the protection of personnel. May not artillery have to play a part in the development of air-fighting also, as in that of tanks? For some think the bomb-dropper will replace the very heavy gun.

A few other points. Scientific calibration in a back area, combined with training and experence on the part of our personnel, enabled us to fire unregistered, which made us more than ever dependent on accurate resection of their positions; note that squared large-scale maps. began to fail us in the last days. The unregistered barrage allowed of surprise as regards the actual moment of attack and the actual target of the spear-head; serious wire could be dealt with by tanks—though, as late as Oct. 13th, 1918, there was talk of cutting new-found wire with field guns. The enemy was on the move, and *at last being pressed all along the line;* he had no time to continue his scientific development of the defensive on a limited front against a limited-objective attack, as exemplified during the 3½ months of the Battle of Flanders (or Passchendaele). Counter-battery work had reached a very high standard. Machine guns had taken up barrage duties in assistance of the field artillery, as well as offensive duties in support of exploitation; but to the very end we had not yet solved the problem of how to deal with enemy machine-guns on defence We had not conspicuously developed high-angle short-range fire for close support, as could possibly have been provided by mobile trench mortars.

H. TRAINING AND PERSONALITY OF JUNIOR OFFICERS, AS WELL AS
N.C.O'S OF THE R.F.A.

As the writer is probably at the end of a long, and by him treasured, connection with the Royal Regiment, he may perhaps be forgiven for uttering the following platitudes.

We have first to deal with professional soldiers. First-class War has taken, so to speak, a turn towards mechanics; whereas we needed a young officer or N.C.O. to ride well and be a horse-master, we now require him to manage a car and to fly. The shooting of a battery and care of the section gun-park, as understood when the writer was a subaltern, is a very different thing from the intricate business of to-day, which requires expert knowledge of equipment (recuperators, etc.), communication-means (wireless), ballistics, and the management of explosives under varying climatic conditions—to mention only four branches of an officer's work. It was suggested in the R.A. Journal some time back that an artillery officer should be capable of acting as "traveller" for armament firms, should be able to show off equipment. More recently an officer wrote an article recommending that the captain should be responsible for the whole equipment of a battery and should not be permitted to reach that rank without passing a course in the "Shops," nor be promoted until he could properly perform his duties. All this shows a tendency to specialised professionalism and to making a Gunner officer what other arms have long believed him to be—a "scientific" man. The writer's recent experience on the Continent was that in the French and German Armies, he is already that to some extent; the French president of the Inter-Allied Commission of Control expressed surprise that a regular artillery officer of considerable seniority had had no factory experience; a very leading German manufacturer of war material, on hearing that the writer was a regular artillery officer, remarked "Das ist schon Etwas" and proceeded forthwith into the realm of advanced science. It seems worth noting as a tendency with regard to the training of the future officer or N.C.O. To go to simpler and quite old-time ideas much might be done (as regards the Regular R.F.A.) in (a) training officers in the tactical handling of a Group first on maps indoors, then visiting the ground, (b) better umpiring of Group and Battery *Tactics* at manœuvres,[1] (c)

---

[1] See General Percin's "Le Massacre", and his earlier book "l'Artillerie aux Manœvres de Picardie en 1910".

training young N.C.O's and recruits by the use of single guns and percussion shells on selected spots close to barracks; these are the writer's—fads?

But practical experience steps in to show us that after a short, all too short, period of first-class war, we no longer have with us our complement of regulars   There is one constant change of personnel in process.  Now some men's characters are obvious at short acquaintance, but in far more cases character appears like the dim outline of a mountain behind the morning's mist; only with acquaintance, as with sunlight, does the mist roll back and disclose some, at any rate, of the truth.   It is generally admitted that the art of command lies largely in putting the right man in the right place; the study of character is a chief duty of a senior regimental officer; there are other ways of dealing with an apparent 'failure' than merely returning him to the base. This leads to the platitude that the commander must be constantly in touch with the personnel under him and must form an opinion for himself of each man—a most difficult thing for a man to do, if not imbued with a sense of the superiority of his own mentality, or who does not hold that seniority is the principal basis of authority; it *should* be so, but only is, when an officer has throughout his service set himself to acquire the knowledge which gives that authority.   The writer wishes not to be sententious—it is this way; if the C.O. does not seek out his new officers, it is very unlikely that they will jostle over one another to seek him.   Whatever the conditions in battle or at rest, whatever its seeming disadvantages—such as personal fatigue when all your mental power is required in the headquarter office—such as apparent waste of time—*never neglect the daily visit* to each unit under your command.

# ARTICLE III.

# A FIELD

# ARTILLERY GROUP

# IN THE SURPRISE.

*Reprinted from the Journal of the Royal Artillery.*
*Vol. L.   No. 4.*
*(By kind permission of the Royal Artillery Institution.)*

CHAPTER I. PRELIMINARY; MORAL.

The late Autumn of 1917 found several divisions of the British Army on the Western front very happy, for they had escaped from the Passchendaele ordeal. Some were on the way to Italy, where things might be better and could scarcely be worse, and which in any case held novelties and romance for such as cared for it. Amongst the happy ones was the old 6th Division, pulled out from months of trench warfare about Lens for their turn at the "push," but whom a lucky fate had headed away on a mysterious errand down South.

The 6th Division, as one of the units of the Expeditionary Force, would, one had thought, have participated in the earliest fighting. However, fear of invasion kept it intact at home for some time, so that it missed the 1914 Retreat—there was a 1918 Retreat, too. It was on the Aisne, but received only the outskirts of the storm called by us the First Battle of Ypres; it missed all but the aftermath of the Second Battle of Ypres. To a long period of trench warfare in "the Salient" had followed a turn on the Somme, where it had the misfortune to meet an enemy strong point, named the Quadrilateral, not far from the notorious village of Guillemont. That encounter explained a considerable change in the personnel of the division, but there followed more trench warfare in the Spring and Summer of 1917, so that considering its antiquity the 6th Division may perhaps have possessed a more marked pre-war flavour than any other in the army, its time on the Somme having been its principal experience of the really bloody battle.

Even now, at Cambrai, it was to find itself at the point of a (new) salient, while enemy hordes chose, in accordance with principle, to batter at the re-entrants; the debacle on its right would not suffice seriously to implicate the division, while the furious German attack on its left rear about Bourlon would scarcely at all affect it.

The 6th Divisional Artillery shared in this emission of a pre-war aroma, which could be detected by any experienced artilleryman in either its wagon-lines or its gun-pits, and gave outward and visible signs of its existence at I Army horse-show in May '17. Such a condition undoubtedly presents more advantages than disadvantages, but there were certain units which had not yet undergone that great metamorphosis which *must* come some day in a long war—comparable to the change which comes over a family when the elder generation is laid to rest.

Within one year, approximately, the effects of battle were to be experienced to the full—in the course of which another Quadrilateral was to figure; the armistice would find this divisional artillery, perhaps not less efficient—for what is lost through casualties may be gained through experience—but profoundly changed in character. In this process, events at the Battle of Cambrai played a very important part—at any rate as far as 2nd Brigade R.F.A. was concerned; and they gave, not only to that unit, but to all present, an invaluable fore-taste of what was to come in 1918; for by November, 1917, the demon of trench warfare had us fairly by the throat, and control from behind was at its height; more than this, we had since July, 1916, been imposing *our* will on the enemy.

CHAPTER II.   THE APPROACH.

In the last days of October, 1917, 2nd Brigade R.F.A was "in rest" near Aire.   The Bde. Commander was engaged (i) in the study of numerous memoranda concerning the nature of the Flanders fighting, and (ii) organising a rough practice camp where the guns of the 6th Divisional Artillery could be calibrated in the old-fashioned way.   These preparations were cut short by an order to march on the morrow—not North, but South; there followed some pleasant days.   We had no idea what was to be our fate or destination; the Caporetto debacle had recently been announced and it was known that several divisions were for Italy, but we were surely marching in the wrong direction for entrainment?   As the march went on, and other movements were noticed besides ours, it was permissible to guess in the manner of Bairnsfather's "Old Bill" that a "blinkin' offensive was coming off"—but where, and how?

Eventually we halted not far from Albert, headquarters of III Army, in an area where houses still partly existed, and in the course of a few days some of us learned that we were to participate in a Surprise—with the assistance of many tanks and a large force of cavalry; that secrecy was all-important; that great hopes were entertained of the operation, the result of which nobody could foretell; and that 6th Division was to be one of those forming the spear-head of the attack.   Further, we learned that the barrage was to be unregistered, fired from guns to be calibrated in the back area by a new method.   Of course the minimum of impedimenta was to be kept with the troops.   We had indeed progressed if all this really came off! For the struggle for the Passchendaele Ridge was still going on and the enemy's attention would be held by this and his eyes fixed on those parts or on Northern Italy.

The new method of calibration, to ascertain the so-called muzzle-velocity (M.V.) of each piece, interested all ranks of the artillery, whatever may have been their doubts as to its efficacy.   The elimination of "registering," as well as of the preliminary bombardment, must undoubtedly wipe out one of the great obstacles to Surprise, which the whole army had long since realised as essential to success, but which it had not been within a long distance of achieving to its satisfaction; the men had never understood why we should keep hammering at the same place after the enemy was once thoroughly prepared, as we had done on the Somme and at Arras and were still doing in Flanders.   Somewhere in Ludendorff's book[1] occurs the remark that the Germans imitated in March, 1918—without tanks,

---

[1] See also article "German Artillery in the Breakthrough," "R.A. Journal," June, 1923.

of course—what we had done at Cambrai; but at the time of the assembly of troops for this Surprise, one was told that we were imitating what the Austro-German army had done on the Caporetto; but to borrow a phrase from the old F.S.R., Part I, the "best type of war is a methodical progression from idea to idea." Then, too, the notion of using tanks *en masse* was not new to the junior ranks, and everyone was keen to see it tried in practice. The massing of cavalry to exploit success was assuredly no new phenomenon—but we hoped that this time they would get their chance (in return for drinking up the water). Lastly, we were to abandon to a certain degree the theory of the limited objective, conceived at Neuve Chapelle, born at Loos, and now grown to full manhood in Flanders.

After seeing some calibration, the Bde. Commander went "on urgent private affairs" to Paris,[1] whence he returned to find 2nd Bde, R.F.A., bivouacked in Manancourt Wood, endeavouring to dry itself after the wettest night march on record.

Here may be mentioned the means adopted to conceal the concentration from the enemy :—

(i)   No troop movements by day.

(ii)  Working parties at night only; all work camouflaged before dawn.

(iii) All troops accommodated in woods; no fresh wood on fires after entering stables (but lights allowed inside tents or shelters); exercise and watering-orders along the fringes of woods.

(iv)  Every unit maintained an aeroplane sentry by day.

(v)   No names mentioned on telephones; new wires forward of a certain line not to be used before zero.

(vi)  No guns on new positions till latest moment possible.

(vii) A quiescent attitude on part of troops holding the line.

At first only battery-commanders were informed as to the positions, which were not taken over by them till 14th; these positions had been chosen by the troops occupying the line, and ammunition (by this time very wet) dumped thereon; they had been allotted numbers and were invariably spoken of by those numbers.

There was a considerable amount of work to be done on the positions *before* zero, in the shape of approaches, preparation of headquarters, floor-emplacements (guns might be sunk axle-deep at

---

[1] Where, besides seeing M. Sacha Guitry in "l'Illusioniste," he enjoyed some most pretty eating; our French friends may not have approved of the gaiety prevalent in England, but they certainly did not cut the quality of their cuisine! The return journey was indicative of the times; rail to Amiens, motor-jump to Corbie, lorry-jump to Peronne, whence, not being able to find floor-space in the "officers' rest-house" established by the B.E.F. Canteen in a ruin, the writer was rescued by an American officer, to enjoy the hospitality of some newly-arrived American Engineers. It is true that he did not get many hours rest in that most pleasant company, but, when conducted by "scooter" next morning along the light railway from Epehy to Fins, he was no emptier for his house had been full. Thence by a luxurious limousine, which certainly never expected such vile treatment, to Equancourt, and from there on his trusty steed to his poor wet brigade, where there was as yet no home.

most), trail logs or fascines, collection of material for work after zero. Obviously some positions, being less exposed, could be better prepared than others.   There were also signal communications to be laid (after the system of command had been decided), observation to be arranged, a visual scheme prepared, alternative positions and routes for advance reconnoitred, ammunition supply, moves of wagon-lines treatment of casualties, etc., to arrange.   In addition, it was essential that officers should know their way about our lines and study the lie of the land in enemy territory; when one remembers that we were all strangers in the district, and that movement by daylight was forbidden, it will be understood that the hours of darkness or semi-darkness were "periods of increased activity."

On the 17th, it was possible to announce the composition of the Right Group under O.C. 2nd Bde. R.F.A.—which as usual meant the splitting up of the Brigade Staff; the location of bridges over our trench system was notified—we were advised to follow tank routes in advance over the enemy system.   On that day also, infantry of 6th Divn. took over defence of the line, while C.R.A. 6th Divn. was to assume responsibility at 17.00 hours on 18th.   He appointed his F.A. Bde. Commanders as his deputies for that purpose.   Arrangements must forthwith be made for the artillery defence, for which Right Group Commander used two batteries from outside 2nd Bde. R.F.A. gave out the necessary S.O.S. Lines, and arranged defensive concentrations, liaison, registration by the two selected batteries (by single rounds), and communications to a certain (formerly battalion) headquarters in the Villiers Pluich—Beaucamp road.   This defensive responsibility entailed O.C. 2nd Bde. R.F.A. leaving his batteries under the senior battery commander, the brigade thenceforth forming a sub-group.   The barrage maps and special instructions had not yet been issued when the Bde. (now Right Group) Commander went up to the line on the afternoon of 18th

A set of instructions was issued by the 6th D.A. late on 17th shewing the final signal and ammunition-supply arrangements.   The instructions dealt with certain other points as follows :—

(a)   Trench Mortars ; task to cease zero + 5' ; personnel to man any captured guns.

(b)   Preparation by R.E. and Pioneers of forward roads and pack tracks, the other side of our trench system ; our artillery told not to use H.E. against any known roads on our line of advance.

(c)   Warning against possible booby-traps in enemy trenches ; this was hardly necessary, but the lessons of the enemy withdrawal in the Spring were not yet forgotten.

(d)   Complete list of Report Centres (selves and neighbours).

(e)   S.O.S. Signals of various Corps and the Cavalry.

(f)   Aeroplanes to give special signals warning us of enemy counter-attacks.

(g)  Water-supply—units to carry biscuit tins.

(h)  Certain instructions *re* care of our own pieces, and information as to Mobile Workshops, I.O.M's., etc.

The above-mentioned signal instructions demanded considerable amplification as to details within the Right Group; personnel had to be found from the batteries for orderly-work, visual stations, transmitting stations, sub-exchanges, and in particular a Forward Communication Party (from which great things were expected); there was wireless this time—not to be used for messages "in clear," of course; a special iron ration issue of cable was given out; operation messages were to be sent, if possible, by orderly.   All this was seen to and settled on 18th.   No doubt great demands were made on the signallers, though such things do sometimes read more alarming than they really are.

His written Operation Order was not issued by Right Group Commander until the last possible moment on 19th.   It announced the extent of the initial attack from Banteux to Havrincourt, and the flanks of the 6th Div. (Villers—Marcoing railway on right and a trench called Coalville Lane on left); gave the enemy opposite us as 27th R.I.R. of 54th *Saxon* Division; 6th Div. to attack with 16th I.B. on right and 71st I.B. on left—18th I.B. in reserve, to advance through 71st I.B.; 29th Div behind 6th Div., and cavalry behind that; 16th I.B. to attack with 2/Y. & L. R. on right and 8/Beds. on left; Right Group supporting 16th I.B. to consist of 2nd, 17th, and 181st Brigades R.F.A.; Field Artillery task involved bombardment of a series of lines —not quite the usual "creeper"—and the use of a deal of smoke; Tanks to assemble behind our trench system and start at zero minus 10; 17th Bde. R.F.A. would be the first to advance; zone calls to be answered by 181st Bde. R.F.A.   The contents of this order were to be communicated to the men after dark on night Y/Z (19/20).   There were the usual number of special instructions for certain batteries outside the normal tasks as given on the barrage map.   Curious to relate, it was only necessary to make one serious amendment after the very last orders had been issued.   Thus we became ready to Surprise. See Position 1 on map.

COMMENTS.—Military records and descriptions of war, unless intended for the front page of a popular journal, seldom bring to the reader's understanding such things as the conditions of the life of the participants; even moral, though pronounced on all sides the most potent factor, generally receives only academic notice.   It is as if we hear at the club that X. "has lost a fish"—interesting to Y., sometimes, perhaps, not unpleasing to Z.—but not disclosing in any way the thrill that X. got when the fish caught hold, the excitement of a few minutes' play blotting out the rest of his world, and his passionate disappointment at the loss.

In the days preceding the assault there was a genuine excitement amongst the men, very different from the anxious foreboding usually experienced.   *All ranks played up for secrecy*—and attained it, aided of course by the cloudy weather which impeded activity in the air, but *aided still more by the passive attitude of the enemy* opposite us. It is true that at the last moment he captured a man or two from one of the newly arrived British Divisions, but fortunately too late to prevent the Break, whatever the results may have been as to summoning of reserves. (Of British reserves there were unluckily all too few, but the writer does not intend here to enlarge the scope of his comments on that point.)

The controlling powers[1] justly endeavoured to decide the minutest details up to zero hour; of course there were bound to be more than the usual number of "ifs," for it was a gamble on massed tanks and Cavalry, comparable to the German gamble on gas in April, 1915. How control was practised after the troops had effected the Break, and what happened to it when the enemy in his turn achieved Surprise, can be gathered to a degree from the ensuing chapters; but some, at any rate, of the controllers crossed the Rhine a full year before their fellows.

The troops used to trench warfare conditions undoubtedly found very trying such things as the rather haphazard arrival of materials, bad storage of ammunition, lack of registration, absence of billets, etc.; in 1918 they were used to all this, but we had not got so far.

An interesting spectacle was the arrival of the tanks by train, their assembly in the woods, and their advance to the line of departure (better known as the "jumping-off place") under what noisy cover a few guns could provide.

Another thing to notice is the relief of troops holding the line prior to a surprise. The sooner it is done, the emptier becomes the area and the better the new troops become acquainted with the country; but, on the other hand, the later it is done, the less chance of capture of individuals from the recently arrived formations; and perhaps this last argument is the most important. The French attack in Champagne in 1917 and the German attack about Rheims on 15th July, 1918, were both vitally affected by the capture of a few men from the attacker's forward troops. Anything which can be done to prevent such a mishap seems permissible, even to an unblushing bolt. The conditions in which the prospective assailant finds himself just prior to the attack afford the enemy a grand opportunity for counter-action, if the latter has but time to arrange such : it is unlikely that that enemy will attack on a large scale—if he did, he would find numerical superiority against him; but he can without insuperable difficulty make a partial offensive on a very limited objective such as seriously to disorganize the attack—vide the German action near the mouth of the Yser in the summer of 1917[2]; or he can retire as the French did on 14th July, 1918, and the Germans did (on a strategic scale) in the Spring of 1917; in either case he can plaster the attacker's assembly with H.E., or perhaps even better in some circumstances with gas. We are anyhow led to the conclusion that if (as the text-books say)

---

[1] See Colonel Bruchmüller's remarks, R.A. Journal, June, 1923.

[2] See "Sir Douglas Haig's Command," Vol. I., p. 354 et seq.

the defender, while hanging on with his teeth and nails, must think of the counter-attack, the attacker can never dare take his eyes off the defence—and there is no earthly reason why the offensive should be the less resolute for that.

\*     \*     \*     \*     \*     \*     \*     \*

In peace time anyone would have described the scene of these operations as an ideal battlefield.  Perhaps there were not so many trenches as usual, but the wire and such trenches as there were made obstacles enough for cavalry.  The principal features of the battlefield at large were :—

(i)   Flesquieres, a village on a hill, without capturing which the attack could not continue; it was held by us still to the last moment in March, 1918.

(ii)  Bourlon Wood, a point d'appui of the first importance on the N.W. flank of the new salient; tanks and H.E. put our infantry into it, and gas drove them out; it possessed two outposts, which were always changing hands—the villages of Bourlon and Fontaine Notre Dame.

(iii) The Canal de l'Escaut, which was held responsible for the failure of the cavalry exploitation, but which was crossed by a Canadian mounted detachment.

(iv)  The villages of Gouzeaucourt, Gonnelieu, and Villers Guislain, pivots of the give-and-take struggle on the S.E. flank of the new salient.

(v)   The towers and spires of Cambrai visible to the N.E.

Of special importance to the 6th Division were :—

(a)   The Grand Ravin which was followed by the Havrincourt—Ribecourt—Marcoing road, a concealed avenue, fairly narrow but unenclosed;

(b)   The cleft, along which ran the roads and railway from Villers Pluich to Marcoing, and which acted as a natural flank to the 6th Divisional area;

(c)   The high ground about La Vacquerie, whence the enemy could easily observe our concentration if carried on in daylight, and our advance if he were not himself attacked;

(d)   The little country town of Marcoing, and the village of Ribecourt, an important road junction;

(e)   Nine Wood, or Bois de Neuf, lying on high ground, in peace no doubt of importance from the point of view of "chasse," but during these times the observation centre of the whole area.

As usual, the villages had, from a distance, the appearance of woods; except along the main roads where there were the usual poplars, there was not a tree to be seen outside woods or villages, the whole area having been intensively cultivated.

CHAPTER III.   THE BREAK.   (November 20/21).

20th.   Zero hour (06.20 hrs.) arrived—"Time and Tide they wait for No Man, No Man, No Man."   Surprise was achieved.

Without waiting for precise information as to events on the flanks, Brigadier 16th I.B. went forward soon after 10.00 hrs., accompanied by Right Group Commander.   There was a hasty visit to the four battalion commanders, all in great heart, to get news; the only fire came from a single 77 mm. gun, obviously at quite close range, and probably one of those captured later N.E. of Flesquieres.

Group Commander then went forward, nearly to Marcoing, and at 12.00 hrs. sent a message to 6th D.A. to the effect that our infantry, probably the 29th Divn., were ascending the slopes beyond the Grand Ravin on their Way to Nine Wood; he could give no information as to events on the right except that the cavalry were advancing, but on the left it appeared that we were not yet established in Flesquieres; the before-mentioned 77 mm. gun had ceased rather before this to annoy us.   Returning at 12.15 hrs. he met the first battery of 16th Bde. R.H.A. (29th Div. Art.) advancing; he requested permission to advance 2nd Bde. R.F.A. and sent for its battery commanders.   The weather had taken a turn for the worse and it was now very wet.

B.C's 2nd Bde. R.F.A. duly arrived for reconnaissance, but brought word that the Bde. was to be prepared to join the cavalry "N.E. of Cambrai"; also that 21st and 42nd batteries had been told to advance alongside 53rd (most advanced) battery, which lay N. of Villers Pluich—Beaucamp road.   Later he received instructions that 2nd Bde R.F.A. was *not* to advance, so he returned to Bde. Hdqtrs., leaving the Forward Communication Party with 16th I.B. Staff.   On arrival at his signal office he found a message that 2nd Bde. might now advance, but it was by this time nearly dark; so he decided to concentrate the Bde. on its gun positions, ready for whatever the next situation demanded; there was some confusion owing to the fact that battery wagon-lines had moved by order of superior authority unknown to battery commanders (3)[1]

Orders issued on the evening of 20th gave the situation as follows : 29th Div. in front line, 6th Div. in support; 2nd Bde. R.F.A might have to move with cavalry or its own infantry; much depended on course of events about Flesquieres; readiness to move at dawn, B.C's. accompanied by battery staffs.   Right Group had ceased to exist as such, for 17th Bde., R.F.A., had joined 29th Div., and 181st Bde., R.F.A. (its own) 40th Div.

21st.   A reconnaissance was made at daylight, in the course of which we learned that Flesquieres was now in British possession; no further orders were received.   6th D.A. Hdqtrs. arrived later to take over (former Right) Group Hdqtrs. accommodation; it was therefore obvious that 2nd Bde., R.F.A. must advance, and a move was made

---

[1] See 'Comments' at end of Chapter.

# MAP TO ILLUSTRATE ARTICLE III.

## ·A FIELD ARTILLERY GROUP IN THE SURPRISE·

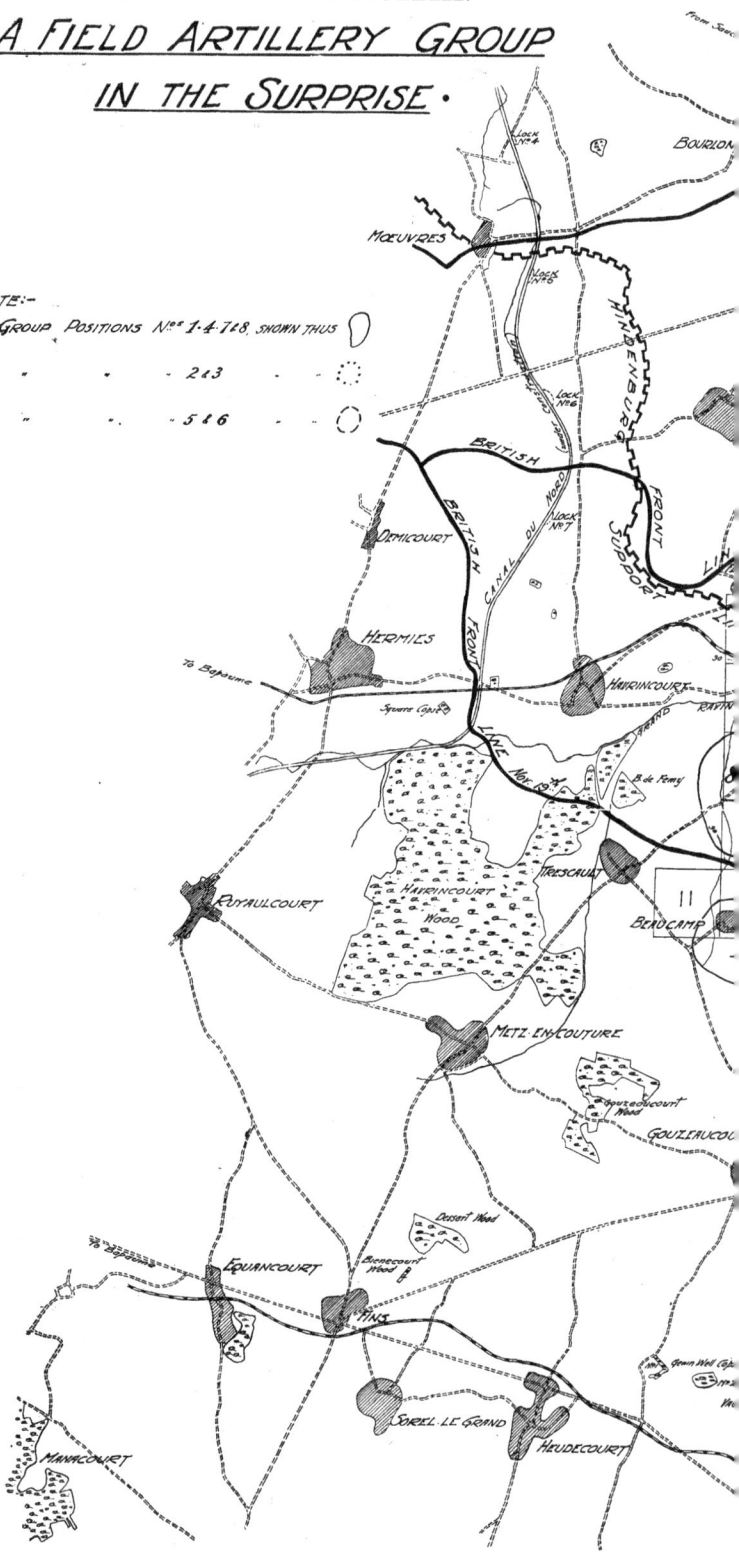

NOTE:-
GROUP POSITIONS Nᵒˢ 1·4·7&8, SHOWN THUS
   "        "        - 2&3  -
   "        "        - 5&6  -

CAMBRAI

FONTAINE-NOTRE-DAME

CANAL DE L'ESCAUT

PROVILLE

LA FOLIE WOODS

BRITISH

CANTAING

FRONT

Lock

LINE

TRUE NORTH

NOYELLES
sur Escaut

8 | 9

Nine Wood

10

14 | 15 | 16

RUMILLY

MARCOING

23

Lock

Nov. 29th

MASNIERES

CANAL DE L'ESCAUT

20 | 21

GREVECOURT
sur l'Escaut

26

6

BRITISH

Nov. 29th

LINE

32 | 33

DEC. 6

HINDENBURG

Bois Lateaux

B. des Chêneaux

VINCELLES

LA VACQUERIE

FRONT

BRITISH

LINE

SUPPORT LINE

Bois de Vaucelles

FRONT

BRANTEUX

CANAL DE L'ESCAUT

BRITISH

GONNELIEU

BANTOUZELLE

LINE

Nov.

VILLERS
GUISLAIN

Honnecourt Wood

HONNECOURT

Canal Wood

Casus Wood

6000    7000    8000 METRES

6000    7000    8000    9000 YARDS

at 10.00 hrs., B.C's parties in front, through Ribecourt. A temporary position (No. 2 on map) was occupied (near the Hindenburg Support Line) about L 20 d.

Bde. Commander then went forward and visited 86th I.B. (29th Div.) and 16th Bde., R.H.A., in Marcoing, where one had found any amount of enemy material, food, trophies, etc.[1] Hearing there that Noyelles was securely in our hands, Bde. Commander advanced 21st and 87th batteries some hundreds of yards, to shorten the range (Position 3 on map); he then visited Nine Wood whence a fine view of the country could be obtained. While there news reached him that Cantaing had been captured by our neighbours. Accommodation for Bde. Hdqtrs. was fixed up in Marcoing, and wagon-lines were ordered forward and later established in or about the village of Ribecourt (3).[2] During the afternoon, while Bde. Commander was at Nine Wood, battery commanders were reconnoitring the forward area in view of the almost certain order to advance. Dispositions were reported to 6th D.A., and were approved, with an important *rider to the effect that it would be advisable to get closer up.*

2nd Bde. R.F.A. Operation Order that night announced that 16th I.B. (6th Div.) was relieving 86th I.B. (29th Div.) forthwith; that 16th Bde. R.H.A. would· be relieved of responsibility for support of (the new) 6th Div. frontage at 09.00 hrs. on 22nd; gave S.O.S. lines for night 21/22 to all batteries; ordered 21st and 53rd batteries to advance at 05.00 hrs. on the morrow (22nd) to L 16 d 2/0 and L 22 a 5/3 respectively, and to complete registration from those positions by 09.00 hrs.; 42nd and 87th batteries to advance, 42nd to near 53rd battery, and 87th to certain quarries immediately W. of Nine Wood, as soon as the 21st and 53rd had "shot themselves in"; located 2nd Bde. Hdqtrs. at L 22 a 9/1.

COMMENTS ON CHAPTER III.

(1) The sad part of this chapter is its brevity. By the evening of 21st all chance of break-through was over; if the advance was to continue, it must be by renewed attacks without the advantage of surprise. The question is, at what moment could the cavalry have been effective? May be there was still a chance on 21st, if the Canal de l'Escaut could be crossed—it *was* crossed by a Canadian mounted detachment on 20th, some of whom are alleged to have penetrated into Cambrai (where they were rounded up), the rest returning the way they came after an exciting ride and an efficient performance. Public opinion on the spot inclined to the view that their best chance of far-reaching success was on the afternoon of 20th; if this was so the cause of failure was the delay before Flesquieres, for which ample troops were available on either flank; the tanks accompanying the troops responsible for the capture of Flesquieres were held up

---

[1] The notepaper found was not yet exhausted when the Germans endeavoured to recapture it on 21st March, 1918. In addition there was some very sour Rhine-wine, and an officer's clothing store with a wealth of decorative hats for souvenirs.

[2] See 'Comments' at end of Chapter.

by, and suffered heavy casualties from, German field-batteries (in the open) E. of, and quite close to, the village. This was probably the best opportunity that cavalry had had since the opening of position warfare; but it was missed, if indeed it ever existed; a barber in Rhineland told the writer in 1919 that he was at that time observing for a German heavy battery, and that, when the German field-guns near Flesquieres were put out of action, there was no one between him and the British and no German infantry that he knew of within miles. With that one must consider the measure of success attained by the above-mentioned Canadian detachment. The writer has never heard what exactly were the orders given to our cavalry for the whole operation[2]; no doubt they will one day be published, but, whatever they were, the chance for effective action was gone by the evening of 21st.

(2)   The great attack of tanks *en masse* had been tried, and very successful it was—and gave an important line as to future handling of tanks, which eventually produced, or much assisted to produce, a decision on the Western front; many people were of the opinion that tanks should never have appeared on the battlefield until they could be used as they were at Cambrai—but let that be. At the time we field-gunners thought that our barrage was redundant and that it even *interfered with the Tanks*, but of course one must consider it as a second string in the way of protection to our infantry—i.e., should the tank enterprise have failed; this is not to say that the field artillery use of smoke was anything but valuable; it is probably an essential to a tank assault, and tanks may in future produce smoke for themselves, like a warship. That tanks can be held up, in limited number, if the moral of the defenders is sufficiently high, is shown by the disaster which befell so many of them at the hands of a few German field-guns (and howitzers) at some hundreds of yards range E. of Flesquieres; it was said[1] that a German artillery-officer continued personally to handle the last of these guns up to the moment when he was shot by the British infantry advancing across the Grand Ravin; we must render this officer the homage due to his gallantry—and can learn something for ourselves from his action; the tank cemetery was optically obvious to those who advanced through Ribecourt on 21st.

(3)   Some points in connection with "wagon-lines" seem worth notice. The shifting of battery wagon-lines unbeknownst to the battery commander is not only administratively inconvenient, but can easily lead to serious inefficiency at a critical moment; it should not occur. The question as to who should originate the order to shift wagon-lines during an advance, whether D.A., the Group Commander, or the battery commander, was raised in Article II, but in any case the battery commander must be warned of the order to move. A very old mistake was made on 21st, the lure of houses (or rather ruins)

---

[1] The incident is, in fact, mentioned in Sir Douglas Haig's despatches.
[2] See now "Sir Douglas Haig's Command," Vol. I., p. 392.

proving once again irresistible; Ribecourt was an important road-centre and a certain target; needless to say we suffered for our temerity, for, as early as the night 21/22, 87th battery wagon-lines were badly shelled; of course at the moment further advance was expected, but————

(4) An impression was prevalent in the forward area that, at the end of a long period of trench warfare, subordinate commanders were more ready to assume control than the controllers were to give it up; that may be a one-sided view.   On the other hand it became obvious at this quite early phase of the war of movement that many individuals amongst the subordinate commanders did not shine with the brilliance expected of them from the experience of the past years, for trench warfare had habituated them to slow decisions, if not to the habit of waiting for orders.

CHAPTER IV.   THE HOLD-UP   (November 22/29).

22nd.   The moves as ordered duly took place; batteries registered, and the usual communication, S.O.S. duties, and liaison, etc., were arranged.   Position 4 on map.   2nd Bde. O.O. issued that evening announced that 16th I.B. (which 2nd Bde. was still supporting) was to consolidate its position, the left battalion swinging up somewhat to meet the neighbouring troops near Cantaing.   But at 17.45 hrs. a message was received from D.A. saying that "6th Div. was to form a defensive flank"—apparently in view of intended attack by our neighbours from Cantaing on the morrow (but there is no copy of this message amongst the writer's records)—and that "all batteries were to withdraw to the neighbourhood of the Hindenburg Support Line."

The only other incidents worth mentioning this day were the severe shelling of 42nd battery wagon-lines and a direct hit[1] during night 22/23 on the house in Marcoing occupied by 2nd Bde. head-quarters.

23rd November was a very busy and decidedly unfortunate day. A reconnaissance for new positions in accordance with last night's message was made betimes.   51st Div., now on our left, attacked Fontaine Notre Dame with tanks; the tanks got beyond the village, but the attack was unsuccessful—probably due to m.g. fire from La Folie woods, which 2nd Bde. R.F.A. was engaged in shelling vigorously throughout the day.   This attack produced heavy hostile fire all over our area, and some gas in Marcoing; 42nd battery suffered severely, losing 3 officers, 5 sergeants, and several others, on its new

---

[1] A young officer from The Shop, applied for by Bde. Cdr., reached his battery wagon-lines to be thus welcomed; he was in the room which received the direct hit that night; at his battery gun-position during the bad time next day; he was sleeping under a wagon between his B.C. and senior subaltern on the night 30 Nov./1 Dec., when one was killed and the other wounded; and was himself severely hit on observation in Nine Wood on 3/Dec.   On his return in time for the Kemmel operations of April 1918, he seemed invulnerable.   Such is the fortune of war!

position (1), another officer was hit on liaison in Nine Wood, and 2nd Bde. Signal Officer severely wounded outside Bde. hdqtrs.; 87th (How.) battery had casualties in the quarries W. of Nine Wood. Batteries had to withdraw, piecemeal, at dusk to their new position (No. 5 on map), while maintaining our defensive responsibilities; it had been promised us that during their withdrawal other R.F.A. units should cover our zone, but the units concerned appear never to have received the order to do so (2). At the same time all wagon-lines, tired of the attention they were receiving from the enemy at Ribecourt, were withdrawn to the neighbourhood of Villers Pluich, which proved later to be an abode of anything but rest. The 4 batteries had now, between them, occupied 16 gun-positions since they left their zero hour points.

On this day it was notified that Bourlon Wood was in British possession.

24th. On 24th, 16th I.B. and 2nd Bde. R.F.A. hdqtrs. moved out together to dug-outs at L 21 a 5/5. A considerable amount of reconnaissance was carried out, night sniping arranged, and other normal trench warfare conditions resumed.

25th. Orders were issued for support of a serious attack by 29th Div. on our right, but this attack did not take place.

It was announced that the line to be consolidated by III Corps ran, high ground in G 21 a — Lock in G 17 d — L 11 c — L 10 b — L 4b 0/5, with posts well in front; it will be seen that the line of resistance ran round Nine Wood. The dividing line between 28th and 6th Divs. ran L 17 c 0/2 — Grand Ravin to L 21 d 8/2 — L 32 c 8/0 — R 7 d 1/0.

Bde. Commander gave priority of battery work as (i) accommodation for personnel, (ii) protection of ammunition, (iii) protection of guns; one must remember it was now winter. The dump to be maintained was fixed at 252 r.p.g. 18-pr. and 204 r.p.g. 4·5″. 24th Bde. R.F.A. on our left, was crossing its fire with 2nd Bde., because of the shape of the ground, and protected right battalion 16th I.B. Two heavy-artillery groups were within call.

Guards Div. was now on our Northern (left) flank, and at 14.00 hrs. a Guards officer told Bde Commander that we held Bourlon village except for a few (surrounded) enemy posts. The Guards' line met 6th Div. about L 4 central.

26th/29th. A readjustment was now ordered, to take place night 26/27. 6th Div. would put two I.B.'s in the Line; 71st I.B. (in relief of 16th I.B.) on right, supported by a Right Group consisting of 2nd Bde. R.F.A. and 112th battery of 24th Bde. R.F.A.; 18th I.B. (in relief of 1st Guards I.B.) on left, supported by a Left Group consisting of 24th Bde. R.F.A. (less 112th battery) and (on 29th November) 277th Army Bde. R.F.A.

Up to the evening of 29th, the daily, and almost all-daily, offensive task of Right Group was the shelling of La Folie Woods in support of efforts by the Guards to capture the village of Fontaine

Notre Dame, an important outpost to Bourlon Wood, the still more important pivot of operations in these parts. The Guards' endeavours did not meet with great success; Fontaine Notre Dame was never long held by us, and Bourlon village was constantly changing hands. Our defensive task was the consolidation of our position at the apex of the new salient, in which the most difficult item to secure was a properly protected O.P. in Nine Wood (3), which was to us what Bourlon Wood was to our neighbours—only that the advanced posts (Cantaing, Noyelles, and Marcoing) were firmly enough established in our possession.

## Comments on Chapter IV.

(1) It is difficult to know why 42nd Battery came under such heavy fire on 23rd; whether it was seen occupying its position, or whether its flashes were visible from some enemy O.P.; personally, the writer believes this fire was in the nature of counter-preparation—directed on an area, rather than on a target. Whatever may have been the cause, the trouble of 23rd was the beginning of the great metamorphosis for this battery: it had but a few days previously got a new captain; almost at this moment its excellent B.S.M. had to go sick; at Marcoing on 23rd it lost 3 subalterns and 5 sergeants—but worse was to come! Events at the battle of Cambrai completely changed the character of the battery, which never again showed its marked pre-war flavour.

(2) The nature of the war of movement had been so forgotten at this period that necessity for strict compliance with an operation order or message was scarcely realised. For instance, on the evening of 23rd the necessary withdrawal of batteries had been most carefully timed so as to maintain possibility of support of the line—a highly important consideration at that moment. Batteries wished to move at the moment most convenient to themselves—all at the same time. We all know there are occasions when a subordinate thinks it best to act otherwise than in accordance with orders, and we know the conditions under which disobedience may be justified: but the last word on the question is that *by disobeying, one lets one's neighbours down.* This is rather harsh criticism; indeed any failure there was, was very likely due to some manner in which the orders were given—i.e., the fault of the orderer rather than the ordered; the matter is mentioned only to lead up to the thesis that in no point was the battle of Cambrai more important than in reminding troops, highly trained before the war to mobility, of the elementary conditions connected with the war of movement.

(3) One may compare our difficulty in employing to the utmost the excellent facilities for observation from Nine Wood to the difficulties doubtless felt by the Germans in using Mount Kemmel during the Summer of 1918.

L

CHAPTER V.    THE COUNTER-ATTACK (Nov. 30-Dec. 6).

30th Nov. Early on the morning of 30th there was heavy firing to the right (South), and a considerable amount of "stuff" fell in the Grand Ravin. After a short time one could see from Group headquarters (in L 21 a) masses of Germans advancing over the heights S. of Masnieres and our own infantry retiring. Later, there was obviously heavy fighting in progress in the direction of Bourlon (the left rear) also.

The enemy had, in his turn, achieved Surprise—Sir Douglas Haig called it "local surprise." As usual, a number of people had expected attack; many people temperamentally expect hostile action; but in this case it would appear that subordinate commanders had definitely warned the authorities that counter-attack was imminent.

Reports of an alarming nature (capture of Gouzeaucourt!!) arrived from the right, and gradually also from behind, but on 6th Div. front it was quiet. Nevertheless, with the concurrence of Brigadier 71st I.B., Group Commander ordered the batteries in the Grand Ravin to withdraw by sections to L 19 d on the slopes N. of Ribecourt and to L 2 6 d on slopes E.S.E. of that village, his principal object being to get direct observation on the enemy, should they continue to advance; additional reasons were (i) the fact that the Grand Ravin was a sure target, (ii) facilities for getting away without traversing Ribecourt. These orders were obeyed by 21st, 53rd, and 87th batteries, but appear to have been misunderstood by 42nd; 112th battery sent 3 guns to L 32 central (W. of Bois Couillet ravine), maintaining the remainder at L 27 d 9/2 on E. slopes thereof; ammunition supply on the new positions was by "echelon" vehicles. Any surplus kit was returned to wagon-lines, which, coming under heavy fire (of course) at Villers Pluich, all moved to Havrincourt Wood.

Towards evening the situation seemed to be stabilised—we heard Gouzeaucourt had been recaptured by the Guards; the defence of our line having to be considered, Group Commander decided to move back to original positions; 21st battery did this, and 87th Hows. (only part of which had, for special reasons connected with the defence of the line, moved); before 53rd could comply, an order came from 6th D.A. that batteries were not to go forward again, so 53rd remained where it was, well placed for eventualities on either side of the Grand Ravin near Ribecourt; 112th battery also maintained its split position. See Position 6 on map.

By midnight communications were thoroughly re-established and ammunition supply seen to, but 42nd battery had lost yet another subaltern wounded.

Owing to the fact that its reports of this period went through the normal channel (O.C. 24th Bde., R.F.A.), no accurate description, unfortunately, can be given of the experiences during period 30th Nov./3 Dec. of 112th battery, commanded by Major W. S. Ironside, D.S.O., M.C., an officer who had landed with 6th Div. in France as a sergeant, and who was killed in command of 112th battery on 2nd

Nov., 1918, near Le Cateau, to the intense regret of the whole division. This battery had enemy infantry within a few hundred yards at one time, it is believed, and on several occasions engaged infantry targets over open sights. As chance would have it, the telephone line from Group Hdqtrs. to 112th never "went dis" and the battery commander continued to discuss the situation through this exciting time with his usual unruffled equanimity. The writer had believed that an account of 112th battery doings appeared in one of the early numbers of "The Gunner"[1] under a series of articles entitled "Some Episodes during battle-fighting on the Western Front (communicated by Major-General H. C. C. Uniacke, c.b., c.m.g.)."

Night 30th Nov./1st Dec. At 01.00 hours on 1st Dec., an enemy shell landed on the wagon under which were sleeping the battery commander and two of the remaining subalterns of 42nd battery. The battery commander was killed and his senior subaltern severely wounded; 42nd battery was now left officered by a newly arrived captain and two, both recently joined, subalterns.

The death of Major N. B. Robertson, d.s.o., was one which the Regiment could ill-afford; he was the very type of a 1914 battery commander. For 42nd battery it spelled (temporary) disaster; the 42nd battery *was* Major Robertson. Everything has the defects of its qualities and the qualities of its defects; the disadvantage of such personality lies in the fact that an awkward time occurs for a unit when that personality departs. Lieut C. H. Wilkinson, m.c., crx. de g., was perhaps the best subaltern the writer had under him during his regimental service in the war; he died of influenza on his way back from New Zealand to rejoin 2nd Bde., R.F.A. in the Spring of 1918.

Immediately on hearing this bad news, Group Cdr. visited 42nd battery, to see that things were for the moment in order, and all batteries (except 112th, which there was not time to do); he also gained personal touch with the F.A Groups on either flank.

Dec. 1/2. There was a good deal doing, one way and another, on 1st. Right Group answered 3 S.O.S. calls—one in the morning in support of 29th Div. on our right, one at 13.45 hrs. in aid of Left Group supporting 18th I.B., a third about Rumilly for 29th Div., in which 112th battery were the chief participants. Our troops to the South had failed to regain the ground as far as Villers Guislain. 29th Div. held to their line, though it was said that the enemy at one time penetrated Masnieres; that night we definitely evacuated Masnieres and the new front line of 29th Div. was about 1,300$^{\underline{x}}$ away from 112th battery position. On the left, the enemy advanced on Cantaing, but was repulsed; there was again very heavy firing in the direction of Moeuvres and Bourlon Wood. In Right Group area, especially in the Grand Ravin, a lot of shells fell, which caused various casualties, including a slight wound to O.C. 53rd battery. 2nd Bde.

---

[1] Vol. 1., Nos. 5 & 7, contain under this heading an account of the experiences of some artillery units lying to our right (S.) on this day of many incidents.

R.F.A. had for the nonce lost its wagon lines and found it hard to maintain battery ammunition dumps.    Communications were not working well this day, and one had to rely to a considerable extent on visual through 53rd.    A new commander appeared for 42nd battery.

After dark Major Robertson was buried to the accompaniment of 4·2 shells, which fell with persistent accuracy just far enough away to the right to allow the party to complete its sad task; it was indeed a soldier's funeral.

Daylight on Dec. 2 disclosed a number of strange batteries in Right Group area, chiefly in the Grand Ravin, where they had arrived during the hours of darkness.    6th Div. frontage (but not as yet Right group frontage) was extended owing to 16th I.B. taking over 87th I.B. ((29th Div.) line.

Dec. 3.    By far the busiest day of this period was 3rd December. The enemy attacked all day on the Flot Farm—Rumilly front.    At 10.45, 13.45, 14.20, 15.10 hrs., Right Group was engaged in answering S.O.S. calls.    At 15.00 hrs. 112th battery said we had retired to West of Marcoing, and at 15.30 hrs. 71st I.B. thought Marcoing was in enemy hands; enemy patrols were reported at 14.45 hrs. to have been seen in Marcoing, having probably worked their way along the canal bank.

Although it turned out later to be incorrect that Marcoing was in possession of the enemy, a conversation with 71st I.B. resulted in a decision to withdraw batteries to the area approximately L 31 b, already reconnoitred by B.C's.    With the approval of 6th D.A., the withdrawal was carried out, well and quickly, 42nd battery remaining in its position, to cover the right flank of our infantry still at Noyelles. Position 7 on map.    An arrangement was arrived at with Left Group to extend their barrage, so that between the two groups the whole 6th Div. front could be properly supported.

After dark, 71st I.B. and Right Group Hdqtrs. withdrew together to Ribecourt.    Between 23.00 hrs. on 3rd and 02.00 hrs. on 4th, Group Commander was able to visit all batteries in position along the Ribecourt—Villers Pluich Road.    With a quiet night, the clearing of ammunition from the old positions and the re-establishment of communications was successfully accomplished.

To the right (S.) the enemy, who had already gained ground on 2nd, this day captured the important heights about La Vacquerie.

At 13.00 hrs. 2nd Bde. R.F.A. suffered further, in that an officer of 53rd was killed and the two remaining subalterns of 42nd battery wounded whilst observing from Nine Wood; the O.P. there had always given cause for concern; some sort of a trench had been dug for it, else the whole party would have been wiped out. Actually 42nd battery had in these 10 days lost its commander and 7 subalterns, amongst the officers only.

Dec. 4/6. On the morning of 4th, C.R.A. 6th Div. met Group Commanders at Boar Copse (Le Bosquet) and announced intended general "withdrawal" to Hindenburg Support Line. The enemy use of gas against Bourlon Wood had proved too much for us. There was to be, after the withdrawal, a Group in support of each I.B.; the present Right Group would become Centre Group, losing 112th battery, but getting the whole 232nd Army Bde. R.F.A., (three 18-pr. batteries, no hows.) instead. In the afternoon the new Boar Copse positions were reconnoitred in detail. Later it was announced that the withdrawal was to take place this night (4/5/).

The retirement of the batteries required careful staffing, adequately to protect the rear-guard[1] which the infantry would leave in position until the new line was properly occupied (03.00 hrs. on 6th). In the event, leading sections of all batteries moved before midnight, to "warm" the new positions, while the bulk of remainder retired between 03.30 and 04.30 hrs. There was much hostile shelling, but the move passed off uneventfully, except for the destruction of one complete gun-team of 53rd battery. Position 8 on map.

Probably the enemy had not discovered our "withdrawal," for 5th was a quiet day; Right Group was duly grateful, there being an endless amount of things to arrange, especially as it was notified that 232nd Army Bde. R.F.A. was to leave Centre Group on replacement by 155th Bde. R.F.A. of which D/155 and B/155 joined (without ammunition) before dawn on 6th.

One had to consider the possibility of still further withdrawal. The British Army was new to "withdrawals" at this period of the war; the experiences of the last few days had been somewhat alarming; many guns had been lost on our right; it was advisable to consider the circumstances under which battery commanders might have to chose between abandoning their guns after taking breech-blocks, etc., or fighting them to the moment of capture. Withdrawal can quite easily become a habit, so at least one seemed to be finding.

The night 5/6 in Ribecourt was about the worst the writer experienced throughout the war. There was no cover other than than from weather and the enemy kept up a terrific fire with large-calibre stuff on the village. Once again, one felt grateful to him for the extreme accuracy of his guns and the good training of his detachments! The points chosen by him as targets (road-junctions, of course) lay on either side of "where our caravan had rested"; each M.P.I. lay just, but only just, far enough away to give a little confidence, which looked like fortitude. There were many casualties on the roads about, and the "padre" nearly left this world of shells and sorrow for a better, brighter, area. At the very worst moment, 01.50 hrs. on 6th, news was received of expected enemy attack, and Right Group was ordered to carry out "Counter-preparation" on a big scale—the first

---

[1] Rearguard did not retire the whole distance, but remained on the line L 28 a 3/8 —Premy Chapel, which eventually became more or less an outpost line with only very distant artillery support.

time this term had come to the writer's notice, except in translated German documents; there was to be heavy harassing fire from 02.00 to 06.00 hrs. and a sort of barrage from 06.00 to 06.30 hrs. All the lines had been broken, and it became necessary for the acting Bde. Signal Officer to use orderlies, whilst arranging visual. Strange to say, none of the orderlies were hit, and visual was established—a most dangerous period for the officer in question, for which he was justly rewarded by a M.C.; it was a really good performance, which resulted in all batteries opening fire by 04.12 hrs.

In the end there was no enemy attack, whatever may have been his intention; enemy fire had stopped almost directly our Counter-preparation proper began; our own shooting was stopped before 07.00 hrs.

During 6th, Centre Group Hdqtrs. moved to a trench dug-out (of a peculiarly "movie" nature) at K 36 a 6/0; Group Commander accompanied 71st I.B. headquarters to another locality, L 32 a 3/3. C/155 and A/155 came into line and the whole 155th Bde. R.F.A. was formed into a sub-group, 232nd Army Bde. R.F.A. also remaining for some considerable time with the Centre Group.

CHAPTER VI.   THE AFTERMATH AND A NEW PRELIMINARY.

From this time on, the air was full of "war and rumours of war," for the Russian tangle meant almost certain attack in force by the Germans on the Western front. Details of defence schemes became matters for grave consideration, and soon the daily delivery began to consist chiefly of ideas how to meet the threat. First question, would the enemy produce tanks?

Apart from this general precautionary attitude, an attempt was expected from the enemy to complete recapture of ground won by us in November. Our new child, Counter-preparation, became an important personage directly she was introduced to us; not only was her name constantly on our tongues and in our correspondence, but also was she in these times a daily deed of dawn.

Trouble occurred at once in connection with alleged "short" shells at the point of the new salient. One eventually concluded that it must be enemy fire from captured 18-prs.; there seemed no other solution of the problem as to their source. In the writer's experience this almost always happened when operations resulted in the formation of a salient; short shells cause bad feeling; it is equally annoying for artillery commanders to be threatened with "disciplinary action" and for the infantry to have aspersions thrown upon their moral. Did the Germans, knowing from experience what happens, deliberately use captured guns against such a salient, at the risk of casualties to troops in their own re-entrant? One would think not; but sometimes, at any rate, it appeared that no British guns had been firing at the moment. A good aeroplane photograph shows both the artillery *and the infantry* where our infantry are, about which there has been known to be uncertainty. The principal trouble in this case seemed to be fire from somewhere W. of Ribecourt on to the ground S. of Premy Chapel; its source was never discovered and complaints were still being received at Christmas.

On 12th December, 19th Div. relieved 6th Div.—headquarters and infantry; that divisional artillery should remain "in" was also not unknown! There is a question, when this happens, whether Father should remain to care for his own children, or whether they should be left to the mercy of a step-papa; an argument for Father remaining is that a divisional artillery brigade without its own C.R.A. is a more hopeless orphan than even an Army Brigade—note what happened on Dec. 26th. The reason on this occasion was the very good one that 19th Div. Art. was still employed elsewhere; the question was settled by C.R.A. 19th Div. taking over the duty; the step-papa behaved in an absolutely model manner—further, he had a remarkable aptitude for getting things the batteries needed. Altogether 2nd Bde. R.F.A. found 19th Div. and V. Corps ( now our masters) very pleasant to serve, which is not invariably the case when strangers are thrust into one another's company.

About this time the Centre Group became once more Right Group, lost this and got that battery, undergoing a hundred-and-one minor modifications to keep one busy. Throughout the period 2nd Bde. R.F.A. and a portion of 155th Bde. R.F.A. remained the Group nucleus.

Other activities of the period were connected with the arrival of Lewis guns for anti-aircraft purposes; anti-tank guns, i.e., guns sited in anticipation of a first-class hostile offensive with tanks, whose chief desiderata were difficulty of detection and a clear field of fire, the final result of which policy proved to be the unnecessary loss of an additional number of guns when the hostile attack came off without tanks on 21st March; attention to reserve positions selected to meet various contingencies; re-entry into the line of "toc-emmas"; employment of a mode of warfare[1] much favoured by C.R.A. 19th Div., but heartily disliked by the infantry, known as "galloping guns," which consisted in the bringing up to the closest range at night of single guns against some predetermined target.

On 26th December 2nd Bde., R.F.A. was relieved.[2]   On 27th it moved to a back area.   Just as it was leaving, there could be heard behind it (in the forward area) a violent bombardment. According to pre-war teaching, one should have marched to the sound of the guns; but war seemed different from that we had studied, and Bde. Commander shamelessly pursued the brigade way Westwards

---

[1] Very fine training for the younger officers.

[2] Bde. Cdr. as senior officer present with 6th D.A. had to decline the disagreeable task of deciding whether 2nd or 24th Bde., R.F.A., should be relieved; for the authorities had decided to retain one in the line, and there was no one of sufficient position present to urge a protest; It was 24th Bde's turn for a rest, but their casualties had been negligeable, whereas 2nd Bde. had lost 13 officers and one of its batteries was terribly shattered.

over roads nearly impassible from frozen snow.  Two or three days later it reached a real haven of rest[1] where it was met by a brusque request to send back representatives to clean up some wagon-lines, while Bde. Commander should at once assume command in the line of another brigade whose lieut.-col. was on leave.  At the risk of the "slight reprimand," Bde. Commander successfully avoided perform-ance of both these "unpleasant duties," for help in being able to do which he gratefully acknowledges thanks to C.R.A 19th Div.

When 2nd Bde. moved eastwards after a wintry but delightful ten day's repose and convalescence, it was to take over a portion of the line where in due course it would receive the full shock of the great German offensive of 1918.

\* \* \* \* \* \* \* \*

The preceding chapters must be vastly uninteresting to the general military public, if looked upon as domestic military history; they may bear another aspect if taken as a framework on which to consider modern developments, such as tanks and tractors, wireless, improved co-operation with aircraft, etc.  The writer has endeavoured to lay out his tale as it appeared at the time and he believes there is no actual discrepancy between the events as herein related and the version given in the official dispatches, just re-read by him with special care. Certainly, in places, the things "look different"; so do short shells to the infantry or artillery!  There is always more than one view from the tower.

Reference has already been made (in Chapter III of this paper) to the then new experience of an attack of tanks *en masse* combined with a barrage; other details in connection with the tactical manage-ment of a F.A. Group in battle have been discussed at length in the previous papers "F.A. Group in Retreat" and "F.A. Group in the General Advance."

But the writer, greatly daring, ventures a few remarks on a rather wider and more general field.

Military History, it has been suggested, takes insufficient account of psychology; historically this battle of Cambrai will rank only as an episode, perhaps as a "might-have-been"; psychologically, it possesses the germs of great interest.  *Firstly*, it was an exploitation of Surprise, which is a psychological weapon.  *Secondly*, it shows that one can create a flank, as was conclusively proved by the "Riga manœuvre," even on a narrow front.  But a break on a narrow front needs a "mass of manœuvre" to exploit it, whereas reserves on a wide front are "local reserves."  There was conflict before the war between the French and German doctrines of war—see Colonel de Grandmaison's "Deux Conferences (Fevrier 1911)"; the French believed in penetration at

---

[1] A Fairy Princess, daughter and heiress of the headquarter chateau, honoured us one night with her company at dinner; she was duly fallen in love with by a sus-ceptible orderly officer, who endeavoured to explain his intense grief at approaching separation with the words "Je pongserai toojore de la feel *de derriere*."

the correct moment of an extended enemy front by a "mass of manœuvre"; the Germans believed in discovery of the enemy mass and its envelopment by an extended line, strong enough everywhere to resist penetration, strongest on one, or on each, extreme flank. British thought favoured the French doctrine because we expected to be numerically inferior, but admitted the advantages of the German doctrine given numerical superiority. The Germans, naturally, began the war on their own doctrine as the French did on theirs; oddly enough, roles were reversed at the end; the Germans now numerically inferior, exploited the French doctrine under the name of " the Riga manœuvre," while the Allies, having marked numerical superiority, though unable to practise envelopment, did what they could by advancing in strength all along the line. At Cambrai we seem once more to have attempted the French doctrine, *but without the necessary mass of manœuvre;* it was in the nature of a bluff with tanks and cavalry.[1] *Thirdly,* Cambrai was of interest, perhaps its principal tactical interest, and the source of eventual success, in the employment of tanks *en masse,* about which no more need be said here. *Fourthly,* the result seemed to settle once for all the question whether cavalry could be used on the Western front.[2] It is true that Germans say now "yes," and endeavour to picture to themselves the vast advantages which would have been theirs, if they had had a strong force of cavalry in March, 1918. But could not their infantry have done what their cavalry might have done? Would not British infantry somehow have stopped those cavalry masses and disintegrated them? One is left with the conclusion that Cherfils' pre-war ideas were only an attractive hypothesis, for cavalry must adopt close formation to penetrate in sufficient strength, and a few machine guns can stop them. To which conclusion all the warring nations seem to have come; but, mark you, there should be interesting developments of Cherfils' theory of employment of strategic cavalry as applied to a large force of tanks and armoured cars.

The last and, as regards field artillery, the most interesting thing to notice was the effect of dissolution of control (with the commencement of movement) on the handling of smaller formations. It was a favourite theme of the writer's before the war that the nearer the battle reached to position warfare, the more important became control; the more movement, the less control and the more co-operation. "Artillery must be controlled, but the principle of co-operation is superior to that of control." We had had little ebb and flux since 1914; at Cambrai we had some, and might have had more. See how the F.A. brigade, enlarged to a Group of ever-varying composition, became the tactical unit of field artillery! Tactically, the most important officer for a field artillery brigade commander was his infantry brigadier; with movement came something very nearly approaching "mixed brigades." It may be that neither infantry nor artillery com-

---

[1] But see "Sir Douglas Haig's Command," Vol. I., p. 386 et seq.

[2] An entirely different set of opinions is put forward in "Sir Douglas Haig's Command." Vol. II., Chapter III.—also page 271 and page 340.

**M**

manders realised the effect of this at once, on administration as well as on tactics. The lesson to be learned is co-operation, not only with gun-fire, but with actual personal good will; it is not usually the junior who has the easiest task in such combinations.

A surprising thing is that from 20th November the writer remembers no personal co-operation with representatives of the heavy artillery until about 7th or 8th December, when the counter-battery staff found it advisable to ask field artillery units in the line to assist in the location of hostile batteries. Can such a state of affairs be for the best?

The waging of war, like every problem really tackled, proved in some aspects easier than one thought it would be from experiences at practice camps; but one was left at the very end of the struggle with an uncomfortable feeling that co-operation between infantry and field artillery had not yet reached a state of perfection;[1] that field artillery, as then equipped and drawn, was not able to provide that degree of close support—especially in the later stages of the battle—that the infantry desires and deserves. On the side of the infantry, perhaps a little more consideration for mundane things like accommodation, a better understanding of the essentials of artillery control, a little better tactical information passed during the battle, might help matters. On the side of the artillery, shrinkage to disappearing point of the number of short shells by means of technical training, and tactically, greater and yet ever greater efforts by more forward action on the part of artillery commanders to give the most immediate support to the infantry in the unforseeable stages of the battle.

A knowledge of how very difficult it is to provide the infantry with this close support in the most efficient manner, is some consolation to the writer for the improbability of ever having again to attempt the task himself. It is true that the first duty of the artillery is to hit, and that ineffective fire is generally worse than useless; *but who knows whether fire somewhere else is being effective or not?* It may happen that fire quickly produced from the right place at the critical moment will achieve decisive influence upon the moral of the attacker, or defender, *or both.* Such a suggestion contains admittedly the germ of artillery immorality; but there is an old saying "Bis dat qui cito dat," and, after all, artillery exists to support its own infantry and frighten the enemy's.

---

[1] Compare opinions expressed by General Percin in his "Le Massacre de notre Infanterie 1914—1918".

www.ingramcontent.com/pod-product-compliance
Lightning Source LLC
Chambersburg PA
CBHW060422100426

42812CB00030B/3271/J